Lyric Orientations

signale
modern german letters, cultures, and thought

Series editor: Peter Uwe Hohendahl, Cornell University

Signale: Modern German Letters, Cultures, and Thought publishes new English-language books in literary studies, criticism, cultural studies, and intellectual history pertaining to the German-speaking world, as well as translations of important German-language works. *Signale* construes "modern" in the broadest terms: the series covers topics ranging from the early modern period to the present. *Signale* books are published under a joint imprint of Cornell University Press and Cornell University Library in electronic and print formats. Please see http://signale.cornell.edu/.

Lyric Orientations

Hölderlin, Rilke, and the Poetics of Community

Hannah Vandegrift Eldridge

A Signale Book

Cornell University Press and Cornell University Library
Ithaca, New York

Cornell University Press and Cornell University Library gratefully acknowledge the College of Arts & Sciences, Cornell University, for support of the Signale series.

Copyright © 2015 by Cornell University

All rights reserved. Except for brief quotations in a review, this book, or parts thereof, must not be reproduced in any form without permission in writing from the publisher. For information, address Cornell University Press, Sage House, 512 East State Street, Ithaca, New York 14850.

First published 2015 by Cornell University Press and
Cornell University Library

Printed in the United States of America

Library of Congress Cataloging-in-Publication Data

Names: Eldridge, Hannah Vandegrift, author.
Title: Lyric orientations : Hölderlin, Rilke, and the poetics of community / Hannah Vandegrift Eldridge.
Other titles: Signale (Ithaca, N.Y.).
Description: Ithaca, NY : Cornell University Press and Cornell University Library, 2015. | 2015 | Series: Signale | "A Signale Book". | Includes bibliographical references and index.
Identifiers: LCCN 2015039290 | ISBN 9780801456954 (cloth : alk. paper) | ISBN 9780801479328 (pbk. : alk. paper)
Subjects: LCSH: Hölderlin, Friedrich, 1770–1843—Criticism and interpretation. | Rilke, Rainer Maria, 1875–1926—Criticism and interpretation. | German poetry—History and criticism.
Classification: LCC PT2359.H2 E43 2014 | DDC 831/.6—dc23
LC record available at http://lccn.loc.gov/2015039290

Cornell University Press strives to use environmentally responsible suppliers and materials to the fullest extent possible in the publishing of its books. Such materials include vegetable-based, low-VOC inks and acid-free papers that are recycled, totally chlorine-free, or partly composed of nonwood fibers. For further information, visit our website at www.cornellpress.cornell.edu.

Cloth printing   10 9 8 7 6 5 4 3 2 1
Paperback printing   10 9 8 7 6 5 4 3 2 1

Contents

A Note on Translations	vii
Acknowledgments	ix
Introduction: On Orientation	1
1. Skepticism and the Struggle over Finitude: Stanley Cavell	16
2. The Anxiety of Theory: Hölderlin's Poetology as Skeptical Syndrome	43
Friedrich Hölderlin, "Blödigkeit," "Das Nächste Beste," "Andenken"	71
3. Calls for Communion: Hölderlin's Late Poetry	84
4. Malevolent Intimacies: Rilke and Skeptical Vulnerability	118
Rainer Maria Rilke, *Sonette an Orpheus* (Excerpts)	147
5. Figuring Finitude: Rilke's *Sonnets to Orpheus*	156
Epilogue: "Desperate Conversation"—Poetic Finitude in Paul Celan and After	193
Selected Bibliography	205
Index	215

A Note on Translations

In attempting to make this volume accessible to non-German-speaking readers, I have endeavored to balance consistency, brevity, and common sense in the use of original and translated quotations. All prose sources are cited in English translation, with the original given when necessary for clarification. Whenever possible I have used published translations; I have identified the few places where translations are my own. The poems of Hölderlin and Rilke with which I work are reproduced in full in both German and English preceding chapters 3 and 5, respectively. When citing the poems within each chapter, I give both German and English for shorter quotations, but dual-language, multiline citations would quickly become unwieldy. I therefore ask for the forbearance of readers without German and refer them to the full translations, which I cite by line number within the chapters.

Acknowledgments

In a project that discusses acknowledgment as a central strategy for placing oneself in the world, it is a particular pleasure to acknowledge those without whom the project could not have taken place. At the University of Chicago, David Wellbery and Eric Santner guided the project through its first stages; their mentoring and teaching have shaped my thinking probably more than I know and surely more than is evident in one monograph. Christopher Wild and Robert Buch provided essential additional perspectives and support, both of the project and of my professional development in general. Finally, the Department of Germanic Studies as a whole, and in particular the members of its student working groups, are the likely origin and certainly the proof of my conviction that intellectual work is not a monologic but a dialogic process.

Such dialogue has continued with colleagues in the Department of German and beyond at the University of Wisconsin-Madison. In March 2014 the project was the subject of a workshop designed to support junior faculty in writing their first books run by the Center for the Humanities. To the participants of this workshop— Sabine Groß, Sara Guyer, Brian Hyer, Mario Ortiz-Robles, Andrew Reynolds, Marc Silberman, and especially Michel Chaouli and John Lysaker, who braved travel to Madison in a snowy March—and to the Center itself I am deeply indebted. Without their input, the project would be less rich and considerably more narrow.

It is, further, a pleasure and a privilege when colleagues are also family members: my father, Richard, and sister, Sarah, read many drafts and discussed many poems and ideas from the beginning of this project and also shared their own work with me. Along with my mother, Joan Vandegrift, they patiently reminded me not to interrupt dependent clauses with further dependent clauses and generally insisted on intelligibility (wherever I miss that goal, it is of course my shortcoming and not theirs). My brother, Jonathan, provided perspective, humor, and reminders that there is life outside academia. Finally, my wife, Marina Sharifi, has supported me in innumerable ways from the very beginning of this project—she is my assurance that in our relations to other minds we live our best-case scenario. This book is dedicated to her with love and gratitude.

I gratefully acknowledge the following rights holders and thank them for their permission to reprint the poems of Celan, Hölderlin, and Rilke:

Anvil Press Poetry, London

"Timidness" and "Remembrance," in Michael Hamburger, *Friedrich Hölderlin, Poems and Fragments*, trans. Michael Hamburger, 4th ed. (London: Anvil Press Poetry, 2004)

Hanser Verlag, Munich

"Blödigkeit," "Das Nächste Beste," and "Andenken," in Friedrich Hölderlin, *Sämtliche Werke und Briefe*, ed. Michael Knaupp, 3 vols. (Munich: Hanser Verlag, 1992)

Insel Verlag, Frankfurt a.M.

Rainer Maria Rilke, *Sonette an Orpheus* I.6, 8, 9, 11, 12, II.12, 18, and 28, in *Rainer Maria Rilke: Gedichte 1910–1926*, vol. 2 of *Kommentierte Ausgabe*, ed. Manfred Engel and Ulrich Fülleborn (Frankfurt a.M.: Insel Verlag, 1996)

Omnidawn Press, Richmond, CA

Friedrich Hölderlin, "What Is Nearest" and "Beginning at the Abyss," in Friedrich Hölderlin, *Selected Poems of Friedrich Hölderlin*, trans. Maxine Chernoff and Paul Hoover (Richmond, CA: Omnidawn Press, 2008)

S. Fischer Verlag, Frankfurt a.M.

Paul Celan, "Die Silbe Schmerz," in Paul Celan, *Die Niemandsrose*, © S. Fischer Verlag GmbH, Frankfurt am Main, 1963

University of California Press, Berkeley

　Paul Celan, "The Syllable Pain," in Paul Celan, *Selections*, ed. and intro. Pierre Joris (Berkeley: University of California Press, 2005)

　Rainer Maria Rilke, *Sonnets to Orpheus* I.6, 8, 9, 11, 12, II.12, 18, and 28, in Rainer Maria Rilke, *Sonnets to Orpheus*, with English translations and notes by C. F. MacIntyre (Berkeley: University of California Press, 1960)

Lyric Orientations

Introduction

On Orientation

> I tried, during those years and the years after, to write poems: in order to speak, to orient myself, to find out where I was, where things were going, to sketch for myself a reality.
>
> —Paul Celan, "Speech on the Occasion of Receiving the Literature Prize of the Free Hanseatic City of Bremen"

This book is an investigation of the powers of lyric poetry with regard to problems peculiar to human subjects in a broadly defined modernity. In exploring these powers, I turn to the poetry of Friedrich Hölderlin (1770–1843) and Rainer Maria Rilke (1875–1926), both of whom—despite the inevitable differences of style and epoch—take poetry to be capable of creating communities of speaking subjects within the context of modern alienation. This alienation appears in different ways in each poet (to put it another way, each has his own modernity story), and thus the proposed communities called together through lyric language likewise look different. But Hölderlin and Rilke share the conviction that modern alienation cannot be overcome, nor communities created, once and for all in any universal event. And both argue that to deny the uncertainty created by the absence of any such event (or to deny the alienation itself) is likewise to deny the particularly human condition of uncertainty and mortality—that is, our finitude.

To show how it is that lyric language can undertake the task of calling communities together, I look outside the German context to the work of the American philosopher Stanley Cavell (b. 1926). In drawing on Cavell, I challenge the idea—perhaps most prevalent in poststructuralist scholarship, but not exclusive thereto—that the uncertainty of any relation between language and world necessarily means that language fails to engage the world. I use Cavell's interlocking discussions of language and subjectivity to investigate how language in and through its formal aspects enables us to engage meaningfully with the world and the other subjects in it. This account of the orienting and engaging capabilities of language likewise helps to explain the extraordinarily ambitious claims Hölderlin and Rilke make for poetry: that it can create political communities, recast human relations to death, or unite the sensual and intellectual components of human subjectivity. I follow out these claims in close readings of Hölderlin and Rilke to show how each, in historically and individually specific ways, takes up the problems of orienting finite, mortal subjects within an uncertain and sometimes hostile world. The vision of language I derive from Cavell (himself greatly influenced by Wittgenstein) shows how the lyric, not despite but because of its unusual, individual, difficult, and sometimes fragmentary language, is ideally suited to undertake this orienting work.

Orientation and Finitude

I use the term "orientation" to describe multiple relations between human subjects and communities, the external world, and other minds as distinguishable but related attempts of those subjects to reach outside or beyond their own finitude.[1] Baldly put, human subjectivity is inevitably confronted by the problem of its own finitude along any of a number of lines: people die and do not know what happens thereafter; they (we) are both part of an external physical world and internally self-consciously aware of our separateness from that world; we cannot ensure that our perceptions and expressions correspond absolutely to anything outside our individual minds; conversely, we cannot be certain that any individual thought derives solely from our own understanding and is not in some way put there by language or culture; moreover, this same uncertainty and finitude governs our relations to other subjects, who may prove to be either not enough or too much like us. In everyday contexts, these remarks are banal—of course subjects are influenced by the contexts in which they find themselves (although how much and how deeply is not so easy to say), and of course we can be quite spectacularly wrong in our assessments of the external world and especially of other minds. But once any of these questions have been raised—whether through abstract or philosophical consideration or in any of the practical, moral, or political situations in which they may arise—they do not seem to be so easy to put to rest.

As my emphasis on finitude and error should make clear, when I use the word "subject" or "human subject" in this project, I refer not to the transcendental, transhistorical rational subject of modern philosophy from Descartes on, but

---

1. As I explain in detail in chapter 1, these attempts necessarily fail—finitude is something that cannot be overcome but must be inhabited—even as the attempts themselves are constitutive of the subjective inhabitation of that finitude.

rather to a self-divided, self-opaque, and historically constituted entity struggling to make sense of its own experience. I am arguing, then, for a picture of subjectivity defined by impossible attempts to exceed its own finitude. Of course, not everyone feels the need for or difficulty of such attempts at every moment, and this is probably a good thing: immersion and absorption in our pursuits remain possible. But we are all liable to moments of rupture and breakdown of conviction in both projects and relationships, even if for some of us such moments do not occur often or with intensity. The inevitability of rupture or self-diremption is the commonality between the portrayals of subjectivity offered by Kant, Nietzsche, and Freud, and continued by their descendants (one might name Adorno, Blanchot, Butler, Deleuze, de Man, Derrida, Guattari, Heidegger, Lacan, or Wittgenstein, to say nothing of—even older—literary presentations of fallenness from assurance and unity). And when such moments of rupture or interruption occur, perhaps the paradigmatic response is to to intellectualize our situation and to overreach for a solution that consists in *knowing* something—how to live, how to respond, what to do—for sure.[2]

The central claim of this book is that lyric poetry offers a mode of response to finitude that neither demands an impossible certainty nor gives up altogether on the drive toward certainty that defines human subjects. I use Cavell's depictions of language and subjectivity to show how it might be that lyric poetry is a vital place where the powers of language in our forms of life are interrogated as possible modes of subject and world orientation. I look to Hölderlin and Rilke to show how orientations in poetic form(s) can *shape* or even *create* orientations to the world and to others that do not exceed or reject but inhabit finitude. My term "lyric orientation(s)" describes the kind of commitments and relations to the world that emerge aesthetically and tentatively out of language use in lyric poetry. The terms "orientation" and "lyric orientation" also emphasize that the relations to the world in and with language created by lyric poetry are processual rather than referential, communal rather than universal, and responsive rather than imposed successfully or unsuccessfully on an external object-world. Such orientation is, to anticipate the Cavellian terms I take up in detail in chapter 1, a matter of acknowledgment, rather than knowledge, a form (among other things) of self-understanding (of one's commitments, responsibilities, temptations, and finitude) that is not like knowledge of an object, in that it involves taking a stand on oneself and one's relations with others in communities of language.

---

2. This response, I argue in chapter 1, leads to an all-or-nothing of knowledge or sheer relativism that I work to undo using lyric poetry. Furthermore, the terms of this binary will be different at different times, as I show in reading problems of finitude in historically specific appearances preparatory to my discussions of Hölderlin and Rilke and as I discuss very briefly apropos the poetology of Paul Celan.

Superficially, the idea that language and world are mutually influential is straightforward, and is represented by the idiomatic tendency to say things about the world by saying things about language, such as "You can't even mention *Werther* and *Twilight* in the same sentence!"[3] But taking the relation between language and world seriously reveals a vision is "as simple as it is difficult, and as difficult as it is (and because it is) terrifying,"[4] because that relation is grounded by nothing more and nothing less than the very agreement in language it seems to require. Cavell arrives at this "vision" through extensive engagement with the later philosophy of Wittgenstein.[5] For Cavell, the relation between language and world runs along the lines of what Wittgenstein calls "grammar." Thus, when Wittgenstein remarks that "a meaning of a word is a kind of employment of it. For it is what we learn when the word is incorporated into our language,"[6] he is emphasizing practical, even material habits and uses—as in the verb "to incorporate" (*einverleiben* in the original German also includes the word for "body," *der Leib*)—over dictionary definitions or names that *refer* to objects. Wittgenstein draws a further distinction between practice and existence, remarking that "children do not learn that books

---

3. Linguist Geoffrey Pullum describes this phenomenon (disapprovingly) as "linguification," where "to linguify a claim about things in the world is to take that claim and construct from it an entirely different claim that makes reference to the words or other linguistic items used to talk about those things, and then use the latter claim in a context where the former would be appropriate." Geoffrey Pullum, "Linguifying," *Language Log* (blog), July 3, 2006, http://itre.cis.upenn.edu/~myl/languagelog/archives/003312.html.

4. Stanley Cavell, "The Availability of Wittgenstein's Later Philosophy," in *Must We Mean What We Say? A Book of Essays*, updated ed. (Cambridge: Cambridge University Press, 2002), 52.

5. Two distinctions seem necessary here: first, the view of language I read as so influential for Cavell is that of the later Wittgenstein, not the view presented in the *Tractatus*. In the *Tractatus*, Wittgenstein remains focused on issues of representation, asking "how words can depict the world" and viewing "language . . . as an abstract system," whereas in the *Philosophical Investigations* and after, Wittgenstein looks at "language as . . . a social practice" and attends to use rather than reference. Wolfgang Huemer, "Introduction: Wittgenstein, Language, and Philosophy of Literature," in *The Literary Wittgenstein*, ed. John Gibson and Wolfgang Huemer (New York: Routledge, 2004), 1–13, at 1. For an extended treatment of the significance of Wittgenstein's modes of writing, see especially Richard Eldridge, *Leading a Human Life: Wittgenstein, Intentionality, and Romanticism* (Chicago: University of Chicago Press, 1997). Eldridge also treats the appearances of philosophical problems or stances as and in literary texts in *Literature, Life, and Modernity* (New York: Columbia University Press, 2008). The second distinction rests on this particular understanding of Wittgenstein: some readers have argued that Wittgenstein *is* narrowly antiskeptical. See, e.g., Anthony Kenny, *Wittgenstein* (Cambridge, MA: Harvard University Press, 1973), 179, 203–18; and P. M. S. Hacker, *Insight and Illusion: Themes in the Philosophy of Wittgenstein*, rev. ed. (Oxford: Oxford University Press, 1986), 208–10, 214, 215–44, 276–77. Kenny and Hacker argue that use or practice is itself a reference-securing intermediary. For them, although use does come first, human beings then establish reference by using words to refer. Other readers read Wittgenstein as skeptical by overlooking the use/reference distinctions in his late work; see, e.g., Marjorie Perloff, *Wittgenstein's Ladder: Poetic Language and the Strangeness of the Ordinary* (Chicago: University of Chicago Press, 1996). Perloff's stance toward Wittgenstein is characterized by remarks like "a trip [through the *Philosophical Investigations*] will gradually make it impossible for us to trust, ever again, the full authority of a given word or group of words to *name* a particular thing" (68). I share with Perloff a sense of Wittgenstein as dismantling any established and automatic "authority" of language, but disagree with her focus on naming and impossibility.

6. Ludwig Wittgenstein, *Über Gewissheit/On Certainty*, ed. G. E. M. Anscombe and G. H. von Wright, trans. Denis Paul and G. E. M. Anscombe (New York: J. & J. Harper Editions, 1969), 10.

exist, that armchairs exist, etc. etc.,—they learn to fetch books, sit in armchairs, etc. etc."[7] In a theory of language based on the referential function of names, in particular, the thought is that books and armchairs are part of a world that is just out there, learned separately, to which language may or may not successfully correspond.[8]

For Cavell, however, drawing on Wittgenstein, language and world cannot be absolutely and ultimately separated into names or signs and their referents. Like Wittgenstein, he attends to the learning of language (and thus, it emerges, of the world) to demonstrate this inseparability:

> Imagine that you are in your armchair reading a book of reminiscences and come across the word "umiak." You reach for your dictionary and look it up. Now what did you do? Find out what "umiak" means, or find out what an umiak is? But how could we have discovered something about the world by hunting in the dictionary? If this seems surprising, perhaps it is because *we forget that we learn language and learn the world together, that they become elaborated and distorted together, and in the same places*. We may also be forgetting how elaborate a process the learning is. We tend to take what a native speaker does when he looks up a noun in a dictionary as the characteristic process of learning language.... But it is merely the end point in the process of learning the word. When we turned to the dictionary for "umiak" we already knew everything about the word, as it were, but its combination: we knew what a noun is and how to name an object and how to look up a word and what boats are and what an Eskimo is. We were all prepared for that umiak. *What seemed like finding the world in a dictionary was really a case of bringing the world to the dictionary*. We had the world with us all the time, in that armchair; but we felt the weight of it only when we felt a lack in it. Sometimes we will need to *bring the dictionary to the world*. That will happen when (say) we run across a small boat in Alaska of a sort we have never seen and wonder—what? What it is, or what it is called? In either case, *the learning is a question of aligning language and the world*.[9]

---

7. Ibid., 62. See also Marcia Cavell, *Becoming a Subject: Reflections in Philosophy and Psychoanalysis* (Oxford: Clarendon Press, 2006), 64–71, for an account of the ways in which this view corresponds to recent work in developmental psychology. In general, my emphasis on the emotional lives of human subjects and use of the term "anxiety" merit some explanation of the differences between my agenda and the field of psychology. In the first place, views of literature that emphasize the therapeutic possibilities of texts tend to produce rather one-sided characterizations of literature as redemptive: "When the recuperative and instructive powers of literature are emphasized, then both its powers to disrupt and its failures to arrive at conclusive doctrinal closure are underplayed." R. Eldridge, *Literature, Life, and Modernity*, 5. Psychology may—Marcia Cavell has argued that it does—aim at precisely the uncovering rather than erasing of signifying stresses of our lives in and with language, but it may also, perhaps especially in the twenty-first century's rush toward pharmacological solutions rather than talking cures, become "the guaranto[r] of the bourgeois dream," serving as a stabilizing force for conditions we should not want to continue. This criticism is leveled by, of all people, Jacques Lacan. Lacan, "The Moral Goals of Psychoanalysis," chap. 23 in *The Ethics of Psychoanalysis*, ed. Jacques-Alain Miller, trans. Dennis Porter, The Seminar of Jacques Lacan, bk. 7 (New York: W.W. Norton, 1992), 303.

8. For more on this view and its consequences in literary studies, see the section "Language, Grammar, and Forms of Life" in chapter 1.

9. Cavell, "Must We Mean What We Say?," in *Must We Mean What We Say?* 19–20; my emphasis.

I take Cavell's questions ("Now what did you do? Find out what 'umiak' means, or what an umiak is?") to emphasize that finding out what an umiak *is* is, in this case, precisely a matter of finding out what it means—how the word is used, what it refers to, who uses it. And that is information about the world; it tells us what an umiak is. The act of "bringing the world to the dictionary" or "bringing the dictionary to the world" in the umiak story describes the testing of the links between language and world in a form of life.

The idea that language aligns with the world is what allows me to propose lyric poetry as a paradigmatic place for sustained, original, and creative testing and contesting of those alignments, which may be called into question or radically disrupted at any time. The wager of this project—made through close readings of Hölderlin and Rilke—is that such testing and contesting offer and explore possible world orientations that neither force a coercive conformity to mere convention nor give up entirely on the possibility of shared attunement in those orientations. It should be apparent from this description of language use that nothing in this project will be construed as offering certain, unequivocal proofs; indeed the fundamental indeterminacy, ambiguity, and sensory complexity of poetry foreclose such proofs, and in doing so make study of the lyric ideally suited to model the kind of language use I describe as world-orienting.

I have selected Hölderlin and Rilke as the poets in whom to seek these orientations because while both poets share at least some of the historically specific forms of problems of finitude with contemporaneous figures and literary or other discourses, they are neither programmatically nor poetically subsumable to any of those discourses or literary movements.[10] Hölderlin and Rilke are among a relatively small group of poets who take up the *problems* addressed in dominant discourses of their epochs but then write *against* those discourses rather than adopting or following the solutions commonly provided by them. Thus Hölderlin writes between German idealism and romanticism, while Rilke investigates the problems raised by empiricism, aestheticism, and modernism without adhering to any of

---

10. Both also have a pedigree as "philosophical" poets, deriving in part from their interest in philosophers (in Hölderlin's case Kant, Plato, Spinoza, and the circle around Fichte in Jena; in Rilke's case Emerson and Nietzsche) but perhaps more from the "philosophical" treatments of their work by Wilhelm Dilthey, Martin Heidegger, Käthe Hamburger, Beda Allemann, Karl Jaspers, Theodor Adorno, and others. While these interpreters vary in the degree to which they take poetry as accomplishing something distinctive as opposed to taking it as an example of philosophical positions, their interest at least makes it plausible to look at Hölderlin and Rilke for poetic treatments of problems typically conceived of as philosophical—problems about which I will contend that much of lyric poetry has something to say by virtue of its language use and *not* by virtue, necessarily or exclusively, of its content. This unusually tight interweaving of philosophical and poetic traditions is one reason for turning to German poets in particular; the other is simply the contingent fact of my training as a Germanist, although I certainly hope that the view of language I use Cavell to develop here is not helpful only for reading German poetry.

them.[11] Where Hölderlin and Rilke are unusual (if not unique), then, is that they are not simply illustrating ideas already formed elsewhere, nor are they appealing to communities already in existence to vouchsafe the orientations their poems strive for. Rather, both seek to orient reader-subjects in language in order to *create* communities in which poetry has a central share in embodying what it means to be language-possessing subjects.

Since both Hölderlin and Rilke wrote in genres other than the lyric, and given my insistence on the (extraordinary) language of the lyric as paradigmatic, a brief reflection on generic specificity seems in order.[12] The probing intra- and intersubjective elements of language I show to be orienting do not appear only in poetry—surely novels, plays, dialogues, and even (sometimes) everyday conversations have moments of such testing and contesting; I hope so. But the lyric, by virtue of its brevity, its material qualities, and its generically sanctioned divergence from conventional speech, may do so more frequently, more directly, and more visibly than other types of language. Considering his own work, the poet Charles Bernstein addresses the seeming distance of poetry precisely from the kind of social and even political engagement I will draw out in Hölderlin and Rilke, and nonetheless insists on its possibilities: "I know it's almost a joke to speak of poetry and national affairs. Yet in *The Social Contract* Rousseau writes that since our conventions are provisional, the public may choose to reconvene in order to withdraw authority from those conventions that no longer serve our purposes. Poetry is one of the few areas where the right of reconvening is exercised."[13]

---

11. For more detailed connections between each poet and the discourses in which the interlocking problems of subjectivity, language, and finitude were taken up in their eras, see the section "Hölderlin's Context and His Cultural Critique" in chapter 2, and the section "Rilke's Epoch and Influences: Problems of Finitude around 1900" in chapter 4.

12. Particularly given that Wittgenstein, the initiator of the view of language I advance here, very seldom mentions literary works and does not take direct interest in questions that have shaped debates on philosophy and literature (Huemer, "Introduction," 3). This is one reason I turn to Cavell, who follows the problems of subjective orientation into a wide range of literary and cultural projects, rather than using Wittgenstein's view of language alone; the second reason is that, as the example of Richard Rorty will show in chapter 1, Wittgenstein's reading of language and skepticism has frequently been misunderstood as appealing to already existing conformist conventionality and as refuting skeptical questioning. Even within Wittgenstein and J. L. Austin, however, the distinction in which "ordinary" language takes part is not that between ordinary and literary, but between ordinary and philosophical language. Cavell makes this point apropos Austin as well when he rejects the literary/ordinary distinction that occasionally appears in literary studies treatments of Austin and opposes it to the philosophical/ordinary distinction: "If in literary studies people have fastened onto the rubric 'ordinary language' as something they take as opposed to literary language, that may or may not be unfortunate depending on what distinction they have in mind; but it must certainly be unfortunate to add to their problems by supposing this distinction either to be enforced or debarred by Austin's work" (Stanley Cavell, "Politics as Opposed to What?," *Critical Inquiry* 9, no. 1 [1982]: 164). Instead, Austin differentiates ordinary and philosophical, not to show them as "two modes or realms of discourse" (164) but rather to claim "that the philosophical is not a special mode of discourse at all; it has no interests of its own (as, say, science or religion or sports or trades have), or it ought not to have. So its departures from the ordinary are not into specialties but, let me say, into emptiness" (165).

13. Charles Bernstein, "Comedy and the Poetics of Political Form," in *A Poetics* (Cambridge, MA: Harvard University Press, 1992), 225.

The "reconvening" I show taking place in lyric orientations is not always directly or visibly social or communal, but understanding the view of language in which language and the world are learned together means that changing a reader's view of language likewise changes her views of and position in the world. I want to emphasize that this is not a weakly therapeutic process of making the reader somehow "feel better" after reading a poem—indeed, many of the poems I treat may have the opposite effect. A poem may show us for the first (or next or thousandth) time just how far amiss our forms of life have gone; it may show us just how inattentive to language we have been; it may remind us of just how much we fall short in our efforts to form free communities with others.

The Pain of Articulation in Paul Celan

In order to demonstrate the paradigmatically lyrical qualities I claim are orienting, and in order to show that lyric poetry addresses the ways our orientations can go awry en route to a reorientation, I turn to a reading of Paul Celan's poem "Die Silbe Schmerz" (The Syllable Pain). In doing so, I demonstrate the ways in which the formal-material as well as semantic structures of the lyric move beyond the binary of failed or successful links between language and world. Instead, Celan's language seeks to reshape those links or relations and thus also to change its readers. Including a discussion of this poem at the oustet also anticipates that the problems I will read in Hölderlin and Rilke—while I take pains to register their historically specific forms—are not unique to 1800 or 1900; they can and do go on through the twentieth and into the twenty-first century in and through poetic form.[14] Conversely, giving a detailed reading of Celan's poem shows the ways in which problems of the fit between language, mind, and world interact at a historically specific point, one in which all of language, subjectivity, and community—precisely the points of orientation toward which finitude strives—are called radically into question by the violence of history.

Die Silbe Schmerz[15]

Es gab sich Dir in die Hand:
ein Du, todlos,
an dem alles Ich zu sich kam. Es fuhren
wortfreie Stimmen rings, Leerformen, alles
ging in sie ein, gemischt   [5]

---

14. Nor is Celan the only poet in whom these issues are continued; other candidates would be Bertolt Brecht (for all the pathos of Hölderlin and Rilke is anathema to him), Ingeborg Bachmann, and Durs Grünbein.

15. Paul Celan, *Die Gedichte: Kommentierte Gesamtausgabe*, ed. Barbara Wiedemann (Frankfurt a.M.: Suhrkamp, 2003), 159–60.

und entmischt
und wieder
gemischt.

Und Zahlen waren
mitverwoben in das [10]
Unzählbare. Eins und Tausend und was
davor und dahinter
größer war als es selbst, kleiner, aus-
gereift und
rück- und fort- [15]
verwandelt in
keimendes Niemals.

Vergessenes griff
nach Zu-Vergessendem, Erdteile, Herzteile
schwammen, [20]
sanken und schwammen. Kolumbus,
die Zeit-
lose im Aug, die Mutter-
Blume,
mordete Masten und Segel. Alles fuhr aus, [25]
frei,
entdeckerisch,
blühte die Windrose ab, blätterte
ab, ein Weltmeer
blühte zuhauf und zutag, im Schwarzlicht [30]
der Wildsteuerstriche. In Särgen,
Urnen, Kanopen
erwachten die Kindlein
Jaspis, Achat, Amethyst—Völker,
Stämme und Sippen, ein blindes [35]

E s   s e i

knüpfte sich in
die schlangenköpfigen Frei-
Taue—: ein
Knoten [40]
(und Wider- und Gegen- und Aber- und Zwillings- und Tau-
sendknoten), an dem
die fastnachtsäugige Brut
der Mardersterne im Abgrund

buch-, buch-, buch- [45]
stabierte, stabierte.

The Syllable Pain[16]

It gave itself into Your hand:
a You, deathless,
at which all of I came to itself. Wordfree
voices drove around, empty forms, everything
entered them, mixed [5]
and unmixed
and mixed
again.

And numbers too
were woven into the [10]
[innumerable]. One and a thousand and what
before and after
was larger than itself, smaller, ripe-
ned and
back- and out- [15]
transformed into
germinating Never.

[Forgotten things
grasped at things to be forgotten], continents, heartinents,
swam, [20]
sank and swam. Columbus,
fall
crocus in his sight, the mother-
flower,
murdered masts and sails. Everything left port [25]

free,
[exploratory],
the windrose flowerd and faded [shed
its leaves], and [an ocean]
bloomed a-heap and a-day, in the blacklight [30]

---

16. Paul Celan, *Selections*, ed. Pierre Joris (Berkeley: University of California Press, 2005), 91–92; modifications to translation in brackets. I have also consulted the translation by Nikolai Popov and Heather McHugh in Paul Celan, *Glottal Stop: 101 Poems* (Hanover, NH: University Press of New England, 2000), 13–14. They translate the title as "Pain, the syllable" (13).

of wild-lubber lines. In coffins,
urns, canopic jars
the little children
awoke: Jasper, Agate, Amethyst—peoples,
tribes and clans, a blind   [35]

L e t   t h e r e   b e

knotted itself in-
to the serpentheaded free-
ropes—: a
knot   [40]
(and counter- and contra- and yet- and twin- and thou-
sandknot), which
the [carnival-eyed] brood
of martenstars in the abyss
spell-, spell-, spelled   [45]
out, out.

In the face of Paul Celan's fragmented language, the claim that lyric poetry performs projects of orientation seems almost perverse: the poem is *dis*orienting. But I argue that this disorientation offers itself as a mode of response to the inscription of history in language and language in history in the wake of the traumas of the twenty-first century, a response that, moreover, foregrounds language both in its content and as a formal-material event. In doing so, it offers a point of entry into Celan's engagement with problems of finitude. After Auschwitz, the problem of the relations between language, mind, and world are radicalized to the problem of how—given what has happened—it is possible to speak at all. In particular, poetry after Auschwitz raises the problem of how a poet can seek—as Celan does—any cohesion of self, any communication with an other, and any universal appeal for poetry without embarking on precisely the totalizing paths that led to the Shoah.[17] That is, how can poetry be poetry and remain honest to the traumas of individual and historical experience?[18]

Crucially, this problem is a dual-directional one: first, the danger emerges that language is unable to hold up under the strain of representing the violence of history. This danger is all too visible in the poem, as it threatens to fall apart into a progression

---

17. I work out Celan's poetological response to this problem in my conclusion; to anticipate very briefly what I discuss there, Celan develops a poetics of individual particularity that, precisely by *way* of its inscription in history and its fragility, is free to seek a free communicative space with an addressee or "you."

18. Of course, the discovery that the world is a hostile or potentially unfit place occurs in both Hölderlin and Rilke as well, along with the problem of how to speak as a finite, particular subject. The greatest historical difference between the three poets is the treatment of language itself in response to these problems.

of stuttering or stammering sounds and letters (or syllables), empty of sense. But the poem also uses the theme of navigation (in the figure of Christopher Columbus) to warn against the concealment of rupture and trauma in smooth narrative trajectories: by calling (directed, controlled, continuous) navigation into question (both formally and thematically), the poem offers an orientation in and to language that builds up its own fragile coherence and remains vulnerable to—even invites—fragmentation and dissolution. "Die Silbe Schmerz" thus not only describes or depicts but undergoes the fragility of language and world after Auschwitz. Because we, as readers, are obliged to undergo the same process of searching for sense in a poetic world of fragmentation and disorientation, our orientation to the world is, I argue, changed by the realization that language can do just *this*, and the concomitant recognition of what our history has done such that this kind of language becomes necessary.

The title "Die Silbe Schmerz" foregrounds both the semantic and the material components of its own language: *Schmerz* (pain) is a word with a meaning, but it is also a (single) syllable, a unit of sound that need not have any semantic content. And the fragmentations and combinations performed by syllabification form several of the central events of the poem. Celan uses single root words with changing prefixes, often with opposite meanings (e.g., *gemischt / und entmischt / und wieder / gemischt*, 5–8; *rück- und fort- / verwandelt*," 15–16; and, most strikingly, *Wider- und Gegen- und Aber- und Zwillings- und Tau- / sendknoten*, 41–42). Similarly, he deploys single verbs with different prepositions, some idiomatic in German and others unfamiliar: thus *abblühen* (to fade or to finish blooming) becomes *blühte zuhauf and zutag* (30), translated by Joris as "a-heap and a-day"; *zuhauf* means "in great numbers" or even "galore"; *zutage bringen* is "to bring something to light or unearth it." Celan also emphasizes individual syllables by interrupting a string of two-syllable words (*Wider-, Gegen-, Aber-, Zwillings-*/"counter-," "contra-," "yet-," "twin-," 41–42) with a further two-syllable word, *Tausend* (thousand), broken after its first syllable. By blurring the distinction between word and syllable, morpheme and phoneme, Celan foregrounds their potential dislocation in what will turn out to be an investigation of the possibilities or impossibilities of language in history, after *this* particular history.

"Die Silbe Schmerz" foregrounds the material character of its language in several other ways, among them frequent transformations of one part of speech into another. Verbs used as participial adjectives are common in standard German, but several instances of adjectives or adverbs used as nouns are more unusual (although still grammatically correct) and locate the agents of the poem in abstractions that contrast sharply with the concrete treatment of syllables described above (e.g., *das / Unzählbare*, "the innumerable," 10–11; *keimendes Niemals*, "germinating Never," 17; *Vergessenes* and *Zu-Vergessendem*, "forgotten things" and "things to be forgotten," 18–19). Moreover, the final sentence of the poem has a quotation as its subject:

ein blindes

E s s e i

knüpfte sich in
die schlangenköpfigen Frei-
Taue—:

The line *E s s e i* is set off by an empty line above and below and is in spaced letters (*Sperrdruck*), marking it as a quotation that recalls the biblical word of creation,[19] a resigned "So be it," an imploring "Let it be so that . . ." or "May it be . . . ," or even a tentative "Unless . . ." (*Es sei denn . . .*). This quotation (creation, command, admission, or condition) knots itself into ropes (*knüpfte sich*, 37), which are then described (or perhaps the action is redescribed) as the proliferation of knots discussed above. Finally, these words (or ropes or knots) are, in a continuation of the poem's syllabification techniques, "spelled / out" (45–46) by a (fictional) constellation, *die Mardersterne* (the martenstars), completing the poem's progress from amorphous *wortfreie Stimmen* (word-free voices, 4) to articulated letters, whose fragmentation into letters or book/staves (*buch-, buch-, buch- / stabierte, stabierte,* 45–46[20]) emphasizes their material writtenness.[21] The poem's attention to language, then, both threatens its communicative coherence and precludes any totalizing sense-making by displaying its own fragility and constructedness on the way to articulation.

The poem thus insists on the telling of history in language: it insists on words as a written or even spelled-out (*buch- / stabierte*, 45–46) formula for what is, what has been, or what will be; this insistence is underscored by the wide-spaced print format, since it emphasizes individual letters. The violence of this inscription appears most directly in a specific world-historical figure, Christopher Columbus, whose feats of navigation initiated centuries of genocide.[22] The navigation theme

---

19. Both Joris and Popov and McHugh translate the quotation as "Let there be," but the German formula from Genesis 1 is *Es werde*, not *Es sei*.

20. Joris translates the lines as "spell-, spell-, spelled / out, out" (45–46). Unfortunately, the words for "letter" and "to spell" are entirely different in English (in contrast to the German *Buchstabe* and *buchstabieren*), and neither has the resonance of "book" (*Buch*).

21. In a reading of the poem as taking part in the legacy of poetic treatments of Columbus, Cecile Cazort Zorach and Charlotte Melin describe this progress toward articulated language as follows: "Celan's poem opens with images of language in a state of primordial fluidity, then advances through a delimiting process of creation to culminate in the stammering articulation of syllables in the penultimate line" (Cecile Cazort Zorach and Charlotte Melin, "The Columbian Legacy in Postwar German Poetry," *German Quarterly* 65, no. 3/4 [1992]: 286).

22. Zorach and Melin read Columbus in "Die Silbe Schmerz" as a figure of "the death-bringing impulses of modern history, for which Columbus (implicitly linked to the diaspora by the events of the Inquisition that coincided with his first voyage) becomes the central icon " (Zorach and Melin, "Columbian Legacy," 288). They highlight that Columbus's departure, in addition to the violence it initiated in the Americas, was concurrent with the expulsion of Spain's Jews (287).

occurs most directly in the images and descriptions surrounding Columbus (from the third strophe on). But it appears subtly from the poem's outset, particularly in the numerous prepositions and prefixes of direction or location: *in* (in, 1, 5, 10, 30, 31, 37), *zu* (to, 3), *davor und dahinter* (before and behind, 12), *rück- und fort-* (back- and forth-, 15), *nach* (after, 19), *aus* (out of, 25), *ab* (from or away, 28, 29, as in "to fade away"), *Gegen-* (against or contra, 41), and *an* (on, 42). Furthermore, the poem's most prominent verbs, including *fahren* (to drive, travel, or go, 4, 35), *kommen* (to come, 3), *gehen* (to go, 5), *schwimmen* (to swim, 21, 22), and *sinken* (to sink, 21), refer to travel, motion, and exploration, whether failed or successful. The figure of Columbus is ambivalent at best: in addition to being the initiator of the European colonial genocide in the Western Hemisphere, he was in fact incorrect in his navigation; many of the prefixes and prepositions point in two directions, rendering unequivocal orientation impossible; masts and sails are murdered by Columbus himself (21–25); the compass rose falls to pieces (28–29); the helmsman or navigator appears to operate at random, producing *Wildsteuerstriche* (wild-lubber-lines, 31); the ropes knot themselves into snakes;[23] the stars are not in the sky but in the abyss (44), suggesting that the journey undertaken here is distorted, everted, out of joint.

This ambivalence returns to the calling into question of the quest to exceed finitude that I read as Celan's temporally and historically specific form of engagement with problems of orientation within that finitude. I have argued that the poem itself offers a fragmentary and vulnerable but nonetheless communicative language in which it registers the wounds and lacks of individual as well as historical experience and memory. In the epilogue, I show that this process of language—first calling attention to its disorienting qualities and then using them to reorient the reader—can be understood with reference to several central elements of Celan's poetology. Here, I offer the reciprocal indexing of language and experience as itself a mode of orientation between mind and world, individual and others; that is, as a preliminary example of what I am calling orientation in, with, and to language and the world as paradigmatically played out in lyric poetry.

In the first chapter, I argue for skepticism as an appropriate point of entry into the general anthropological problems of finitude I read as paradigmatically treated by lyric poetry. The second and fourth chapters locate Hölderlin and Rilke in the respective discourses engaged with the struggle over finitude in their eras, thus framing those problems in temporally specific ways, before showing how both poets write against the solutions proposed by those discourses, giving individually specific responses to the problems of finitude identified by their contemporaries. The third and fifth chapters then draw on the projects and goals for poetry delineated

---

23. "The 'Freitaue'... appear 'schlangenköpfig,' a term that echoes the serpentine image of evil and victimization from Celan's 'Todesfuge'" (Zorach and Melin, "Columbian Legacy," 289).

in response to the problems of finitude to show how such projects and the struggles they express are taken up in poetic form. The volume concludes by returning to Celan, to sketch the difficulties Celan identifies for poetic production and to explain how those difficulties may be read as further instantiations of the problems of orientation within finitude in a new historical horizon, demonstrating that efforts at acknowledgment and the inhabitation of finite subjectivity can and do go on through the twentieth century.

1

SKEPTICISM AND THE STRUGGLE OVER FINITUDE

Stanley Cavell

To show in detail how lyric poetry has the capacity to orient finite human subjects within the horizon of modern alienation, this chapter offers a fuller account of that finitude and responses to it as worked out by Stanley Cavell. Giving this account thus presents the most general form of the problems that poetry, in my reading, can address in unique and exemplary ways by linking language, finitude, and community. It is these problems that Hölderlin and Rilke pick up in their own historically and individually specific discourses, and that I track through their poetry as demonstrating the orienting capacities of lyric language. This chapter argues for skepticism as an appropriate point of entry into the general anthropological problems of finitude I read as paradigmatically treated by lyric poetry. I make this case by raising counterintuitions to Cavell and then developing his and my own responses to them.

Briefly put, philosophical skepticism is one particularly virulent form of a more general epistemic rationalism (often—unfairly—associated with the European Enlightenment). By the twenty-first century, this rationalism ramifies into a scientism that divides the world into an all-or-nothing of certain (rational) knowledge and total uncertainty or relativism. Cavell is certainly not the first to challenge dominant models of rationalism, or the first to do so by an appeal to language,[1] just as Hölderlin and Rilke are hardly the only poets who seek links between mind and world in language. But Cavell *is* unique in combining an account of language's challenge to narrow rationalism (and all that challenge entails) with an account of the necessity (and necessary failure) of the yearning for certainty of which assorted rationalisms (epistemology, behaviorism, scientism[2]) are the most intellectually sanctioned expressions. Thus, although the drive for certainty is both impossible and (often) dangerous, that drive and its failure are essential to human subjectivity's mode of inhabiting its own constitutive finitude.

I present Cavell's discussions of skepticism, in its two paradigmatic forms of skepticism about other minds and skepticism about the (existence of) the external world, as the modern, secular appearances of the struggle against human finitude that poetic language seeks to inhabit.[3] I demonstrate that and why these

---

1. Indeed, much of Cavell's work is the writing of his own genealogy in this tradition: "Cavell cites less than two dozen authors over and again throughout his writing: those who for him constitute an alive part of the accepted British and American tradition—Plato, Descartes, Hume, Mill, Wittgenstein, and J. L. Austin; a major part of the Continental tradition—Kant, Hegel, Rousseau, Luther, Kierkegaard, Marx, Nietzsche, Freud and Heidegger . . . ; a claimed American tradition—Thoreau and Emerson; Blake and Wordsworth; Beckett, here by virtue of the long essay on *Endgame*; and Shakespeare, especially *King Lear* and *Othello*, tragedies which for Cavell play out essential features of the philosophical problems most on his mind. (The absence of women from this list is a measure of the failure of these traditions and an indicator of what we cannot rely on them for.)" Charles Bernstein, "Reading Cavell Reading Wittgenstein," *boundary 2* 9, no. 2 (Winter 1981): 297. In the German context, one might add Johann Gottfried Herder and Johann Georg Hamann.

2. Scientism here is understood as "the belief that only knowledge obtained from scientific research is valid, and that notions or beliefs deriving from other sources, such as religion, should be discounted; extreme or excessive faith in science or scientists. Also: the view that the methodology used in the natural and physical sciences can be applied to other disciplines, such as philosophy and the social sciences" (*Oxford English Dictionary*, online ed., s.v. "scientism," http://www.oed.com/view/Entry/172696?redirectedFrom=scientism#eid). I hope the use of scient*ism* makes clear that I do not take any of my or Cavell's arguments for or against skepticism to be attacks on *science* as it is currently carried out and where practices of doubt and seeking certainty are and should be in place. (Although I would also reflect that the frustrations of lab work might deter scientists more than anyone from "excessive faith in science or scientists.")

3. The terms "modern" and "secular," of course, link Cavell to scholarly narratives of modernity as secularization, as the failure of cultural institutions to sustain conviction, and/or as entailing increasing doubt and contingency familiar from (although of course not identical in) Max Weber, Niklaus Luhmann, Charles Taylor, Reinhart Koselleck, and others. When I describe skepticism (both in the sense of professional skepticism and in the sense of radical contingency) as the modern, secular appearance of a fundamental anthropological habitus, I am not arguing for a particular beginning point or narrative of modernity defined by philosophy; indeed, as Cavell himself points out in his readings of Shakespeare, precisely the problems he identifies as those of skepticism appear earlier than their epistemological articulation: "Skepticism as manifested in Descartes's *Meditations* is already in full existence in Shakespeare, from the time of the great tragedies in the first years of the seventeenth century, in the generation preceding that of Descartes" (Stanley Cavell, *Disowning Knowledge in Seven Plays of Shakespeare*, updated ed. [Cambridge: Cambridge University Press, 2003], 3). To this I would add that skeptical questioning is not always fully secular (as becomes evident in Hölderlin), and that because I contend that striving against finitude toward certainty is a fundamental anthropological behavior, prior to philosophical epistemology it will be found in other places, e.g., perhaps the problem of the discernment of spirits in religious visions or the topos of vanitas (the belonging of human subjects—or better, souls—to another world) or debates surrounding election/salvation.

questions cannot be answered or closed once and for all while showing how the view of language I use Cavell to develop in the chapter's final section offers new possibilities for reading lyric poetry and for understanding the lyric as an exit from the self-incurred constraints of the all-or-nothing of certainty and relativism.

Professional Skepticism and Human Finitude

Given that Cavell opens his most detailed considerations of skepticism (in *The Claim of Reason*[4]) by way of highly technical presentations of epistemological argumentation in Anglo-American philosophy, skepticism seems, on the face of it, too technical, too narrow, and too academic to be any kind of representation of a fundamental subjective habitus. Richard Rorty, in a review sympathetic to many of Cavell's aims, raises this question by way of Cavell's (in his view insufficiently explained) connection between "professional" skepticism and the "sense of the contingency of everything" that Cavell reads in Kant and romanticism (among other places).[5] Rorty agrees with Cavell on the centrality of Wittgenstein but would be perfectly happy to "leave Ayer and Price [the traditional epistemologists Cavell discusses in *The Claim of Reason*] in the care of Austin and Ryle [their challengers] and hasten on to the serious thinkers across the water," by whom he means Kant, Wittgenstein, and Heidegger.[6]

Because this stance has an innate plausibility (as Cavell puts it, how *can* the virulent problems of misunderstanding or misreading others be related to "that dreary discussion of invented surfaces of things and possible or impossible dreams or hallucinations that passes for philosophical investigation of our world"?[7]), it is worth looking at Rorty's alternative to see how a position that simply abandons skepticism and gets on with the business of coping with "the contingency of everything" works. Rorty shares with Cavell the view that philosophy as a cultural practice whose goal is the uncovering of natures or essences is doomed to failure, but, unlike Cavell, he therefore feels that philosophy of this sort should take its place alongside other cultural practices that subsequent cultural developments have rendered outdated or undesirable.[8] In a pragmatist acceptance of the "contingency of everything," he "defends the standard pragmatist claim that criteria for preferring some

---

4. Stanley Cavell, *The Claim of Reason: Wittgenstein, Skepticism, Morality, and Tragedy*, new ed. (Oxford: Oxford University Press, 1999).
5. Richard Rorty, "Cavell on Skepticism," in *Contending with Stanley Cavell*, ed. Russell B. Goodman (Oxford: Oxford University Press, 2005), 16. (The essay was originally a review of *The Claim of Reason* published in *Review of Metaphysics* and was then reprinted in *Consequences of Pragmatism* in 1985.)
6. Rorty, "Cavell on Skepticism," 15.
7. Stanley Cavell, "Responses," in Goodman, *Contending with Stanley Cavell*, 159.
8. See Richard Eldridge, "Philosophy and the Achievement of Community: Rorty, Cavell, and Criticism," *Metaphilosophy* 14, no. 2 (April 1983): 111–12.

practices to others can be found within, and only within, the history of culture."[9] On his account, abandoning the search for knowledge of essences leaves the level of cultural practices untouched—one can choose from among practices without much difficulty.

Again, this view is appealing, especially given that most of us most of the time do seem to choose between cultural practices while wearing the sense of our contingency lightly (this is what Rorty means when he says that if traditional philosophy is put in its place, relativism as a problem dissolves).[10] But Rorty's assumption that cultures simply develop better and better criteria for choosing cultural practices all the time ignores the "cases (surely there must be cases) in which later practices are not to be preferred to earlier ones,"[11] or situations in which cultural conflict "*cannot* be resolved simply by appealing to existing social practices," precisely because "the heart of the controversy is the genuine and serious conflict of competing social practices."[12] And in a second (related) problem for Rorty's view, he never asks why traditional philosophizing would arise in the first place, as, for example, in the case of skepticism, "how [traditional epistemology's] preoccupations could ever have seemed to express our fundamental concerns about our relation to the world and I and others in it, which . . . is to ask how modern skepticism (in Descartes and Hume and Kant) can (have) come to seem the fundamental question of philosophy."[13] The force of this question increases in light of responses to skepticism that

---

9. Ibid., 114.
10. "The reason relativism is talked about so much among traditional Platonic and Kantian philosophers is that they think being relativistic about philosophical theories—attempts to ground first-level theories—leads to being relativistic about the first-level theories themselves. If anyone really believed that the worth of a theory depends upon the worth of its philosophical grounding, then indeed they would be dubious about physics, or democracy, until relativism in respect to philosophical theories had been overcome. Fortunately, almost nobody believes anything of the sort" (Rorty, *Philosophy and the Mirror of Nature*, 3, cited in R. Eldridge, "Rorty, Cavell, and Criticism," 112).
11. R. Eldridge, "Rorty, Cavell, and Criticism," 114.
12. Richard J. Bernstein, "Philosophy in the Conversation of Mankind," *Review of Metaphysics* 33, no. 4 (June 1980): 769.
13. Cavell, "Responses," 159. Note that here Cavell has shifted away from the Anglo-American philosophy of the 1950s and 1960s, perhaps as part of a sense that while the underlying conviction of this type of epistemology remains active, the particular appearances of it in Ayer and Price have lost their weight, making some of the introductory material to *The Claim of Reason* more historically specific than it need be. Charles Bernstein reflects that "*The Claim of Reason*, in the course of its reading of the *Investigations*, also makes a full-scale case in opposition to the assumptions of the predominant tendency in professional philosophy in England and North American, that is, analytic philosophy. On this account, it may seem to those already sympathetic to Cavell's position that he spends an inordinate amount of time refuting what is obviously wrong from the first. I suspect Cavell, in part, may share that view, and it may partly explain why this work, a large section of which was written almost twenty years ago, has taken so long to come out. Cavell notes in his preface that he would not now attempt what I assume to be this aspect of the project" (C. Bernstein, "Reading Cavell Reading Wittgenstein," 301). This shift does *not* mean what Rorty thinks it should—namely, that we should just get on with Wittgenstein as telling us to attend to nonphilosophical problems—because Rorty misreads "the Wittgenstein of the *Investigations* insofar as he thinks that Wittgenstein there urges us to stop thinking about essences and natures altogether, as though we could stop" (R. Eldridge, "Rorty, Cavell, and Criticism," 124).

refer to Kant in particular and philosophy in general as the initiators of cultural and/or individual crises.[14]

Perhaps the central strategy of Cavell's philosophizing is to ask this question—why *would*, how *could* anyone say such a thing or think it was interesting?—nonrhetorically. Because Rorty hears the question as a dismissal, he overlooks or elides the possibility that traditional philosophizing "appears on the historical scene for the sake of help with practical problems."[15] And the absence of—not even a case against or disagreement with—this view in Rorty is the reason he cannot see a connection between narrow skepticism and the problems of finitude, between "professional philosophy" and "the education of grown-ups." (In fairness to Rorty, much of professional philosophy—at least at the time in which he and Cavell are writing—not only forgets this connection but works to sever it; uncovering and tracing back this forgetting and the reasons for it occupy much of Cavell's attention for large swathes of his career.[16])

Cavell's answer to the question of why professional epistemology or narrowly skeptical questioning gets started is that skepticism is "a place, perhaps the central secular place, in which the human wish to deny the condition of human existence is expressed."[17] That is, philosophical skepticism is a particularly virulent and intellectually reflective form of a fundamental anthropological habitus. The "condition of human existence" is the one of finitude I described in the introduction; what skepticism takes issue with is the commonsense view that that finitude is (or could be) overcome by having *successful* knowledge about others or about the external world, if we could only get that knowledge to be good enough or really settle the conditions for having it.[18]

---

14. The most famous such response in the German context is of course the so-called Kant crisis of Heinrich von Kleist, expressed in a letter to his fiancée that discusses the impossibility of unfiltered access to the external world: "If everyone saw the world through green glasses, they would be forced to judge that everything they saw was green, and could never be sure whether their eyes saw things as they really are, or did not add something of their own to what they saw. And so it is with our intellect. We can never be certain that what we call Truth is really Truth, or whether it does not merely appear so to us. If the latter, then the Truth that we acquire here is not Truth" (Kleist to Wilhelmine von Zenge, 22 March 1801, in *An Abyss Deep Enough: Letters of Heinrich von Kleist with a Selection of Essays and Anecdotes*, ed. and trans. Philip B. Miller [New York: Dutton, 1982], 95).

15. R. Eldridge, "Rorty, Cavell, and Criticism," 115.

16. Furthermore, Cavell's undoing of this self-forgetfulness may be responsible for the most common misreading of his work—namely, that he seeks to *refute* skepticism. For a summary of this misinterpretation and a direct account of what it is Cavell does instead—i.e., acknowledge the *truth* of skepticism—see Richard Eldridge, "'A Continuing Task': Cavell and Skepticism," in *The Persistence of Romanticism: Essays in Philosophy and Literature* (Cambridge: Cambridge University Press, 2001), esp. 189–93.

17. Stanley Cavell, *In Quest of the Ordinary: Lines of Skepticism and Romanticism* (Chicago: University of Chicago Press, 1988), 5.

18. Hence the collapse into the all-or-nothing of certain knowledge vs. relativism that I described in the introduction, and the problem of relativism for philosophy that Rorty points out. Cavell's insight is that, despite its problematic search for knowledge, skepticism gets something right about our relations to the world: "What is valuable in skepticism is its refusal to accept the common sense view of the nature of our grip on the world—a view which regards that grip as most fundamentally cognitive, regarding the existence of material objects (for example) as something which we know for certain or in which we believe" (Stephen Mulhall, "Wittgenstein and Heidegger: Orientations to the Ordinary," *European Journal of Philosophy* 2, no. 2 [1994]: 154).

Skepticism attacks the success of that knowledge by pointing out that the grounds given for it are insufficient, but accepts the idea of cognitive *knowledge* as the ideal mode of relation to others and to the world. In doing so, the skeptic "shares in the mistake of the commonsense philosopher; but his attack upon the latter is essential in the sense that a correct understanding of our relationship to the world requires that we dispense with a commonsense understanding of that relationship."[19] Furthermore, the skeptic is at least honest, in Cavell's view, about her dissatisfaction with human finitude, and thus expresses a wish to overcome that finitude that neither traditional philosophy nor commonsense belief can put to rest.[20] Cavell calls the combination of this honesty with the awareness that, as a matter of knowledge, our relations outside finitude fail, "the truth of skepticism." But "to acknowledge the truth of skepticism is not the same as admitting that skepticism is true, for this would constitute a further escape into a new inverted metaphysics of certainty, namely relativism."[21] Being certainly uncertain would be a position as stable as that of commonsense belief; as Cavell shows in detail in his readings of tragedy, the skeptical position opens the self-protective possibility of denying any relation to the world or to others because our knowledge of them is imperfect.[22]

It is therefore unsurprising that the skeptic, faced with the uncertainty of finitude, persistently shifts back to problems of knowledge: "The real problem with skepticism, according to Cavell, is that we attempt to convert the way we inhabit the human condition into a theoretical problem and this prevents an acknowledgment of the limitedness of the human glimpsed in skepticism."[23] And one may, like Rorty, feel that Ayers and Price offer only a thin sense of this limitedness; what Cavell's attention to skepticism shows is that the all-or-nothing of knowledge as world-relation that the skeptic advances is a specialized form of a more general cultural scientism: "Scientism is the demon that haunts analytic philosophy—the

---

19. Mulhall, "Wittgenstein and Heidegger," 156.
20. Thus, for Cavell, "philosophy is best regarded as defined not by the knowledge of natures which people have obtained, but rather by the wish for such knowledge, expressed not only in the claiming of it, but also in the proposing of a method for acquiring it. As we try to realize this wish, we had better think hard about the fact that this wish has persisted unsatisfied throughout our history" (R. Eldridge, "Rorty, Cavell, and Criticism," 119).
21. Simon Critchley, "Cavell's 'Romanticism' and Cavell's Romanticism," in Goodman, *Contending with Stanley Cavell*, 48.
22. The denial and avoidance of others, especially, is the form of skepticism Cavell sees as taking place in Shakespeare's tragedies: to give the most obvious examples, Othello and King Lear, unable to withstand or acknowledge the love of Desdemona and Cordelia, respectively, demand *knowledge* or proof—of love, of innocence—as a way of avoiding the demands of what Cavell calls *acknowledging* others. See Cavell, *Disowning Knowledge*, chaps. 2 and 3. I discuss the *King Lear* essay in some detail in my reading of Rilke's novel *The Notebooks of Malte Laurids Brigge* in the section "Crisis: *The Notebooks of Malte Laurids Brigge*" in chapter 4.
23. Critchley, "Cavell's 'Romanticism,'" 48. Critchley points out that "the theoreticism of skepticism is only a problem for modern, epistemological skepticism and the same claim cannot simply be made for ancient skepticism, which was not merely theoretical doubt about the truth of certain metaphysical theses but a practical doubt about the whole of one's life, a full existential *epoche*. In this light, Cavell's work might be viewed as a tacit recovery of the ethos of ancient skepticism" (48–49).

belief of science that its empirical method of prediction and control of phenomena provides the only legitimate claim to knowledge and certainty."[24] This view opens the (scientific/cognitive) knowledge-or-nothing binary I raised at the outset; Cavell enables us to see the intellectualizing of human finitude as an attempt to overcome that finitude and thus to deny the human condition. In what follows I turn to his treatments of external world and other minds skepticism to show how such intellectualizing takes place, what it forecloses, and how *acknowledging* that finitude can shift our relations to language, others, and the world. Once this shift has taken place, lyric poetry can be understood as a paradigmatic place for acknowledgments of finitude that recognize the temptation and impossibility of certain knowledge without subsiding into irrationalism or unreason.

From Knowledge to Acknowledgment

Skepticism's truth, along with its falsifying intellectualization of that truth, appears perhaps most directly in Cavell's treatment of other minds skepticism, and particularly in the essay "Knowing and Acknowledging,"[25] where Cavell lays out in detail a case for the failure of ordinary language philosophy to refute the skeptical claim that two persons cannot have "the same pain."[26] Again, this is the kind of academic, arcane example to which Rorty objects; again, Cavell traces the philosophical problem back to a problematic way of inhabiting an accurately identified condition, that of our separateness from but obligation to others.[27] In response to the claim that two people cannot have "the same pain," Cavell agrees with the skeptic's admission that we have ways of describing pain ("e.g. throbbing, dull, sharp, searing, flashing")

---

24. C. Bernstein, "Reading Cavell Reading Wittgenstein," 301. Bernstein conects this point to Habermas's distinction between kinds of knowledge in *Knowledge and Human Interest*, where Habermas "usefully contrasts two forms of knowledge—the dialogic or hermeneutic and the monologic or scientific. He differentiates the two modes by their interest component, pointing to prediction and control as the knowledge-constitutive interest of the scientific mode" (Bernstein, 300). Cavell, instead of distinguishing kinds of knowledge, distinguishes between knowledge and *acknowledgment*, as I discuss below.

25. Stanley Cavell, "Knowing and Acknowledging," in *Must We Mean What We Say? A Book of Essays*, updated ed. (Cambridge: Cambridge University Press, 2002), 238–66.

26. Cavell's other example in the essay is whether two people can see the "same" color; although this question has less immediate moral implications, it nonetheless raises the same questions of privacy and separation along the lines of an interrogation of what "sameness" means here. See Cavell, "Knowing and Acknowledging," 242–45.

27. In "Cavell on Skepticism," Rorty discusses only the arguments about external world skepticism; in fact the connection between professional philosophical questioning and lived experience is stronger in the case of skepticism about other minds, because while people in general do not walk around wondering if their tomatoes are hollow, we *do*, in everyday life, take the position that we cannot without evidence trust the actions and intentions of others, much less know how their minds exist: "There is no everyday alternative to skepticism concerning other minds. . . . I already know everything skepticism concludes, that my ignorance of the existence of others is not the fate of my natural condition as a human knower, but my way of inhabiting that condition; that I cannot close my eyes to my doubts of others and to their doubts and denials of me, that my relations with others are restricted, that I cannot trust them blindly. . . . I live my skepticism" (Cavell, *Claim of Reason*, 432).

and "so you can say, if you like, that if one pain gets identified by these criteria with the same results as another (same place, same degree, same kind) then it is the same pain. But it also seems to me not *quite* right, or these criteria of identity are not quite enough, to make intelligible saying 'the same.'"[28] That is, it is the skeptic and *not* his challenger (often an ordinary language philosopher) who seems to be more in touch with when and how we use the phrase "the same" to describe pain.

The skeptic is justified in persisting in his language because he has gotten hold of something fundamental that his challenger ignores about the pain of others: "[The skeptic] begins with a full appreciation of the decisively significant facts that I may be suffering when no one else is, and no one (else) may know (or care?); and that others may be suffering and I not know, which is equally appalling";[29] furthermore: "The fundamental importance of someone's having pain is *that* he has it; and the nature of that importance—namely, that he is suffering, that he requires *attention*—is what makes it important to know where the pain is, and how severe and what kind it is."[30] Pain, as a behavior, seems to be expressive of something, and the skeptic, in asking what kind of pain it is, recognizes that the significant fact is that what is being expressed demands to be addressed.[31]

In response to this demand, however, the skeptic shifts from questions of acknowledgment (pain needs to be acknowledged) to questions of knowledge: "But then something happens, and instead of pursuing the significance of these facts, [the skeptic] is enmeshed—so it may seem—in questions of whether we can have the same suffering, one another's suffering."[32] And in arguing with the skeptic about whether or not we can have the same pain, the antiskeptic permits the skeptic's shift to the idea "that the problem of knowledge about other minds is the problem of certainty. At the same time, he neglects the fundamental insight of the skeptic by trying single-mindedly to prove its non-existence—the insight, as I wish to put it, that *certainty is not enough*."[33] To recapitulate, the skeptic identifies something crucial about our relation to others by way of the question of pain ("there *are* special problems about our knowledge of another; *exactly the problems the skeptic sees*"[34]); he then converts those problems to the realm of knowledge and certainty; the antiskeptic, in attempting to refute the skeptic, accepts this shift and thus shares in the skeptic's conversion of "metaphysical finitude" to an "intellectual lack."[35]

---

28. Cavell, "Knowing and Acknowledging," 245.
29. Ibid., 247.
30. Ibid., 245.
31. "What [the skeptic] wants to know—namely, what it is we go on in the idea that behavior is expressive—is the right thing to want to know" (Cavell, "Knowing and Acknowledging," 262); thus, "the skeptic's problem, unlike the anti-skeptic's, is directed to what I spoke of earlier as our natural interest in the occurrence of pain, namely, *that* a given man has it" (248).
32. Cavell, "Knowing and Acknowledging," 247.
33. Ibid., 258; emphasis in original.
34. Ibid.
35. Ibid., 263.

Cavell, conversely, accepts the problems the skeptic raises about knowing others, but he rejects the intellectualizing of those problems as problems of certainty. He returns to the idea that pain makes a claim or demand on its observers, and turns (unusually for discussions of other minds) to a declaration of knowledge addressed to another person: what do I mean when I say, "I know *you* are in pain"?[36] Following the strategies of ordinary language philosophy, he explains that this remark is not an expression of certainty (it doesn't mean "I checked—you really are in pain": what could I possibly check to confirm this?) but of sympathy, and this sympathy admits the claim made on me by another's pain.[37] This claim is what, for Cavell, demands to be acknowledged, and acknowledgment, rather than the search for certainty, is what shows I understand your pain: "It is not enough that I *know* (am certain) that you suffer—I must do or reveal something (whatever can be done). In a word, I must *acknowledge* it, otherwise I do not know what '(your or his) being in pain' means. Is."[38] To retreat from acknowledgment to knowledge, from action to the quest for certainty, is to fall short of the claim made on me by another, and to retreat from the possibility of inhabiting our finitude in our lives with others.[39]

The difficulty of acknowledgment, however, is that it necessarily does without certainty; it does not follow automatically upon knowledge of another's having precisely *this* pain. For this reason, "sympathy may not be forthcoming. So when I say that 'We must acknowledge another's suffering, and we do that by responding to a claim upon our sympathy,' I do not mean that we always in fact *have* sympathy, nor that we always ought to have it. The claims of suffering may go unanswered."[40] Precisely because acknowledgment requires action ungrounded by certainty, the temptation arises to return to questions of knowledge, to retreat from the claim made on me by the other by asserting his separation from me.

Cavell follows out this temptation in his treatment of skepticism about other minds in *The Claim of Reason*, where it appears as a question of the relation between minds (private, hidden) and bodies (public, expressive). He tracks two inverse fears (or, as they appear in light of the denial of acknowledgment, hopes)

---

36. Ibid.
37. Ibid.
38. Ibid. Likewise, "acknowledgment goes beyond knowledge. (Goes beyond not, so to speak, in the order of knowledge, but in its requirement that I *do* something or reveal something based on that knowledge.)" (257).
39. Cavell's notion of acknowledgment and the claims of the other upon me that are not based on knowledge or certainty marks a coincidence of his thought with that of Emmanuel Levinas, as Critchley points out: "Cavell's proximity to Levinas can be seen in the way in which the problem of skepticism (which is also extensively discussed by Levinas) opens a noncognitive relation to the other as a distinctively *ethical* insight. The Cavellian need to accept the limitedness of human cognition, the need for the acknowledgment of the other's separateness from me and my own irreducible separation can be placed alongside Levinas's account of the ethical relation to the other exceeding the bounds of knowledge" (Critchley, "Cavell's 'Romanticism,'" 54). One might also see an initial point of divergence from Heidegger in the primacy of ethics over ontology implied by the shift from knowledge to acknowledgment.
40. Cavell, "Knowing and Acknowledging," 263.

about the relation of minds and bodies: first, the idea that the body is inessential, and thus a veil or block to a more direct or genuine communication of minds; and, second, the notion that a body may hide an inhuman or nonexpressive mind, which Cavell addresses via the thought experiment of a "perfect automaton." In the first view, Cavell understands the thought of veiling not (as it is presented) as an expression of the relation between the mind and the body, but as an attempt to relocate the experience of our separateness from others into a (merely) physical realm. The fantasy of body as barrier asserts that if the body can be understood as inessential, *knowledge* of another mind could eradicate any separation between us: when I know another fully, she will no longer be other to me. Cavell explains that "in the fantasy of it as veiling, [the body] is what comes between my mind and the other's, it is the thing that separates us."[41] As long as I hold onto the assertion that bodies keep me from knowing other minds, I may deny the claim made on me by the acknowledgment of another by insisting that I have inadequate knowledge of her.

The ostensible fear that the body veils an expressive mind is reversed in the fear that others as they appear to me may be just a "something" in a body; here, too, Cavell asks how this fear comes about and what it expresses. Cavell uses the thought experiment of a perfect automaton—an extreme instance of body as veil—to ask after "the nature of the worry, if it is a real one, that there may at any human place be things that one cannot tell from human beings."[42] That is to say, what hope or fear might be behind the question "But is X really *human*?" The thought that something nonhuman could produce human expression contains both the threat that I may never know whether something is human and the hope that if I fail to know or be known it is not my fault. If knowledge of other minds is impossible, I may disavow the responsibility for others because they are unknowable and thus (potentially) alien.

Claiming the worries about the body as block to communication or guise of something alien also introduces the fear or hope that all humans, including me, may be something in human guises, and thus enables me to deny my responsibility for my own expression. As Cavell puts it, "Suppose I become convinced . . . that my body is a guise, not my original. I am harboring the idea that this body is 'mine' in something like the way my clothes are mine; but it is not—what shall I say—*me*."[43] To refuse to acknowledge my body is to dismiss a great part of my expressive capacities as not really belonging to me, only to my body. That dismissal amounts, Cavell argues, to taking myself as unintelligible and withholding my intelligibility from others. He continues Wittgenstein's insight that being intelligible to others is not a matter of their (universal, provable) *knowledge* of me; rather, "I wish to paint my conviction that I am intelligible to others, my capacity to present myself for

---

41. Cavell, *Claim of Reason*, 369.
42. Ibid., 416.
43. Ibid., 381.

acknowledgment, as my believing myself."⁴⁴ "Believing oneself" requires admitting the expressivity of the body. If the self cannot be reduced to the mind, if the body refuses to melt away, I must accept the expressions of my body as meaning what I mean, and as potentially readable to others.

And yet, there can be no absolute proof that I am intelligible or that I am acknowledging others correctly: I cannot attain the fantasized *knowledge* that would erase the other's separate identity, and the body cannot be sloughed off en route to full mental transparency. For that reason, nothing stops me from denying that I or they can mean anything at all. *Acknowledging* that I cannot erase the separation between myself and others, that I cannot finally and completely *know* them, and nonetheless taking the risk of reading them and being read by them, is what Cavell calls "let[ting] yourself matter." He elaborates:

> To let yourself matter is to acknowledge not merely how it is with you, and hence to acknowledge that you want the other to care, at least care to know. It is equally to acknowledge that your expressions . . . are yours, that you are in them. This means allowing yourself to be comprehended, something you can always deny.⁴⁵

The possibility of directing these expressions as best we can, admitting that they may go awry, and accepting those of others while knowing that we may get them wrong is all we have of our own subjectivity. That subjectivity strives for—claims—its own ability to communicate and be understood as rational and human in and through its expressions. We may still be self-divided or self-opaque; admitting the possibility of (more or less) successful subjective expression hardly saves us from that.

Although denials of the other or of my accessibility to her will portray themselves as a matter of ignorance, the shift from acknowledging to knowledge is at bottom a maneuver of avoidance: in converting a call for acknowledgment into a claim of knowledge and then denying all possible bases of that claim, I force the demand of the other into the all-or-nothing of knowledge and certainty. Cavell sees this avoidance as the central gesture of (Shakespearean) tragedy, where avoidance as a denial of the other is carried to fatal conclusions.⁴⁶ Even in less extreme situations, following out the skeptical desire for certain knowledge of others makes us "dealer[s] of those small deaths of everyday slights, stuttered hesitations of acknowledgment, studied reductions or misdirections of gratitude, that kill intimacy and maim social existence."⁴⁷ From this standpoint, skepticism looks like an idea we would be better off without—if the yearning for certainty that underwrites

---

44. Ibid., 393.
45. Ibid., 383.
46. See again his reading of Othello in the final section of *The Claim of Reason*, as well as in *Disowning Knowledge*.
47. Cavell, "Responses," 159.

it leads to a denial of the humanity of persons, surely at least the commonsense view that I can know some people well enough to get on with social life is preferable. Readings and misreadings of others are of course staples of literary plots, both comic and tragic; the happy endings of marriage plots often appear to be precisely this kind of commonsense retreat to a community of two once a few misunderstandings have been cleared up. Lyric poetry, particularly in its most "hermetic" strains, may seem to give up on knowing or being-known altogether in favor of a single subject that can at least say what it wants. Literature—if understood as simply a series of interacting plots, themes, codes, forms, patterns—seems able to get along without any recourse to skepticism or quests for certainty.

Skepticism and/in the Ordinary

So why *not* just give up on the quest for certainty expressed in skepticism? If skepticism were only the misplaced and distracting set of scruples belonging to a class of professional philosophers that Rorty interprets it to be, it is true that we would be better off without it. But understanding that the skeptic gets ahold of crucial truths about the finitude of human subjectivity means understanding that to abandon skeptical yearning entirely would likewise be to abandon those truths while accepting without question the knowledge-or-nothing binary the skeptic establishes. Cavell argues for the necessity of skeptical questioning, of acknowledging both its truths and its temptations, in order to prevent the ossification of commonsense views into conventionality and injustice. In literary contexts, to abdicate the quest for certainty deprives us of the possibility of explaining the absurdly ambitious goals both Hölderlin and Rilke (and I would argue not only they) have for their poetry, as well as cutting off the possibility of claiming any relation to a literary work beyond observation or perhaps mere personal preference; poetry becomes a cryptogram to be decoded, rather than an interlocutor in a shared human concern.

The yearning for certainty expressed in skeptical questioning can lead to the transformation of convention into what Cavell calls the ordinary, in which our relations both to other minds and to the external world undergo the transformation from epistemologizing to inhabiting finitude for external world skepticism that I discussed above.[48] Finally, Cavell's considerations of the ordinary open onto the view of language based on convention I draw out of his readings of Wittgenstein to

---

48. Cavell also raises the possibility of acknowledgment vs. knowledge in response to external world skepticism in the first two sections of *The Claim of Reason* in his discussions of traditional epistemology and his close reading of the steps of arguments against (our knowledge of) the existence of the external world. I do not discuss these sections in detail, first, because of what Cavell calls the primacy of skepticism about other minds, and, second, because Cavell's interrogation of those steps can easily sound like a refutation of skepticism—which it is not meant to be—when taken out of the context of *The Claim of Reason* as a whole. Against this misinterpretation, see again R. Eldridge, "Cavell and Skepticism," 189–93.

ground my claim that lyric poetry works to shape and create orientations to others and the world; I can now add that those orientations are matters of acknowledgment, rather than knowledge.

Distant as such thinkers may seem from German poetry and philosophy, Cavell finds the problems of the ordinary, language, and skepticism interwoven in American transcendentalism.[49] Thoreau and Emerson take up the problem of subjective relations to the external world in a specifically post-Kantian form, thus treating external world skepticism as the problem of relations to things in themselves: "Epistemologically, [*Walden*'s] motive is the recovery of the object, in the form in which Kant left that problem and the German idealists and the romantic poets picked it up, viz., a recovery of the thing-in-itself; in particular, of the relation between the subject of knowledge and its object."[50] But rather than beginning from a hierarchical subject/object division in which the self-conscious subject somehow has to encompass or reach the object, both Thoreau and Emerson critique the category of the thing-in-itself. That is, both thinkers contend that for all his attention to our relation to the external world, Kant fails to give an account of its externality, as such. Specifically, Kant leaves "unarticulated an essential feature (category) of objectivity itself, viz., that of *a world apart from me in which* objects are met. The externality of the world is articulated by Thoreau as its nextness to me."[51] In Cavell's reading of Emerson, our nearness to the world and the possibility (terrifying to the skeptic) that what we see in the world is only what we put there attests to our intimacy with the world. When Emerson remarks that "the universe wears our color,"[52] he acknowledges that the universe is (the skeptic would say, only, merely) what we make it. For Emerson and Thoreau, in Cavell's reading, the weight of that definition shifts: "The universe *is* what constantly . . . answers to our conceptions."[53] We have access to the world not through knowledge of its existence but precisely in that it is that which responds to our questioning.

---

49. Contra this apparent distance, there are in fact several points of direct connection between American transcendentalism and German thought and poetry: Emerson and the other contributors to the *Dial* were persistently interested in both Kantian philosophy and the poetry and science of Johann Wolfgang von Goethe, while Rilke himself read Emerson. Indeed, it is possible to use transcendentalism to understand Goethe's scientific texts as a project of world reclamation from the dehumanizations of modern rationalism, rather than as an inaccurate embarrassment. I have argued elsewhere that on this point, Goethe is less pre-Kantian than he often sounds. See Hannah Vandegrift Eldridge, "'Forms of Knowledge/Knowledge of Forms: The Epistemology of Goethe's West-östlicher Divan and Cavellian Skepticism," *Goethe Yearbook* 20 (2013): 147–65. For Rilke's readings of Emerson, see Marilyn Vogler Urion, "Emerson's Presence in Rilke's Imagery: Shadows of Early Influence," *Monatshefte* 85, no. 2 (Summer 1993): 153–69.

50. Stanley Cavell, *The Senses of Walden—An Expanded Edition* (Chicago: University of Chicago Press, 1992), 95.

51. Ibid., 107.

52. A remark that corresponds precisely to and reverses the import of Kleist's fear of "green glass in front of our eyes" in his Kant crisis. (See note 14 above.)

53. Cavell, *Senses of Walden*, 128.

American transcendentalism (here Emerson's "Circles," in particular) thus offers a reversal of the Kantian description of knowledge. In Emerson, the intellectual or conceptual parts of knowledge are receptive, come from outside of us, while the intuitive (perceptive) elements are spontaneous.[54] This reversal once again acknowledges the truth of skepticism: "The answer does not consist in denying skepticism, but in reconceiving its truth. It is true that we do not know the existence of the world with certainty; our relation to its existence is deeper—one in which it is accepted, that is to say, received."[55] Cavell's "favorite way of putting this is to say that existence is to be acknowledged."[56] (Of course, this may *not* happen—the observation that his culture's mode of relation to the world is one of inattention and denial drives a great part of Thoreau's discussions in *Walden*.) But to someone worried that we have no access to things in themselves, this definition of our relation to existence provides no help at all. Just as Cavell shows Wittgenstein to take the thesis of skepticism "as *undeniable*, and so [to] shif[t] its weight,"[57] he here shows Thoreau and Emerson's mode of Kantian response to be that of asking us to live in the world as those creatures who ask a world to answer them.

This relationship of acknowledgment to the external world, as with other minds, requires more than ("goes beyond") knowledge, and here, again, it is unsurprising that we often fail to live in a way that acknowledges our commitments to others and the world. If our orientations were a matter of (certain) knowledge, functioning on their own without our intervention or agreement, it would be possible to determine them once and for all and then set them aside. Thoreau diagnoses his culture—that is, American culture in the decades before the Civil War[58]—as having forgotten that it is responsible for choosing and ratifying its institutions, and thus having lost interest in its own experience, distracted by businesses of daily life (presented in *Walden* as worries about acceptability, social judgment, and economy) that are not truly necessary. Thoreau's departure for Walden Pond is, then, an attempt to wrest himself away from those businesses and to ask "questions which some would call impertinent."[59] These questions mean to interrupt the "quiet desperation," "silent melancholy," and "savage torpor" that Thoreau contends "result in part from our refusal to take an interest in our experience."[60] Asking these questions is, centrally,

---

54. Ibid., 129.
55. Ibid., 133.
56. Ibid.
57. Cavell, *Claim of Reason*, 45.
58. Cavell uses the first-person plural in discussing readers of Thoreau, thus implicitly including the late twentieth century in Thoreau's diagnoses of his era. In the early twenty-first century one might fairly say, I think, that the conditions of democracy based on mere convention and spectacle and of alienation from everyday life have—if anything—intensified, while also recognizing limited progress in the realms of individual expression and freedom (or at least the extension of what freedom there ever was to a somewhat greater number of individuals).
59. Cited in Cavell, *Senses of Walden*, 46.
60. Michael Fischer, *Stanley Cavell and Literary Skepticism* (Chicago: University of Chicago Press, 1989), 117.

Thoreau's first step toward a reclaiming of the everyday or ordinary that could underwrite a renewal of community in language.

Because we may find we have no answers to Thoreau's "impertinent" questioning, because skepticism reveals that we do not have the *knowledge* we crave in our relation to the world, because we have not performed the placing and shaping of acknowledgment, the turn to the ordinary begins with an experience of strangeness, alienation, and loss—or, in my terms, of disorientation. For Cavell, as for Emerson and Wittgenstein,

> the everyday is not a network of practices or forms of life to which we can return by leaving our colleges and taking a turn in the street or a job in Woolworth's. Rather, the turn to the everyday demands that philosophy becomes *therapy* or, to use Cavell's words, "the education of grownups." That is, it becomes a way of addressing the crisis of late modernity where the everyday is concealed and ideologically repacked as "common sense," what the later Husserl rightly saw as *Lebensweltvergessenheit*. . . . The ordinary is not a ground, but a goal. It is something we are in quest of, it is the object of an inquest, it is in question.[61]

Thus Thoreau's (first-person) parable of having lost "a hound, a bay horse, and a turtle-dove," and the travelers to whom he speaks who "seemed as anxious to recover them as if they had lost them themselves,"[62] "fully identifies his audience as those who realize that they have lost the world, i.e. are lost to it."[63] Acknowledging the truth of skepticism means first losing the commonsense relation to the world and then discovering that the certainty skepticism sought is not available either. Cavell describes this as a condition of "worldlessness," suspended between the conventionalism we have lost and the ordinary we cannot fully or permanently attain.[64]

That the ordinary is opposed both to inattentive daily life and to philosophical distractions marks perhaps the strongest point of similarity between Cavell's readings of Emerson and Wittgenstein and the philosophy of Martin Heidegger.[65] This connection is treated extensively by Cavell himself in his discussions of Heidegger's

---

61. Critchley, "Cavell's 'Romanticism,'" 38.
62. Henry David Thoreau, *Walden* (New York: Penguin Books, 1986), 53.
63. Cavell, *Senses of Walden*, 53.
64. Cavell discusses human worldlessness at length in *In Quest of the Ordinary*, 33–40.
65. Jennifer Anna Gosetti-Ferencei treats Heidegger's conceptions of the everyday in relation to phenomenology and modernist literature (including Rilke) in her 2007 monograph, *The Ecstatic Quotidian: Phenomenological Sightings in Modern Art and Literature* (University Park: Pennsylvania State University Press, 2007); in particular, she describes Heidegger's discussions of *Verfallenheit* as diagnosing everyday life as suffering from "denial of the fragility of everydayness" (35). Her general project is to find an "affirmative side" (4) to what has been characterized as the defamiliarization or alienation of modernist works, wherein defamiliarization renders the everyday ecstatic (see, e.g., 14). I return to her discussions of Heidegger's concepts of *Vorhandenheit* (presence-at-hand) and *Zuhandenheit* (readiness-to-hand) in my treatment of things in Rilke's *Notebooks of Malte Laurids Brigge* (see the section "Crisis: *The Notebooks of Malte Laurids Brigge*" in chapter 4).

and Emerson's perfectionism;[66] Cavell also acknowledges that Heidegger was central to his reading of *Walden* (even as *The Senses of Walden* ends by criticizing Heidegger).[67] This therefore seems an appropriate moment to recognize the numerous ideas and approaches both Cavell's project and mine in this book share with Heidegger as perhaps the most prominent philosophical proponent of poetic language and (in)famous reader of Hölderlin, even as I ultimately turn to Cavell's rather than Heidegger's view of language and subjectivity. The Heidegger of *Being and Time* shares with Cavell thematizations of anxiety and finitude (in being-toward-death), the centrality of language, and the attempt to change an inauthentic or inattentive everydayness into an inhabitation of the ordinary.[68] Particularly in his treatment of the ordinary or everyday, Heidegger shares with Wittgenstein and Cavell the awareness that our relation to the ordinary can become inauthentic either by way of inattentiveness or by way of its subjection to categories authorized by traditional philosophy.[69]

But there is also a fundamental difference in Heiddegger's and Cavell's (and here, Wittgenstein's) conception of the ordinary: Heidegger (again, the Heidegger of *Being and Time*) inherits from Husserl the "idea that the goal of philosophical inquiry is the uncovering of the underlying structures of phenomena as an essential part of grasping them in their Being as phenomena, and so of uncovering Being as such."[70] For all that Being must be approached by way of *Dasein*,[71] for all that Being may be unreachable, "in *Being and Time*, [Heidegger] attempts to provide a fundamental ontology (an account of the underlying existential structure) of Dasein as an essential preliminary to any adequate revival and engagement with the even more fundamental question of the meaning of Being."[72] Orientation to the

---

66. See Stanley Cavell, *Conditions Handsome and Unhandsome: The Constitution of Emersonian Perfectionism*, The Carus Lectures, 1988 (Chicago: University of Chicago Press, 1991), esp. chap. 1.

67. "I criticize Heidegger ... yet it is hard for me to think I would have come to my sense of *Walden* without having studied Heidegger" (Cavell, "Responses," 175).

68. "What Heidegger opposes to this average everydayness is his conception of authentic Being-in-the-world: Dasein achieves this mode by resolutely anticipating its death as its ownmost non-relational possibility, as something which lays claim to it as an individual Dasein, thus tearing itself away from the 'they'" (Mulhall, "Wittgenstein and Heidegger," 150).

69. "The focus upon an entity in its everydayness is intended as a way of avoiding the imposition of traditional or time-hallowed philosophical categories which effectively prejudge the question of the Being of any given entity. In this sense, Heidegger's concept of the everyday is opposed to that of the philosophical; it is that which philosophy represses but that without which philosophy cannot begin to move towards its goal of understanding Being" (Mulhall, "Wittgenstein and Heidegger," 149).

70. Mulhall, "Wittgenstein and Heidegger," 148.

71. *Dasein* ("being there," sometimes translated as "presence") is Heidegger's term for "the distinctive *mode* of Being realized by human beings" or "Heidegger's term for the distinctive kind of *entity* that human beings as such are," although there is some debate about this. See Michael Wheeler, "Martin Heidegger," in *The Stanford Encyclopedia of Philosophy*, Spring 2013 ed., ed. Edward N. Zalta, http://plato.stanford.edu/archives/spr2013/entries/heidegger/. Since "one way of asking the question of the meaning of Being" is to ask "What does 'to exist' mean?" it is not possible to give a definition of "Being" in Heidegger along the lines of "Being is ..."

72. Mulhall, "Wittgenstein and Heidegger," 161.

world in language or in the ordinary is not, for Wittgenstein or for Cavell, a preliminary, however essential, to "even more fundamental question[s]"—orientation reaches all the way down; there is no more fundamental structure to be disclosed.[73] *Dasein*—or what Rilke will call *Hiersein*, being *here*—is all there is.

This structure of our relation to Being in Heidegger also underwrites the differences between his conception of poetic language and Cavell's (which I adopt). Like Cavell, Heidegger links language and finitude; unlike Cavell, Heidegger sees both in service to the revelation of Being: "Implicit and inevitable . . . is the tendency for temporality and language to press toward one another, becoming the joint medium through which Being is concealed and revealed."[74] Heidegger's conception of language thus entails a certain submission or even annihilation of the subject: "Proximity to Being will be registered by a submission to the 'speaking of Being'—to the way in which Being gives itself to language and to *Dasein*."[75] Heidegger sees the (rational, calculating) subject, as part of the subject/object distinction of traditional metaphysics, as a locus of hierarchically composed ego and will.[76] In Heidegger's picture, the poet is not and cannot be an agent—he is the "conduit of reception" of the poetized, "the *essence of what is to be said*."[77] Because Heidegger works to overcome a (for him) overly metaphysical conception of subjectivity, rather than (as I use Cavell to do) to see fragile and finite subjects as the inhabitants of an impossible yearning in which they recognize themselves, Heidegger does not see that "poetic language, as creative, enacts truth as a process of withholding emergence, a process whose element of withholding is due not principally to the self-concealment of Being, but to the finitude of the poetic self and of poetic subjectivity."[78]

---

73. As is perhaps obvious from the title of his article ("Wittgenstein and Heidegger: Orientations to the Ordinary"), Mulhall does not see this distinction.

74. Stephen Melville, *Philosophy beside Itself: On Deconstruction and Modernism* (Minneapolis: University of Minnesota Press, 1986), 53.

75. Ibid.

76. "Poetic language, as the errant-truthful historical founding and reception of Schicksal, is said to be opposed to subjectivity's ego-centrism and will" (Jennifer Anna Gosetti-Ferencei, *Heidegger, Hölderlin, and the Subject of Poetic Language: Toward a New Poetics of Dasein* [New York: Fordham University Press, 2004], 48). Gosetti-Ferencei points out that this view is also wrong of Hölderlin in particular: "What Heidegger believes is the simple unity of the essential in poetic language obscures the thoroughly modern philosophical problematic to which Hölderlin's work is inextricably tied. This problem involves the unique paradoxes of subjectivity" (103).

77. Gosetti-Ferencei, *Heidegger, Hölderlin*, 67.

78. Ibid., 140–41. For all the similarities between her language here and mine, Gosetti-Ferencei's project is to use Hölderlin to rescue Heidegger's robust view of poetic language from his own subject-free ontology. She thus advances the claim that "Heidegger's theory of language, when not overwhelmed by the destiny of *Seinsgeschichte*'s sending, offers a new orientation for thinking in the collapse of epistemological, transcendental truth claims, and in the failure of the Enlightenment to secure, alongside the notions of human rights and autonomous freedom, a reconciliation with nature or earth against which it points the human" (142). This goal, although I am in sympathy with much of it, has two problems: first, it involves a large amount of reading Heidegger against himself, which is, second, deemed worthwhile (rather than just discarding his view altogether) based on the claim that "Martin Heidegger's theory of language, in particular in his interpretations of the poet Friedrich Hölderlin, has

I draw out implications of the Cavellian (rather than Heideggerian) view of language below and in my readings of Hölderlin and Rilke; first, I want to return to the idea of a lost or forgotten ordinary or everyday in Emerson and Thoreau to connect it to community and, more specifically, to the idea of convention that grounds language use for Wittgenstein and Cavell. In *Walden*, as Cavell reads it, Thoreau sees the recasting of our relation to ourselves (as beside ourselves in a potentially positive sense) and to the world (as neighbors, of acknowledgment) as opening the possibility of a similar recasting of our moral and political lives with others. (Thoreau often figures this work as a form of bodily labor, e.g., in his discussions of sowing and harvesting; he thus also reflects on its potential failure, when the harvest does not yield fruit: "I am obliged to say to you, Reader, that the seeds which I planted ... did not come up."[79]) Thoreau's writing of *Walden* thus presents itself as a moral, political, and poetic project of freeing language and community from their enslavement to unreflecting conformity.

In Thoreau's diagnosis, we have reduced our words to a particular institutional context through which *we* no longer mean anything with them at all. The rapid play of metaphor and punning in *Walden* (particularly around metaphors of finding/ founding and metaphors of economy, worth, and value) is thus Thoreau's attempt to orient us away from our shallow and enslaved understandings of our words: the loss of meaning in democratic institutions is a symptom of "our faithlessness to

---

brought poetry to the forefront of philosophical thought after more than two millennia of nearly unanimous, but also highly problematic, ejection of poetry from the realm of knowledge and truth" (xi). Heidegger is hardly the only champion available for this project, and there are good reasons for not taking him as a model for the reading of poetry. First, Heidegger uses Hölderlin for a specific purpose and in a specific way that has more to do with his own philosophizing than with Hölderlin. See, e.g., Manfred Riedel, "Seinserfahrung in der Dichtung: Heideggers Weg zu Hölderlin," in *"Voll Verdienst, doch dichterisch wohnet der Mensch auf dieser Erde": Heidegger und Hölderlin* (Frankfurt a.M.: Vittorio Klostermann, 2000), 20–21. Second, as Gosetti-Ferencei herself points out, Heidegger excludes Hölderlin's Kant reception as the means to rid "the poet of subjective traces in order to submit to his figuration to the Seinsgeschichte" (Gosetti-Ferencei, *Heidegger, Hölderlin*, 63), with the effect that he ignores Hölderlin's poetological work (64–65)—hardly a model for taking the problems that poets present seriously. Third, Heidegger's method of reading produces an excessive focus on the single word and thus ignores the formal shapings distinctive of poetry as opposed to other discourses: as Paul de Man remarks, "Heidegger's own language has come in for severe criticism, not without reason, for the manner in which it reduces the original text to a relentless philosophical discourse that bypasses the complexity and the nuances of the statement; at no point does Heidegger reveal an awareness of the expressive value of Hölderlin's highly deliberate formal structurization" (Paul de Man, "Patterns of Temporality in Hölderlin's 'Wie wenn am Feiertage ... ,'" in *Romanticism and Contemporary Criticism: The Gauss Seminar and Other Papers*, ed. E. S. Burt, Kevin Newmark, and Andrzej Warminski [Baltimore: Johns Hopkins University Press, 1993], 55). Finally, the bulk of Heidegger's readings of Hölderlin fall in the most politically suspicious time span of Heidegger's career, between the Rhektoratsrede in 1933 and his unedited reprinting of "Was heißt Metaphysik?" in 1953 with its infamous "sentence in which the 'unrealized' or hidden verity of National Socialism was first invoked" (George Steiner, "Heidegger, Again," *Salmagundi* 82/83 [1989]: 49). The publication of the "Black Notebooks" in March 2014—which Gosetti-Ferencei did not have the benefit of consulting—has raised even more questions about the possibility of separating Heidegger's Nazism from his philosophical thought.

79. Thoreau, *Walden*, 209.

our language."⁸⁰ Thoreau, in his metaphors, "is doing with our ordinary assertions what Wittgenstein does with our more patently philosophical assertions—bringing them back to a context in which they are alive. It is the appeal from ordinary language to itself."⁸¹ This is what I will argue Hölderlin and Rilke are doing, aided perhaps in ways Thoreau is not by the formal complexity and density of lyric poetry; Thoreau wants to "seek a justness [... of writing], its happy injuries, ecstasies of exactness," that will "feel like a discovery of the a priori, a necessity of language and of the world, coming to light.... That these words should lay aside their differences and join upon this ground of sense, proposes a world which mocks the squalor and cowardice of our imaginations."⁸²

Language, Grammar, and Forms of Life

This seems like a lot for language to accomplish, and Thoreau's project may seem to be merely literary—it is, after all, based on our reevaluation of our words and our standing in language. But Thoreau's point is precisely that we have the same sense of mere literariness about our lives.⁸³ We treat our lives as though they do not really matter; part of the task of *Walden* is the undercutting of the "mereness" of the literary. I contend that this undercutting is enabled by a view of language use like the one Cavell reads out of Wittgenstein. Cavell draws on Wittgenstein's later views of language to argue that "we learn language and learn the world *together*."⁸⁴ This view defines itself in opposition or resistance to a cultural conviction as old as Plato—namely, the conviction that language ideally is or ought to be a system of *reference* to a reality that somehow exists by itself, apart from being perceived and talked about, and that names of objects, in particular, can be true or false of reality, which in turn simply and actually divides up into categories that can be named with an accuracy that philosophy ought to investigate.⁸⁵

For Cavell, however, following Wittgenstein, "learning a language is not learning the names of things outside language, as if it were simply a matter of

---

80. Cavell, *Senses of Walden*, 66.
81. Ibid., 92.
82. Cavell, *Senses of Walden*, 44.
83. "We do not believe in our lives, and so trade them for stories; their real history is more interesting than anything we now know" (Cavell, *Senses of Walden*, 81).
84. Cavell, "Must We Mean What We Say?," 19. As I explained in the introduction, this is an accepted but not universal view of Wittgenstein's post-*Tractatus* depictions of language. See note 5 in the introduction.
85. For a full reading of this conviction, see Bernard Harrison, "Imagined Worlds and the real one: Plato, Wittgenstein, and Mimesis," in *The Literary Wittgenstein*, ed. John Gibson and Wolfgang Huemer (New York: Routledge, 2004), 94. Harrison explains this conviction as one that language is "empty of reality, a mere notation." In this picture, reality "just does divide up into certain categories of nameable elements, and it is the business of philosophical inquiry ... to determine the identity and nature of those categories of elements" (94).

matching up signifiers with signifieds, as if signifieds already existed and we were just learning new names for them. . . . Rather, we are initiated by language into a socious, which is for us the world."[86] Hence, for Cavell, the continued interest and importance (*pace* Rorty) of ordinary language philosophy, particularly Austin: "The philosophy of ordinary language concerns itself with everything that we talk about in language. In this sense, philosophy speaks of nothing but language, and Austin in particular has lots to say about differences language marks."[87] Austin's distinctions—specialized and particular as they may seem—bespeak the relation "between language and the world, but not in the traditional analytic terms of realism or correspondence . . . [but rather] in terms . . . of a *harmony* between words and world."[88] Finding out something about language thus entails finding out something about the world; discovering something about what Wittgenstein calls grammar means uncovering something about what he calls a form of life. And so whatever lyric poetry discovers about language, it will also discover about the form of life from which it emerges; changing language also entails changing a form of life.

Moreover, the connections between grammar and forms of life found the intelligibility of language: we can understand other speakers because language is not arbitrary. Thus "Wittgenstein's relation of grammar and criteria to 'forms of life'" shows that "human convention is not arbitrary but constitutive of significant speech and activity," and thus that "mutual understanding, and hence language, depends on nothing more and nothing less than shared forms of life."[89] But this vision of language runs into several difficulties: first, although we learn and use words in practical contexts and generally do seem to agree on how they can be extended or projected from one meaning or context to another, this happens without the underpinning of universal *rules* that ground and legislate the correct use of language. And any view that suggests that language can communicate just because, in general, it does so will seem alarmingly unstable:

> Nothing insures that this projection will take place (in particular, not the grasping of universals nor the grasping of books of rules), just as nothing insures that we will make, and understand, the same projections. That on the whole we do is a matter of our sharing routes of interest and feeling, modes of response, senses of humor and of significance and of fulfillment, of what is outrageous, of what is similar to what else, what a rebuke, what forgiveness, of when an utterance is an assertion, when an appeal, when an explanation—all the whirl of organism Wittgenstein calls "forms of life." Human speech and activity, sanity and community, rest upon nothing more, but

---

86. C. Bernstein, "Reading Cavell Reading Wittgenstein," 299.
87. Sandra Laugier, "Rethinking the Ordinary: Austin *after* Cavell," in Goodman, *Contending with Stanley Cavell*, 97.
88. Ibid., 98.
89. Cavell, *Claim of Reason*, 168.

nothing less, than this. It is a vision as simple as it is difficult, and as difficult as it is (and because it is) terrifying.[90]

Wittgenstein's vision is terrifying precisely because it reveals the degree to which communication, teaching, talking, and all the manifold activities human subjects complete in language rest on nothing more than what Cavell calls *convention*.

Moreover, because there are no universal rules governing language use, the temptation emerges to deem all usage merely private, or as arbitrary as if it were private, particularly because language use does change over time, idiom, and circumstance:

> The meaning of words *will*, of course, stretch and shrink, and they will be stretched and be shrunk.... It is a wonderful step towards understanding the abutment of language and the world when we see it to be a matter of convention. But this idea, like every other, endangers as it releases the imagination. For some will then suppose that a private meaning is not more arbitrary than one arrived at publicly, and that since language inevitably changes, there is no reason not to change it arbitrarily.[91]

From this perspective, efforts to enforce communicability may read as coercive; it may seem sensible to give up on communication altogether in the interest of an expressive community of a single subject, which can at least say what it wants. But understanding language use as based on convention, which may be challenged (Cavell's word is "convened upon") at any time begins to suggest the ways in which poetry, as a genre that often works on the edge of what is linguistically permissible while deploying and challenging conventions of understanding, can seek orientations in language that are neither coercive nor solipsistic.

One response to the absence of rules for reference and meaning is the turn to criteria as a means to control and universalize both language and knowledge. The thought would be that if we have really settled criteria (signs, signals, behaviors) for calling something by a given word, then it ought to be possible to get to universal agreement that a given word applies in a given situation. Cavell again uses the example of another person's pain, considering the case of a person who, in a situation that we might logically suppose to be painful, exhibits all the criteria of being in pain—whimpering and screaming, wringing his hands, and so on—who nonetheless insists that he is only "calling his hamsters."[92] Should the hamsters in fact appear in response to such behavior, we had better believe him. But the worry such a scenario (in an extreme version) presents is that we can never know if someone really is in pain—he may be faking it, he may be deranged, or he may be calling

---

90. Cavell, "The Availability of Wittgenstein's Later Philosophy," in *Must We Mean What We Say?* 52.
91. Cavell, "Must We Mean What We Say?," 42.
92. Cavell, *Claim of Reason*, 88.

his hamsters. Criteria will not solve the problem of another person's pain or enable us to have knowledge of it (rather than, as I argued above, to acknowledge it); and therefore, "criteria are disappointing. They do not assure that my words reach all the way to the pain of others."[93] Criteria and convention, then, are crucially not controls on our *knowledge* of the world, of ourselves, or of others.

Because language functions without appeals either to an external world of referents or an internal system of criteria, "it may be hard to make out that the weaving of language here is something more than a shuttling of fortune."[94] And this, indeed, is the conclusion arrived at in literary-theoretical approaches that proceed from the "unreliability" of language. Bernstein sees Cavell and Jacques Derrida (in *Of Grammatology*), in particular, as similar "in respect to getting rid of the idea that words refer to metaphysical absolutes, to universals, to 'transcendental signifieds,' rather than being part of a grammar of shared conventions, a grammatology."[95] Both see that it is correct that, by the standard of universal rules, language is unreliable.

Where Derrida and Wittgenstein (in Cavell's reading) differ is in their response to this unreliability:

> What Derrida ends up transforming to houses of cards—shimmering traces of life, as insubstantial as elusive—Wittgenstein locates as *meaning*, with the full range of intention, responsibility, coherence, and possibility for revolt against or madness without. In Wittgenstein's accounting, one is not left sealed off from the world with only "markings" to "decipher" to but rather *located* in a world with meanings to *respond to*.[96]

Being "sealed off" is both the fear (that I cannot reach the world or others) and the desire (therefore I am not responsible for others or the world, and they cannot reach me) of skepticism as an expression of the yearning to transcend finitude as I read it above. Here I want to emphasize Bernstein's insight that Derrida, like the skeptic, misinterprets what Bernstein calls "the lesson of metaphysical finitude," that is, the confrontation of individual subjects with their own delimitedness: where Derrida sees only "codes" or "marks," and denies the possibility of presence, Cavell takes the lesson from Wittgenstein that any kind of "presence" (to continue Derrida's term) we may have comes only from shared grammar in a form of life.[97]

---

93. Ibid., 79.
94. Ibid., 94.
95. C. Bernstein, "Reading Cavell Reading Wittgenstein," 304.
96. Ibid.
97. Ibid. Bernstein argues further that Derrida thus "ends up in a situation comparable to the traditional epistemologist in *The Claim of Reason*, who misunderstands the implications of the discovery that the experience of knowing things in terms of their presence to us does not mean these things are 'transcendentally' present and so imagines there is something wrong with presence itself, that it is illegitimate or failed, as if presence could only be of this kind" (304). Richard Eldridge and Bernard Rhie make this point with almost startling directness: recalling "Cavell's oft-repeated point that there is in

38 Lyric Orientations

I discuss the notion of language's "unreliability" or "indeterminacy" at some length not because Cavell's usefulness emerges only in contrast to it, nor because it is necessarily the predominant view in literary studies,[98] but because adherence to it absolutely prohibits an understanding of lyric poetry as performing the kinds of orientation for which I argue. I therefore offer at least a preliminary case against this view in order to show how my work gets past the kind of knowledge-or-nothing binary that poststructuralism, like professional skepticism, accepts. Moving from discussions of the unreliability of language to its effects on literary interpretation, Paul de Man discusses "indeterminacy" particularly clearly in his introduction to *Allegories of Reading*, where he treats the final question of Yeats's poem "Among Schoolchildren."[99] Reading the question "How can we know the dancer from the dance?" first literally/grammatically and then rhetorically, de Man holds that the literal reading expresses despair about the possibility of *distinguishing* dancer from dance, creator from artwork, whereas the rhetorical reading celebrates the organic unity of artist and artwork unfolded throughout the poem.[100] For de Man, the presence of two contradictory and yet connected readings indicates the fundamental indeterminacy of literary texts; despite his own virtuosity in reading Yeats and Proust, he asserts that the end stage of critical interrogation of a text is inevitably a "state of suspended ignorance."[101]

This "undecidability" or "unreliability" of language, particularly literary language, highlights the precipitousness with which deconstructive reading moves

---

fact nothing more human than the desire to transcend the human (to become, even, somehow inhuman or post-human)," they point out that "far from actually succeeding in leaving behind (by deconstructing) the category of the human, we believe that poststructuralist antihumanism is itself but another (very sophisticated) expression of one of the deepest and most characteristic human impulses—the wish humans have always had to transcend their own finitude" (Richard Eldridge and Bernard Rhie, "Cavell, Literary Studies, and the Human Subject: Consequences of Skepticism," in *Stanley Cavell and Literary Studies: Consequences of Skepticism*, ed. Eldridge and Rhie [New York: Continuum, 2011], 5).

98. Indeed, I share the reaction of Hans Adler and Sabine Groß when they point out, in response to the claims of cognitive literary studies to rescue the field from poststructuralist theory, that such an approach "accord[s] poststructuralism—with its admittedly high visibility and demonstrated potential for arousing opposition—too much weight. Setting up versions of poststructuralism as the enemy . . . ignores the prevalence of other types of literary study that, in terms of publication output, vastly outnumber deconstructive and poststructuralist analyses and theoretical essays" (Hans Adler and Sabine Groß, "Adjusting the Frame: Comments on Cognitivism and Literature," *Poetics Today* 23 [2002]: 202).

99. Paul de Man, *Allegories of Reading: Figural Language in Rousseau, Nietzsche, Rilke, and Proust* (New Haven, CT: Yale University Press, 1979), 11–12.

100. De Man, *Allegories of Reading*, 11–12. Cavell points out quite rightly that de Man performs his "literal" reading too narrowly, since "How can we know the dancer from the dance?" cannot, in fact, be unproblematically reduced to "How can we *tell dancer and dance apart?*" (Cavell, "Politics as Opposed to What?," *Critical Inquiry* 9, no. 1 [1982]: 170). Cavell suggests a further reading—namely, that Yeats's interest in knowing *from* asks a different question: "How can we know the dancer from, meaning by means of, the dance; how is that the dance can reveal the dancer"? (171). This interpretation is in line with Cavell's interests in problems of knowing versus acknowledging others based on behavior. Cavell also connects these problems of knowing with de Man's refusal of referentiality in favor of rhetorical/figural criticism. Cavell, "Politics," 172; compare with de Man, *Allegories of Reading*, 3–4.

101. De Man, *Allegories of Reading*, 19.

from the observation that multiple, even contradictory readings may be plausible for any given passage of text to the assertion that language is fundamentally unreliable, that misreading and misunderstanding are necessary or inevitable.[102] But there is no reason to assume that the plurality of possible interpretations points to the hopelessness of communication and the unreliability of language; quite the opposite: the multiplicity and complexity of literary texts make them particularly suited to the investigation of expressive possibilities.[103] In rejecting the kind of universal, rule-grounded underpinnings for language that Cavell and Wittgenstein agree we must do without, poststructuralist thought misconstrues the implications of that rejection and forces language into an all-or-nothing that denies the possibility that linguistic attunement and convention might provide the kinds of world orientation that I investigate in poetry.

If, however, we turn to the Wittgensteinian view of use rather than reference, the idea that we learn language and the world together already suggests how recasting our relation to or in our language might reorient our relations to the world and to others. As the deconstructive and skeptical views emphasize, the difficult part of this view is the discovery that

> the radical absence of any foundation for the claim to "say what we say" . . . is not a mark of any absence of logical rigor or rational certitude in the procedure that arises from this claim. . . . This is the meaning of what Wittgenstein says about our "agreements in judgment" and in language: it is not founded on anything but itself, on *us*.[104]

This may make it sound as though Wittgenstein and Cavell want to solve all our problems of language use and world orientation simply by getting everybody to speak good English (German)—a kind of conformist/prescriptivist reading of Wittgenstein's "grammar."[105] The question might—and indeed should—arise of

---

102. Martin Stone, "On the Old Saw, 'Every Reading of a Text Is an Interpretation': Some Remarks," in Gibson and Huemer, *Literary Wittgenstein*, 200.

103. "The 'indeterminacy' which is the correlate of critical pluralism in literature is not—*pace* de Man—any sort of defect or failure. To the contrary, that literature lends itself to multiple and divergent readings is apparently one of the things we most value about it" (Stone, "On the Old Saw," 202).

104. Laugier, "Rethinking the Ordinary," 86.

105. Hence the misunderstanding that Cavell's and Austin's emphasis on "what we say" or "what we would normally say" represents a "form of 'commons-room' authoritarianism" (R. Eldridge and Rhie, "Consequences of Skepticism," 3). Laugier sees this as part of Rorty's misinterpretation of Cavell and Wittgenstein: "'The acceptance of our form of life,' immanence, does not afford us a pat response to philosophical problems. Wittgenstein certainly would not have appreciated certain talk nowadays of supposedly Wittgensteinian inspiration, in which 'the acceptance of our form of life' becomes a flight from every investigation or questioning of our forms of life, and a pretext for talk about the end of philosophy. Rorty's reading and use of Wittgenstein is clearly guided by this sort of 'conformist' interpretation of form of life" (Laugier, "Rethinking the Ordinary," 86); "The strength of Cavell's analysis in chapter 5 of *The Claim of Reason*—and what fundamentally distinguishes it from Rorty's analysis of community and convention—is that it makes us revisit the profoundly problematic character of every appeal to convention, and the difficulty therefore of locating a 'conventionalism' in Wittgenstein" (89).

just who the "we" in "what we say" is; more broadly, how is the community whose agreement (how documented?) grounds language use identified, and what are its limits and scope? *Whose* form of life is it? Especially given that I claim repeatedly that lyric poetry in general, and the poetry of Hölderlin and Rilke in particular, do something for (to?) their readers, it may seem necessary to get some hard data about who those readers were or are, perhaps via reviews or publication statistics or library subscriptions or book fair catalogs. Or perhaps the claim that poetry orients readers needs some information about how readers read—what are the cognitive processes involved, what are the medial and sociohistorical conditions of reading in play?[106] But here the question of how communities of use come about—of how any single "I" can say "what *we* say"—joins the problems of ordinary language philosophy to the problems of skepticism and its truth. Cavell's work shows a repeated awareness that the "agreements" discussed in Wittgenstein (and in Austin) are founded on neither, as it were, polling data, nor universal rules.[107]

Instead, just as the skeptic, in her discovery that certain knowledge is not available or enough, gets hold of a crucial truth about human finitude, "the lack of any external foundation for our agreement in language" tells us something fundamental about our language use and the communicative rationality we use it to claim.[108] As both Sandra Laugier and Simon Critchley point out, Cavell's attention to the fragility of "forms of life" goes beyond the "breathtaking cultural and political complacency of much that passes for Wittgensteinian philosophizing."[109] In recognizing that nothing grounds the claim of "what I say" other than an individual voice asking for agreement, "Cavell shows at once the fragility and the depth of our agreements, and he seeks out the very nature of the necessity that emerges, for

---

106. That literary studies does not, in general, take account of how "normal" readers read is a main critique leveled at it by certain types of scholarship influenced by the natural sciences, most particularly neuroaesthetics. For example, David S. Miall argues that literary interpretation tells us little about how ordinary readers read and blames literary scholarship for "a decline in reading." See David S. Miall, "Experimental Approaches to Reader Responses to Literature," in *New Directions in Aesthetics, Creativity, and the Arts*, ed. Paul Locher et al. (Amityville, NY: Baywood Press, 2006), 176–78. Even if literary scholarship is to blame for a decline in reading, it is doubtful that Miall's turn to neuroscience is going to help: sentences such as "The neuropsychological work reported here supports the theorized function of foregrounding in literary response, suggesting that RH [right hemisphere] processes facilitate a reconceptualization, analogous to the solution of an insight problem, that occurs downstream from the initial response" are not exactly a clarion call for literary reading (Miall, "Neuroaesthetics of Literary Reading," in *Neuroaesthetics*, ed. Martin Skov et al. [Amityville, NY: Baywood Publishing, 2009], 239).

107. "The agreement of which Austin and Wittgenstein speak does not have the character of an intersubjective agreement: it is not founded on a 'convention' or on any actual act of agreeing, entered into by already civilized speakers.... But what is this agreement? Where does it come from, and why should we give it such authority? That is the problem for Cavell. In all his work, he raises the question: what permits Austin and Wittgenstein to *say what they say about what we say?*" (Laugier, "Rethinking the Ordinary," 85). Of course, data about who uses what language in what way, and even some efforts at universal rules about languages, do have an informative and intellectually rigorous place, which is linguistics, not ordinary language philosophy.

108. Laugier, "Rethinking the Ordinary," 86.
109. Critchley, "Cavell's 'Romanticism,'" 38.

Wittgenstein, from our human form of life."¹¹⁰ The response Cavell, with Wittgenstein, calls for in answer to any of the myriad ways in which our forms of life with language can go awry is not the discarding of criteria or the declaring of language to be arbitrary, but rather, "a convening of my culture's criteria, in order to confront them with my words and life as I pursue them and as I may imagine them; and at the same time to confront my words and life as I pursue them with the life my culture's words may imagine for me: to confront the culture with itself, along the lines in which it meets in me."¹¹¹

Hence the importance of (individual) voice or voices in all of Cavell, Wittgenstein, Kant (on aesthetic judgments), and Austin (in his investigations of ordinary language). What I say, or what we say, are matters for *Übereinstimmung* ("agreement," but including the word for "voice," *Stimme*):

> A judgment of taste demands universal assent, "and in fact everyone expects this assent [*Einstimmung*]." What sustains this pretension is what Kant calls a universal voice (*allgemeine Stimme*). In Wittgenstein as in Kant, this is a voice that is to be understood in terms of the idea of agreement: *übereinstimmen* is the verb employed by Wittgenstein to describe our agreement in language (PI, 241–42).¹¹²

But because there are no universal rules governing any of "grammar," judgments of beauty, or "what we say," this agreement is always one that must be sought rather than assumed. Likewise, communities in which such agreement might take place are not defined by criteria or external features (still less by rules), but by the acknowledgment of others: "The question of community . . . is not one issue but a whole complex of interrelated public and private issues. . . . A community consists of any or all of those persons who have the capacity to acknowledge what others among them are doing."¹¹³

As for communities of readers, neither Hölderlin nor Rilke writes for some nebulously defined "ordinary" reader (and indeed, Hölderlin in particular found very few readers in his lifetime). Both poets, per the readings of their poetologies that I perform in chapters 2 and 4, quite deliberately undertake to *denormalize* their readers' reading experiences in the name of changing their relationships to language and to the world—and at least as matters currently stand, none of cognitive experiments on readers, reader surveys, historical publication information, study of libraries, or sociologies of reading will be able to give much information about that. In claiming that something happens in a poem for (or even to) the reader, the

---

110. Laugier, "Rethinking the Ordinary," 86.
111. Cavell, *Claim of Reason*, 125.
112. Laugier, "Rethinking the Ordinary," 94.
113. Lyn Hejinian, "Who Is Speaking?," in *The Language of Inquiry* (Berkeley: University of California Press, 2000), 34. Hejinian's further ruminations on community, however, call attention to the fact that those convening are not groups (how established or determined?) gathered in advance of convening on language and then polled retroactively for their agreement (36–37).

only evidence I can offer is my own experience of reading, together with the invitation to my readers to share in that experience and to value in the poems what I find important in them. Historical, linguistic, or philological information can all be helpful—indeed essential—in avoiding errors of interpretation and increasing understanding of complicated poetic language. Even so, none of the information they offer will be able to *prove* that a poem does what I say it does for any given reader.

In addition to its arrogance, this claim entails a certain vulnerability, one that Cavell addresses in three essays on philosophy and criticism, "Aesthetic Problems of Modern Philosophy," "A Matter of Meaning It," and "Music Discomposed." He concludes "Aesthetic Problems of Modern Philosophy" with a reflection on the fundamental difference between philosophy (modern philosophy, aesthetic philosophy, or—what I take my readings to perform—criticism) and proof: "Philosophy, like art, is, and should be, powerless to *prove* its relevance; and that says something about the kind of relevance it wishes to have. All the philosopher, this kind of philosopher, can do is to express, as fully as he can, his world, and attract our undivided attention to our own."[114] The (occasionally disorienting) lyric orientations I find in Hölderlin and Rilke—again, processual rather than referential, communal rather than universal, and responsive to rather than imposed on an external object-world—share the tenuous status of language use and relations to others in Cavell's Wittgensteinian picture of language. They are grounded on nothing more, and nothing less, than the search for an agreement that may always fail.

---

114. Stanley Cavell, "Aesthetic Problems of Modern Philosophy," in *Must We Mean What We Say?* 96.

2

THE ANXIETY OF THEORY

Hölderlin's Poetology as Skeptical Syndrome

This chapter has two primary objectives: first, to show that the skeptical arguments of the human subject with itself "over its finitude" find a place in Hölderlin's thought, and, second, to delineate the relationships between Hölderlin's theoretical writings and his poems. Having done so, in chapter 3 I will be able to use Hölderlin's own vocabulary for describing the stakes and achievements of poetry to read that poetry as seeking orientations within human finitude without reducing it to illustrated examples of theoretical or philosophical ideas (mine or Hölderlin's). This chapter addresses the objectives I have set forth (first) by recharacterizing the problems of skepticism (in the broad sense in which I discussed it in chapter 1) in the temporally specific vocabulary Hölderlin uses to diagnose his era as in need of new strategies for the overcoming of finitude, and (second) by drawing out a contradiction, previously ignored by scholarship on Hölderlin, that runs through his theoretical texts: why do Hölderlin's poetological texts try to do what, by their own lights, they cannot?

Hölderlin makes a strong distinction between discursive or theoretical and poetic language;[1] given that he assigns to poetry the task of mediating between the

---

1. I am using the word "discursive" in the vulgar-Kantian sense to describe argumentation proceeding through conceptual reasoning; since not all poetry is completely nondiscursive all of the time, I will typically use "theoretical" to describe language that is predicated exclusively on argumentative reasoning by way of abstract claims.

antinomies of mind and world, nature and freedom, and given that he states repeatedly that this mediation can only be articulated in poetic language, why does he continue to attempt to effect this mediating work in theorizations of the possibilities of and procedures for writing poetry? I suggest that this contradiction derives from Hölderlin's struggle with the truth of skepticism, understood as a recognition that human subjects inevitably strive to have certainty (whether about the world, other minds, or the divine) that they cannot possess—and, moreover, that this dissatisfaction with the uncertain state of our knowledge is constitutive of human subjectivity.[2] The paradox of Hölderlin's theoretical texts conditions both the themes discussed and the stylistic or metatextual features of the texts themselves.[3] In what follows, I will analyze these features at some length to show the problems of finitude at work both in the content and in the form of Hölderlin's theoretical texts.

Finally, taking the self-contradiction of Hölderlin's texts seriously as a symptom of the struggle with the native dissatisfactions of subjectivity in its quest for certainty shifts the relation between his poetological texts and his poetry, enabling me to use Hölderlin's own language to elucidate the ways in which his poetry takes up the tasks of finding and testing the boundaries between language, mind, and world as matters of (unassured, processual) orientation toward acknowledgment rather than (certain, permanent) knowledge. Previous scholarship has either taken it for granted that the theoretical texts (if only we could understand them) provide an ideal rubric for reading Hölderlin's poetry, or it has discarded them as vestigial remnants of Hölderlin's philosophical studies that are irrelevant for his poetry.[4]

---

2. Cavell's account of the necessity of both striving and dissatisfaction, together with his linking of both to our condition as creatures possessing language, is the reason I continue to have recourse to his vocabulary of skepticism and acknowledgment, rather than simply shifting fully into Hölderlin's—sometimes inconsistent and opaque—vocabulary.

3. The latter, in particular, have not been taken into account by a scholarship that seeks to link Hölderlin's writings to any of a number of contemporary discourses, including but not limited to idealism, pietism, and receptions of Hellenism. Hölderlin did quite obviously participate in these discourses, and knowledge of them is a great help in understanding the historical specificity of his language and his projects. That specificity can, however, be limiting as well as explanatory, as it makes Hölderlin's project more historically conditioned than it needs to be. Still more problematically, the temptation arises in this mode of scholarship to use these external discourses as a way of decoding Hölderlin's texts such that the contradiction I highlight here disappears. On Hölderlin's relation to idealism, see Dieter Henrich, *Der Grund im Bewußtsein: Untersuchungen zu Hölderlins Denken (1794–1795)* (Stuttgart: Klett-Cotta Verlag, 2004); and Lawrence Ryan, *Hölderlins Lehre vom Wechsel der Töne* (Stuttgart: Kohlhammer Verlag, 1960). On his relation to pietism and revolution, see Gerhard Kurz, *Mittelbarkeit und Vereinigung: Zum Verhältnis von Poesie, Reflexion und Revolution bei Hölderlin* (Stuttgart: Metzler Verlag, 1975); and Priscilla Hayden-Roy, *"A Foretaste of Heaven": Friedrich Hölderlin in the Context of Württemberg Pietism* (Amsterdam: Rodopi, 1994).

4. In the former group, see, e.g., Dieter Burdorf, "Mikrologische Lektüre: Am Beispiel eines Bruchstücks aus dem Homburger Folioheft," in *Hölderlin und Nürtingen*, ed. Peter Härtling and Gerhard Kurz (Stuttgart: Metzler Verlag, 1994), 191–202; Dietrich Uffhausen, "Bevestigter Gesang: Hölderlins hymnische Spätdichtung in neuer Gestalt," in *Neue Wege zu Hölderlin*, ed. Uwe Beyer (Würzburg: Königshausen und Neumann, 1994), 323–45; Ulrich Gaier, "Hölderlins vaterländischer Gesang 'Andenken,'" *Hölderlin Jahrbuch* 26 (1988/89): 175–201; Martin Anderle, *Die Landschaft in den Gedichten Hölderlins: Die Funktion des konkreten im idealistischen Weltbild* (Bonn: Bouvier, 1986); Gerhard Kurz, "Das Nächste

I contend that the theoretical texts are indeed useful for reading Hölderlin's poetry in that they show us what poetry strives for, but not what it will look like or how it should be written. Taking Hölderlin's poetics as working within the difficulty of acknowledgment allows me to address the simultaneously historical and ontological, epistemological and moral, questions of fit between mind and world that the texts yearn to resolve.[5] It also allows me to understand Hölderlin's poetry not as philosophy rendered in verse, but as the expression of a yearning—with its frustrations and fulfillments—that is most fully articulated in poetry.

Hölderlin's Context and His Cultural Critique

Johann Christian Friedrich Hölderlin was born in 1770—the same year as Ludwig van Beethoven and William Wordsworth—in Lauffen am Neckar in Württemberg.[6] At the time Württemberg was a member of the loose conglomeration of duchies and principalities under the Holy Roman Empire;[7] this lack of national unity becomes a theme in Hölderlin's poetry. Hölderlin was educated at a

---

Beste," in *Interpretationen: Gedichte von Friedrich Hölderlin*, ed. Gerhard Kurz (Stuttgart: Reclam, 1996), 166–85; Michael Franz, "Hölderlins Gedicht 'Andenken,'" in *Friedrich Hölderlin*, special issue of *Text + Kritik*, ed. Heinz Ludwig Arnold and Andreas Döhler (Munich: e:t+k, 1996), 195–212; to some extent, Dieter Henrich, *The Course of Remembrance and Other Essays on Hölderlin*, ed. Eckhart Förster (Stanford, CA: Stanford University Press, 1997). In the latter group, see, e.g., Roland Reuss, *"Die eigene Rede des anderen": Hölderlins "Andenken" und "Mnemosyne"* (Frankfurt a.M.: Stroemfeld/Roter Stern, 1990); Cyrus Hamlin, "Die Poetik des Gedächtnisses: Aus einem Gespräch über Hölderlins 'Andenken,'" *Hölderlin Jahrbuch* 24 (1984/85): 119–38; Götz E. Hübner, "Nach Port-au-Prince: 'Andenken' als Hölderlins geschichtspoetologisches Vermächtnis," *Le Pauvre Holterling* 9 (2003): 43–54. This divide also follows, to some extent, the divide between the *Große Stuttgarter Ausgabe*, edited by Friedrich Beißner, and the *Frankfurter Ausgabe*, edited by Dietrich Sattler; the former tends to present somewhat artifically completed versions, while the latter tends too far in the other direction and offers such a proliferation of versions, drafts, and fragments that it becomes difficult to decipher the text. For this reason, I cite from the Munich edition: Friedrich Hölderlin, *Sämtliche Werke und Briefe*, ed. Michael Knaupp, 3 vols. (Munich: Hanser Verlag, 1992), which emphasizes readability, but not at the cost of creating coherence where none exists. All German versions of the texts cited in this chapter are from the Munich edition, hereafter cited as MA, followed by volume number and page number, so that the originals may be easily located.

5. One of the virtues of the view of language that I derive from Cavell's readings of Wittgenstein is that it helps to make these extremely ambitious goals for poetry comprehensible, even given Hölderlin's lack of audience in his own day: if changing the reader's orientation in language changes the world, it is not so far-fetched for poetry to take on the task of making world and subject more fit for each other.

6. David Constantine, *Friedrich Hölderlin* (Oxford: Clarendon Press, 1988), 1.

7. Prior to the French Revolution and the Napoleonic wars, the eighteenth-century Holy Roman Empire of the German Nation consisted of 462 more or less sovereign political entities, including secular states, imperial city-states, and church-held ecclesiastical territories. See, e.g., Eric Dorn Brose, *German History, 1789–1871: From the Holy Roman Empire to the Bismarckian Reich* (Oxford: Berghahn Books, 1997). For the specific situation in Württemberg, see Otto Borst, *Geschichte Baden-Württembergs: Ein Lesebuch*, ed. Susanne Quarthal and Franz Quarthal (Stuttgart: Theiss Verlag, 2004), esp. chaps. 8 and 9, for the effects of the Enlightenment and Revolution, as well as the at-best-ambivalent figure of Duke Carl Eugen (1737–93). On the transformation of (some) Catholic cloisters into Evangelical "Klosterschulen," see Borst, chap. 10.

Lateinschule in Nürtingen (where his family moved on his mother's remarriage) until the age of fourteen, and then at a Klosterschule in Denkendorff.[8] At the age of eighteen he began studying theology at the Tübinger Stift; because his education (from Denkendorff onward) was funded by the state, it was mandated that he should become a pastor in Württemberg, an obligation Hölderlin went to great trouble to avoid.[9] Instead, he repeatedly took up positions as a house tutor, first in Waltershausen and Jena, then in Frankfurt, Hauptwil (Switzerland), and Bordeaux (France).[10] Both Jena (1794–95) and Frankfurt (1796–98) were decisive: in the former, he studied philosophy at the university and worked out ideas that would remain influential in his poetry; in the latter, he fell in love with Susette Gontard, the wife of his employer.[11] She reciprocated; they were discovered, and Hölderlin resigned or was dismissed;[12] they continued to meet secretly for two years thereafter while Hölderlin lived (on an allowance from his mother, which she deducted from his patrimony)[13] and wrote in Homburg (1798–1800).[14] Following his employment in Hauptwil (1801) and Bordeaux (1802), he returned to his mother's house in Nürtingen before his friend Isaac von Sinclair secured him a position as court librarian in Homburg (1804–6).[15] In 1806 Hölderlin suffered a mental collapse and was institutionalized in the clinic of Dr. Ferdinand Autenrieth in Tübingen from 1806 to 1807. In 1807 Hölderlin was given three years to live and was released into the care of a Tübingen carpenter who had admired his

---

8. Constantine, *Friedrich Hölderlin*, 2.
9. Ibid., 2–3. Constantine describes the effects of this commitment on Hölderlin as follows: "Until the end of his life, Hölderlin remained under the supervision of Württemberg's educational and church authorities, the Consistorium; and for all his movements, his jobs as house tutor 'abroad', he had to seek official permission. He was legally bound, from the age of fourteen, to a particular career; and thus bound also to orthodox belief. It is true that many of his fellows in the same predicament successfully resisted or evaded these requirements, and Hölderlin himself, until his mental collapse, was fending them off with some confidence; but the obligation or threat remained, more or less close; it coloured his view of his own homeland, became a constituent of the image of himself as a wanderer debarred from returning and settling in his native country. The immediate representative of this obligation was not, however, a bureaucratic body, but Hölderlin's mother. She was a pious woman who wanted secure prospects for her eldest son. On both counts it answered particularly well that he should enter the Church. Hölderlin's relations with his mother were very adversely affected by the obligation she put upon him and which he was bound to resist. She acted properly according to her lights, and so did he according to his" (3).
10. I draw these dates from Constantine's "Chronology of Hölderlin's Life and of Contemporary Events," in *Friedrich Hölderlin*, 394–95.
11. Constantine, *Friedrich Hölderlin*, 61ff.
12. The precise circumstances are unclear (see Constantine, *Friedrich Hölderlin*, 80).
13. Constantine describes the Hölderlin/Gok family finances as follows: "From various sources, chiefly from his father, Hölderlin was to come into a considerable inheritance. His mother invested the money shrewdly and undertook that she would neither use the principal nor the interest to defray the cost of his upbringing but would pass on to him the whole enhanced amount—on one condition: that he remained obedient" (Constantine, *Friedrich Hölderlin*, 4). Hölderlin never requested and she never released the patrimony; although his brother and sister attempted to reduce his share of the inheritance after their mother's death, the court ruled against them and Hölderlin was wealthy when he died (300).
14. Constantine, *Friedrich Hölderlin*, 105.
15. Ibid., 268–72.

earlier work; in fact he lived until 1843, becoming something of a local tourist attraction.[16] During the thirty-six years of his illness his half brother was the only member of his family who visited him, and that only once. None of his family attended his funeral.[17]

Within this brief outline, there are several key points for understanding Hölderlin's thought and his poetry. First, his education in Tübingen was influenced by the events that resonated throughout Europe at the end of the eighteenth century: the outbreak of the French Revolution in 1789 and the critical philosophy of Immanuel Kant. Hölderlin's access to Kant came through Immanuel Carl Diez, a teacher at the Stift, and was mediated (for Diez and his students) through the works of Karl Leonhard Reinhold and Friedrich Heinrich Jacobi.[18] Hölderlin shared both his Kantian and his revolutionary enthusiasms with his schoolmates Hegel and Schelling, and both enthusiasms put him in opposition to the institutional culture of the Stift, which was funded by the conservative Duke Carl Eugen[19] and remained under the jurisdiction of the Lutheran Church's Consistorium, which objected to the Kantian elevation of reason over revelation and viewed the revolution as a potential disruption to the comfortable relation between church and state in Württemberg.[20] Although Hölderlin's poetry, especially in Denkendorff, uses some pietist diction and images, the strains of pietism to which Hölderlin was exposed fit neatly with the institutional church that Hölderlin rejected, making it likelier that pietistic language in his works derives in general from sentimentalism's deployment of this diction, and its use in Klopstock, in particular, whom Hölderlin strove to emulate in his earliest poetry.[21] Later he transferred his admiration to Friedrich Schiller, whose appeals to ancient Greece and engagement with Kantian philosophy influenced Hölderlin's

---

16. Ibid., 299–300.
17. Ibid., 300 and 313.
18. On Reinhold and Jacobi as mediators of Kant in general, see Dieter Henrich, "Die Anfänge der Theorie des Subjekts (1789)," in *Zwischenbetrachtungen: Im Prozess der Aufklärung*, ed. Axel Honneth et al. (Frankfurt a.M.: Suhrkamp, 1989), 106–70. For Reinhold and Jacobi as Hölderlin's "Textfilter" in approaching Kant, see Manfred Frank, "Hölderlins philosophische Grundlagen," in *Hölderlin und die Moderne: Eine Bestandaufnahme*, ed. Gerhard Kurz et al. (Tübingen: Attempo-Verlag, 1995), 174–94.
19. The duke "paid [the *Stift*] six official visits during four years and regarded it very much as his" (Constantine, *Friedrich Hölderlin*, 20); on Carl Eugen's education reforms, see Borst, *Geschichte Baden-Württembergs*, chaps. 8–9.
20. On the orthodox Lutheran Church's (and its pietist subsection's) anti-Kantian sentiment, see Hayden-Roy, *"A Foretaste of Heaven."* Hayden-Roy's overarching argument is that the influence of pietism on Hölderlin has been greatly overstated without attention to the specific strains of pietism to which Hölderlin was exposed, specifically the more conservative segments of Württemberg pietism, which, she argues, have less in common with his thought that the speculative branches. She offers compelling evidence that overlaps in theoretical or philsophical concerns between Hölderlin and Friedrich Christoph Oetinger had more to do with their cultural situation of response to and critique of late Enlightenment and Kantian dualisms (8–17).
21. Indeed, views Hölderlin adopted/adapted from Klopstock's Moravian pietism often place him in opposition to the Württemberg pietism with which he grew up (Hayden-Roy, *"A Foretaste of Heaven,"* 17).

own development, and who found Hölderlin his first house tutor position and published parts of *Hyperion*.²²

It was through the tutorship secured for him by Schiller that Hölderlin was able to study philosophy in Jena,²³ where he met Schiller and Goethe and attended Fichte's lectures.²⁴ Hölderlin's presence in Jena in 1794–95 together with his time with Hegel and Schelling in Tübingen situates him in the initial scenes of post-Kantian philosophy in Germany. Since Hölderlin's engagement with idealism, in particular with Fichte, is crucial for the development of his thought, I discuss it in detail in my elucidation of the internal dynamics of Hölderlin's poetology. Hölderlin also met Novalis at the home of Immanuel Niethammer, a professor of philosophy, but despite the geographical and to some extent temporal proximity to the circle of Jena romantics (the Schlegels would arrive in 1796, Tieck and Brentano in 1798), there is a curious lack of contact between Hölderlin and the members of the Jena/Berlin romantic circle until Clemens Brentano's enthusiasm for the first strophe of "Bread and Wine," published as "Night" (in an almost certainly unauthorized version) in 1807, after Hölderlin's mental collapse.²⁵

This lack of contact is the more perplexing because both Hölderlin and the Jena romantics were deeply influenced by Fichte's philosophy, in particular its "quest of the absolute,"²⁶ and the longing to overcome human finitude I have used Cavell to characterize as paradigmatic of human subjectivity. Cavell himself describes the struggle for acknowledgment as "the romantic quest [he is] happy to join" in *In Quest of the Ordinary*,²⁷ and reads Wordsworth and Emerson as among those who also undertake romantic revolutions in language and the recovery of the world. Nor is Cavell the only one to see romanticism as involved in the struggle over finitude: romanticism begins from and perpetuates a "relentless and obviously impossible drive to overcome the finitude of the human condition."²⁸ This drive, and the recast relations toward and within human subjectivity and its surroundings, are a

---

22. Constantine describes Hölderlin's relation to Schiller as embarrassed and dependent (Constantine, *Friedrich Hölderlin*, 54). In his letters to Schiller Hölderlin expresses gratitude and poetic admiration and performs elaborate processes of self-criticism (see, e.g., Luigi Reitani, "'Mit wahrster Verehrung': Hölderlins Rechenschaftsbriefe an Schiller," *Hölderlin Jahrbuch* 34 [2004/5]: 143–60), while in letters to friends he criticizes Schiller's aesthetics for not daring to depart sufficiently from Kant (e.g., his letter to Christian Ludwig Neuffer of 10 October 1794, in which he remarks that Schiller "has ventured a step less beyond the Kantian borderline than he should have done in my opinion"; Friedrich Hölderlin, *Essays and Letters*, ed. and trans. with an intro. Jeremy Adler and Charlie Louth [New York: Penguin, 2009], 34).
23. Constantine, *Friedrich Hölderlin*, 46.
24. Ibid., 47.
25. Ibid., 200.
26. Louis Dupré takes this quest as the unifying attribute of European romanticism (and as the title of his comparative study thereof: *The Quest of the Absolute: Birth and Decline of European Romanticism* [Notre Dame, IN: University of Notre Dame Press, 2013]).
27. Stanley Cavell, *In Quest of the Ordinary: Lines of Skepticism and Romanticism* (Chicago: University of Chicago Press, 1988), 9.
28. Dupré, *Quest of the Absolute*, 4.

central part of Hölderlin's poetology and of the stance toward finitude that, in the view of language I advance, poetry can seek to address but never alleviate entirely.

Thus, Hölderlin and this broad form of romanticism share with Jena romanticism a beginning with and departing from Kant and Fichte, a concern with the self-relation of the subject, and an attention to the recuperative work of language. But the Jena romantics offer fundamentally different responses to the finitude of the subject, the work of language, and the relation between poetry and philosophy.[29] The Jena romantic relation between language and subjectivity is perhaps most clearly expressed in Novalis's famous "Monologue," in which language speaks only of itself: "It is the same with language as it is with mathematical formulae—they constitute a world in [themselves]—their play is self-sufficient."[30] The play of these formulae exceeds all control of a speaking subject, and only in its freedom from subjective control can language "mirror . . . the strange play of relationships among things."[31] This is precisely the view of language I challenged in chapter 1; in what follows I show the extent to which it is foreign to Hölderlin's poetics. In Jena romanticism, the understanding of language as uncontrolled and self-referential play leads to the interrelated themes of the fragment and irony or *Witz* (wit).[32] Like Hölderlin, the Jena romantics see the absolute as unreachable; unlike Hölderlin, they seek to express that unreachability in the deliberate incompletion of the fragment; irony, then, in the properly romantic sense, is the reflection of the fragment

---

29. In a footnote to their now-canonical work on romanticism, *The Literary Absolute*, Philippe Lacoue-Labarthe and Jean-Lucy Nancy offer a preliminary characterization of the overlaps and distinctions between Hölderlin, Jena romanticism, and idealism: "It would be a long and difficult task to specify the place Hölderlin occupied or the role he played in the genesis of romanticism or idealism, between 1794 and 1796 (or even beyond). . . . He still maintains relatively close relations to Schelling and Hegel and, like most everyone else at the time, is influenced by Fichte (whose lectures at Jena he may have attended). His first essays, especially those on the poetics of genres, are inscribed within, or, more accurately, begin to establish the future speculative dialectic. . . . In particular, the idea of a completion of philosophy on the level of aesthetics alone—and not on the level of knowledge, as Schiller affirmed at the time and as Hegel will always affirm—seems due to Hölderlin alone. . . . But none of this, it is true, will prevent Hölderlin's irreversible withdrawal from a 'constellation' to which . . . he never really belongs. Nor, above all, as his work on Greek tragedy and Sophocles indicates, will it prevent him from putting into question the dialectical model [of idealism] whose matrix he helped produce" (Philippe Lacoue-Labarthe and Jean-Luc Nancy, *The Literary Absolute: The Theory of Literature in German Romanticism*, trans. and ed. Philip Barnard and Cheryl Lester [Albany: SUNY Press, 1988], 131–32). The task of fully elaborating Hölderlin's relation to idealism has been undertaken to great effect by Dieter Henrich in the decades since the publication of *The Literary Absolute*. See Henrich, *Der Grund im Bewußtsein*; Henrich, *Hegel im Kontext* (Frankfurt a.M.: Suhrkamp, 1971); Henrich, with David S. Pacini, *Between Kant and Hegel: Lectures on German Idealism* (Cambridge, MA: Harvard University Press, 2003); Henrich, *Grundlegung aus dem Ich: Untersuchungen zur Vorgeschichte des Idealismus; Tübingen—Jena 1790–1794* (Frankfurt a.M.: Suhrkamp, 2004).

30. Novalis, "Monologue," trans. Joyce Crick, in *Classic and Romantic German Aesthetics*, ed. J. M. Bernstein (Cambridge: Cambridge University Press, 2003), 214–15.

31. Ibid. One way of putting this is to say that Novalis is a better Heideggerian than Hölderlin; that Heidegger chose Hölderlin as the bearer of precisely the view that Hölderlin rejects represents one of the great—nonromantic—ironies of the history of philosophy.

32. See Simon Critchley, *Very Little . . . Almost Nothing: Death, Philosophy, and Literature*, 2nd ed. (London: Routledge, 2004), 134.

on its own incompleteness against the (only imagined) completion of the absolute, while *Witz*, conversely, is a momentary and involuntary flashing forth of coherence and fullness.[33] This deliberate fragmentation, then, differs greatly from the failure or incompletion or repeated revisions of many of Hölderlin's late poems, which have given him a reputation as a poet of fragmentation.

Finally, Jena romanticism undertakes to undo precisely the distinction between poetry (or nondiscursive language generally) and theory (or what the Jena circle will call "criticism") that Hölderlin insists upon, and that creates the paradox that marks his theoretical texts. Lacoue-Labarthe and Nancy modify Madame de Staël's criticism of romantic literature (that it is literary theory and not literature) to reflect that "[what the Jena romantics] invent is theory itself as literature, or, in other words, literature producing itself as it produces its own theory."[34] Hölderlin, by contrast, leaves Jena in 1795 and describes himself as fleeing the "tyrant" of philosophy, writing to (the philosopher!) Niethammer in February of 1796: "I miss having you to talk to. Even now you are still my philosophical mentor, and your advice to beware of abstractions is as precious to me as it was before, when I let myself get caught in them whenever I was at odds with myself. Philosophy is a tyrant, and I suffer its rule rather than submitting to it voluntarily."[35] In leaving Jena and the study of philosophy, Hölderlin is declaring himself once more for poetry as the proper mode of inhabiting finitude and accommodating the desire of that human finitude to transcend itself. But as Niethammer's advice to be on guard against abstractions and Hölderlin's description of having allowed himself to be entangled in them to the point of self-diremption show, the temptation of theoretical certainty is still alive in Hölderlin's thought and work. This temptation is the one that structures the dynamics of Hölderlin's thought; it is also the expression of the unfulfillable but paradigmatically human desire to exceed finitude once and for all that, in Hölderlin's case, leads to paradox.

The Dynamics of Hölderlin's Thought

I contend that the paradox running through Hölderlin's theoretical texts appears as a symptom of anxiety about the political, moral, and aesthetic problem of finding a

---

33. Ibid. To be clear, this is only the *programmatic* stance of Jena romanticism, to which perhaps only Friedrich Schlegel adhered rigorously throughout his—barely distinguishable—theoretical and literary texts. One might plausibly argue that the greatest works of romanticism—Novalis's *Hymnen an die Nacht*, Brentano's *Godwi* and much of his poetry, Eichendorff's poetry and his *Aus dem Leben eines Taugenichts*, the novels of Jean Paul or, controversially, E. T.A. Hoffmann—end up, against this program, expressing something like subjective experience interested in its own expression and language use. Apropos Hölderlin, see Constantine's remark that even in Hölderlin's earliest poetry "there is nothing slight or trivial, very little that is even ordinarily light and pleasing in his first verses; nothing urbane or witty, ironic, lascivious, or playful" (Constantine, *Friedrich Hölderlin*, 12).
34. Lacoue-Labarthe and Nancy, *Literary Absolute*, 12.
35. Hölderlin to Immanuel Niethammer, 24 February 1796, in Hölderlin, *Essays and Letters*, 67–68.

modern world to be a home for finite human subjectivity. Moreover, this worry is a temporally specific form of more general anxieties about human finitude symptomatic of a modernity in which previous locations for addressing such anxieties (e.g., family structures, religious institutions, feudal societies) have lost their ability to sustain conviction. In his discussion of the forms taken by skepticism and its attendant anxiety in the post-Kantian landscape, Cavell describes skepticism as the human subject's "argument with . . . itself (over its finitude)."[36] It is this argument that I want to follow in Hölderlin's theoretical texts, whose contradiction I understand as struggling to acknowledge the desire for infinite knowledge and at the same time the impossibility of that knowledge: the interest in ensuring full connectedness to the world or to other minds both investigates and succumbs to skeptical anxiety. These texts, moreover, highlight the stakes of poetry in Hölderlin's view: far from subscribing to language-centered or solely self-referential views on the nature of poetic production, he holds that poetry undertakes unifications that are at once political, religious, moral, individual, and more generally anthropological. Taking up Cavell's term, I understand these yearned-for unifications as matters of acknowledgment—of the subject's own finitude, of its distance from and yet responsibility to others, and of its own responsibility for the forms of life and language of a speaking community.

Hölderlin's philosophical engagement with finitude appears most directly in his engagement with German idealism, whose primary task was to achieve access to things-in-themselves (denied by Kant's critical philosophy) by deducing what Dieter Henrich has called the *Grund im Bewusstsein* (grounding in consciousness).[37] This ground or grounding would at once unite the human subject and assure knowledge of the external world. Hölderlin, however, realizes that such knowledge, qua knowledge, is impossible and that the idealist approach has important consequences for the subject and its access to the external world. The grounding sought by idealism, located in the human subject, was to ensure continuity between mind and world, thus also undoing the Kantian antinomies of reason and sensibility, nature and freedom. Linking these antinomies unequivocally and permanently, in turn, would guarantee that the mind can reach beyond itself, whether to the absolute, to the external world, or to other minds, thus relieving the anxiety of finitude. I contend that Hölderlin understands relatively early in his career that the act of locating the possibility of access to the external world in an adequate conception of the human mind is itself an attempt to make the problem of fit between mind and world a matter of knowledge (rather than, as I worked out in chapter 1, *acknowledgment*),[38] and that such knowledge is impossible. The search for a ground

---

36. Cavell, *In Quest of the Ordinary*, 5.
37. Henrich, *Der Grund im Bewußtsein*. Hölderlin's stance with regard to Kant and especially Fichte's *Wissenschaftslehre* is worked out by Frank, "Hölderlins philosophische Grundlagen."
38. See the section "From Knowledge to Acknowledgment" in chapter 1.

in and of consciousness moves everything inside the subject; if that move is successful, then there is nothing *other* to the subject, nothing separate, which is precisely skepticism's goal—and so, Hölderlin realizes, the world disappears. This quest for certainty—here via the knowledge of the unity of the subject—once more "converts metaphysical finitude into an intellectual lack," performing the shift from knowledge to acknowledgment characteristic of (but not limited to) skepticism.

This realization is the locus of his critique of idealism, leveled primarily at Fichte's "absolute I" and its grounding of consciousness in the positing of that I by itself.[39] Hölderlin argues that, followed to its logical conclusion, Fichte's system not only dissolves the external world but negates the subject itself. Hölderlin writes to Hegel while attending Fichte's lecture course in Jena that "[Fichte's] absolute I (= Spinoza's substance) contains all reality; it is everything, and outside it there is nothing; therefore for this absolute I there is no object, for otherwise all reality would not be in it."[40] Hölderlin then traces the consequences of the Fichtean absolute I with respect to consciousness, explaining that the Fichtean positing of a not-I by the absolute I (for Fichte the foundational act of consciousness) is incoherent: "But a consciousness without an object is not conceivable, and if I myself am this object then as such I am necessarily limited, even if only in time, and therefore not absolute; therefore no consciousness is conceivable in the absolute I."[41] The inclusion of *alle Realität* (all reality) in the absolute I means that there is no external object for consciousness; the I itself cannot be the object of that consciousness because then it would be (as an object) limited, therefore not absolute. Finally, because there can be no object for consciousness, Hölderlin concludes that the absolute I cannot be conscious or self-conscious, and is thus nonpresent to itself: "And insofar as I have no consciousness I am (for myself) nothing, therefore the absolute I is (for me) nothing."[42] The location of all reality inside an absolute subject, intended to ensure access to the world by anchoring it in a subjective mind, in fact not only dissolves the external world but also negates the subject itself.[43]

Despite this critique, Hölderlin insists on the importance of philosophy for modern culture as a whole and Germany in particular; like much of idealism, he

---

39. In reading Hölderlin's critique of Fichte *as* his engagement with idealism, I am neither identifying idealism as a whole with the Fichte of the 1790s nor claiming that Hölderlin's primary contribution is in avoiding Fichte's mistakes. Whether or not Hölderlin gave the impulse to later idealist thought in Hegel and Schelling, he dropped largely out of contact with Schelling by 1795 (with the exception of a letter begging for contributions to a literary journal in 1799) and with Hegel by 1801, and certainly knew nothing of their philosophical works after 1806. I elaborate Hölderlin's Fichte critique here in some detail because it illuminates the dynamics of Hölderlin's own thought.
40. Hölderlin to G. W. F. Hegel, 26 January 1795, in Hölderlin, *Essays and Letters*, 48.
41. Ibid., 48.
42. Ibid., 48.
43. This is not to say that Hölderlin understands any of Fichte, Hegel, or Schelling as saying that the absolute I is equivalent to an individual or personal subject; instead, Hölderlin uses Fichte's assertion that the absolute is subject-*like* to show the circularity of its self-positing and to hold that the absolute is occluded and unknowable, at least in theoretical knowledge.

views the acceptance of the laws of reason as having direct moral and thus political consequences. More specifically, although he is critical of the circularity of the positing of the subject by itself, Hölderlin adapts two of Fichte's main principles. First he maintains the idea of a *Wechselwirkung* (interaction, mutual influence) between opposed components as the principle of their unification (in Fichte's case I and Not-I; in Hölderlin, this will become a poetological principle of dynamic opposition). And second, Hölderlin ends his critique by reclaiming the Fichtean idea of *Streben* (striving) as a fundamental principle of human activity—precisely the kind of striving that Cavell understands as characteristic of the human subject's constitutive attempt to overcome its own finitude. Hölderlin gives a reading of the drive toward the infinite and to the ideal as what separates humans from animals, in a letter to his half brother in which he explains that it would be less human to live without such striving:

> Why don't they [humans] live like the deer in the forest, content with little, limited to the ground, the food at their feet, where the connection with nature is like that of the baby to its mother's breast? Then there would be no anxiety, no toil, no complaint, little illness, little conflict, there would be no sleepless nights etc. But this would be as unnatural for man as the arts he teaches the animals are to them. To push life onwards, to accelerate nature's endless process of perfection, to complete what he has before him, and to idealize—that will always be the instinct that best characterizes and distinguishes man, and all his arts and works and errors and tribulations stem from it.[44]

This striving is a necessary component of human subjectivity for Hölderlin, and is part both of his engagement with idealism and of his recognition that human subjects constitutively strive to exceed their own finitude.

Moreover, Hölderlin particularizes his argument for the necessity of philosophy to the state of (nationless) German culture around 1800. Idealist philosophy is a necessary corrective to what Hölderlin describes as a German tendency of each individual to focus only on his own particular circumstance: "Everyone only feels at home where he was born, and only rarely do his interest and ways of thinking give him the ability or inclination to go beyond it."[45] Philosophy, in particular idealist philosophy, tends too far in the opposite direction, but in doing so helps compensate for the Germans' ostensible original limitedness:

> Now, as the Germans found themselves in this state of anxious narrow-mindedness they could come under no more salutary influence than that of the new philosophy, which takes the universality of interest to an extreme and discovers the infinite

---

44. Hölderlin to Carl Gock, 4 June 1799, in Hölderlin, *Essays and Letters*, 135.
45. Hölderlin to Carl Gock, 1 January 1799, in Hölderlin, *Essays and Letters*, 119.

striving of the human breast. And even if it does orient itself too one-sidedly towards the great autonomy of human nature, still it is the only possible philosophy *for our time*.⁴⁶

Hölderlin reiterates shades of his critique of Fichte—contemporary philosophy accords too much to the rational subject and pays insufficient attention to the external world—but explains that precisely this defect is a necessary condition of the philosophy of his era.

The difficulty with this philosophy, and the political program of rational (presumably) democracy it implies, resides in the fact that it can only conceive the ideal in terms of duty and necessity, rather than in terms of harmony and unification: "Apart from anything else, the disadvantage intrinsic to a political and philosophical education is that it may well connect people to the fundamental, incontrovertibly necessary conditions of law and duty, but how close are we then to the harmony of human kind?"⁴⁷ Philosophy can lead each subject to his duty, understood as necessary under the (freely accepted) law of reason, but cannot unify numerous subjects in a community bound by anything other than rationality or self-interest. It is thus unable to alleviate the anxieties of finitude, despite its drive toward systematicity and the absolute.

The task of unification—philosophical and political, intersubjective and intrasubjective, between nature and freedom, between reason and sensory perception—falls, in Hölderlin's view, to poetry. It is this view of poetry that prompts Hölderlin's rejection of the idea of poetry (or aesthetics more generally) as play (*Spiel*):

> I was saying that poetry unites people differently from the way play does; that is, if it is genuine and has a genuine effect, it unites them with all their manifold suffering and happiness and aspiration and hope and fear, with all their opinions and errors, all their virtues and ideas, with all about them that is great and small more and more to form a live, intricately articulated, intense whole.⁴⁸

This criticism is in part directed at Hölderlin's poetic mentor, Schiller, who in his aesthetic letters shares the terminology of drive and varying interplay (*Trieb* and *Wechselwirkung*) that Hölderlin draws on from Fichte, but unites the two contrasting drives of human subjects (in his view the "sensuous impulse," *Sachtrieb* or *Stofftrieb*, and the "formal impulse," *Formtrieb*) via the idea of a *Spiel*trieb (play impulse), which is itself aesthetic.⁴⁹ Hölderlin, by contrast, makes the idea of unification in

---

46. Ibid., 120.
47. Ibid., 123.
48. Ibid., 122.
49. Friedrich Schiller, *On the Aesthetic Education of Man*, trans. with intro. Reginald Snell (Mineola, NY: Dover Publications, 2004), 74. The relationship between Hölderlin and Schiller is, at least on Hölderlin's side, vexed and complex, and exceeds the scope of my argument here. For a detailed treatment, see Reitani, "Hölderlins Rechenschaftsbriefe an Schiller."

poetry not merely a theme but a formal principle by way of a reconception of mutual influence or interdependency (what Fichte and Schiller call *Wechselwirkung*) as the active placing or positing of oppositions. The idea of active opposition as a necessary component of unification appears as a fundamental theme in Hölderlin's poetological texts, in which he attempts to spell out the procedures for poetry to perform its unifying work.

And in this attempt the contradiction with which I opened this chapter reappears: Hölderlin's texts attempt to perform the unifying work they themselves assign to poetry and not to discursive language. Hölderlin adheres at least in part to the idealist view that unifying the diremption of the human subject is part of linking mind and world. (Unlike idealism, he does not locate either unification solely within the mind.) Because Hölderlin asserts that the repair of human dividedness is the task of poetry, he makes the quest for fit between mind and world the task of finishing a poem; poetry is the place where the constitutive striving of the human subject and the impossibility of its fulfillment are played out. And finally, Hölderlin's attempts to depict the object of our constitutive striving lead him to attempt to elaborate discursive procedures for the writing of successful poetry. Because Hölderlin is alive to the anxious desire expressed in skepticism, his texts, against their own precepts, attempt to depict the certainty (of the subject, of our relation to the world or to other minds) they deny to discursive language.

Read in this light, Hölderlin's poetological texts represent his version of the skeptical fantasy of a private language.[50] In the desire for a language—not a code, not a translation—spoken only by one person, containing everything necessary for coherence within itself, the skeptic expresses the wish that communication might be unnecessary for intelligibility: if language itself offers all that is needed for understanding, then if I fail to understand or make myself understood, it is not my fault. Hölderlin's theoretical sketches, analogously, are driven by the desire to secure the success of any poetic enterprise in advance so that the process of unification and the perception of an aesthetic whole can be moved outside the poem itself. If such a system could be worked out, then poetic failure—the lack of cohesion in drafts or fragments, the loss of particularity in the unification of oppositions—would no longer haunt poetic labor.

---

50. Cavell considers Wittgenstein's so-called private language argument as a linguistically inflected version of skepticism about other minds, specifically about communication. The standard reading of Wittgenstein understands him to assert that the idea of a complete language (not a code, not a translation) understood only by one person is antithetical to what a language is. See, e.g., Stewart Candlish and George Wrisley, "Private Language," in *Stanford Encyclopedia of Philosophy*, Winter 2011 ed. (article published 26 July 1996; substantive revision 29 September 2010), http://plato.stanford.edu/archives/win2011/entries/private-language/. Cavell, by contrast, reads the desire that a language be fully internally motivated as a fear either of inexpressiveness or of uncontrolled or unintended expressiveness. See Stanley Cavell, *The Claim of Reason: Wittgenstein, Skepticism, Morality, and Tragedy*, new ed. (Oxford: Oxford University Press, 1999), 352.

Poetics of Anxiety: Key Features

Hölderlin's attempts to delineate that, how, and why poetry is the proper location for the joining of mind and world are thus caught between the activity of striving for an impossible certainty in the relation of mind and world and the recognition that such certainty is impossible from within human finitude. In order to look more carefully at this tension—and the resultant paradox that his texts attempt to do what they prohibit—I identify six central features from his theoretical drafts. Three of these features are, loosely speaking, thematic; the other three can be described as metatextual. The thematic features elucidate the interplay between philosophical and poetological questioning, discursive and poetic language. They likewise take up the problems of diremption and unification that emerge from the specifically post-Kantian form of problems of finitude—namely, worries about fit between mind and world. And finally, these features will appear in poetry both as *themes* (filled in with specific content) and as organizing or formal *structures* whose successful deployment links poetry to the stakes for human mindedness explicated but not prescribed in Hölderlin's poetics.

1. The idea of *Vereinigung* (*unification*, or "making one") of oppositions appears in the texts as both a philosophical and a poetological principle. Hölderlin sometimes shifts to the term Zusammenhang (understood literally as the hanging together of opposed or disparate moments, which I translate as *continuity*). Both poems and subjects are understood as divided or disparate in their relations to themselves and to the world or nonaesthetic life, and they thus need to be unified or to have their discrete parts revealed as fully continuous.
2. Hölderlin takes the previous principle of unification or continuity to occur via a process of *opposition*, *Entgegensetzung*, in an active sense of setting elements against each other. This placing activity itself both acknowledges the separateness and finitude of its components and offers a hope for their eventual continuity.
3. He develops a robust and specialized notion of the temporality of poetic (and so subjective) development. His idea of *dynamic temporality* begins with the realization that the yearning for full connection to the external world and other minds can be fully expressed only in the course of poetry—whereupon he retheorizes the progression of poetry into a series of moments that must each occur at a specified place in the systematized parts of a poem.

Three stylistic or metatextual features appear as a direct result of the skeptical anxiety that drives the texts to attempt to achieve what they cannot, and as such bear witness to the unspoken desire to resolve questions of subjectivity and poetry permanently. They bespeak an anxious drive toward totality: the quest for certainty needs to have every stage of poetic or subjective development spelled out in poetic technique to ensure the overcoming of human finitude and the bridging of the gap between the mind and the external world. Moreover, these features underscore that Hölderlin's poetological or theoretical texts do *not*, as has been assumed, represent either a complete poetology or a philosophical system within or beyond idealism.[51] Since these metatextual features are frequently the most obvious things about the texts (making it all the more surprising that they have so often been ignored), I will typically give only brief examples of their presence after elucidating the less transparent thematic issues.

4. Hölderlin calls repeatedly for a *further step* for the completion of his oppositional structures, either remarking in the texts that something more is required or noting in paratexts that the text does not achieve its goal.
5. The drive toward totality prompts an ever-increasing *proliferation* of terms and conditions in each text: much of the difficulty of Hölderlin's writing derives from his tendency to put every potential correlative to a statement in between its beginning and its end.
6. And in consequence, the texts themselves are *incomplete*—even when Hölderlin does not mark the lack of achieved ending they break off, sometimes midsentence. Hölderlin (unlike, e.g., the Jena romantics) is not programmatically fragmentary: his texts postulate and strive toward a completed state that they almost never attain. The need to elaborate every step and every possible term makes it impossible for his texts to fulfill the tasks they set themselves.

Hölderlin's Theoretical Oeuvre

In what follows, then, I give a developmental account of Hölderlin's theoretical texts from 1794 to 1800 as the questions of finitude he treats expand from epistemology to religion to poetry, genre, and history. Tracking these features—and the paradox from which they emerge—through Hölderlin's theoretical texts enables me to show that the problems of finitude appear both as truths to be acknowledged and as forces working anxiously on the texts themselves; here, as elsewhere, the problems of finitude find a place in the emotional life of the subject. Moreover, taking both the paradox of Hölderlin's texts and their metatextual features seriously represents a significant departure from previous treatments of his poetological texts: it has frequently been assumed that if only we could decipher Hölderlin's

---

51. This assumption underpins the methodologies of Gaier and Ryan; both authors attempt to use Hölderlin's own earlier or later texts to fill in gaps or contradictions in any given document. Ryan, for example, asserts that his first task will be to present the *theory* of tones in its coherence, not only as a coherent whole but as a craftsmanly/poetic expression of a theory of mind centered on poetry (Ryan, *Hölderlins Lehre vom Wechsel der Töne*, 3). While the texts' difficulty is registered, the reasons for that difficulty are not reflected upon. Moreover, both Gaier and Ryan (among others) succumb to the desire to pursue every singular detail, frequently rendering the explication nearly as obscure as the original.

poetological writings, they would yield a full system for reading his poetry. I contend instead that trying to paste them together into a complete poetological system elides both their central characteristics and the paradox in which they are inscribed. Most importantly, avoiding this drive to systematicity within the scholarship while nevertheless not discarding Hölderlin's poetological writings allows me to understand the theoretical texts as delineating the (immensely high) stakes for poetry in Hölderlin's view *without* attempting to read them as successfully prescribing what such poetry will look like. Instead, I track the development of Hölderlin's engagement with problems of finitude as they unfold in his texts, enabling me to turn in chapter 3 to readings of his poetry as attempting to achieve the stakes Hölderlin himself establishes.

My account thus begins with Hölderlin's recognition of the limits of human *knowledge* as expressed in theoretical discourse, arising in a fragment referred to as "Being and Judgment,"[52] written in 1795. Hölderlin attended Fichte's lectures in the winter semester of 1794–95,[53] and "Being and Judgment" points to the problematic circularity in Fichte's positing of the "I" by itself, the critique I sketched above.[54] The significance of Hölderlin's critique for my purposes is that he withholds access to the absolute from discursive knowledge, claiming that only in intellectual intuition do we have access to *"being as such" (Seyn schlechthin).*[55] The statement that the absolute is not reachable in discursive knowledge is the kind of move I have characterized as acknowledging the truth of skepticism—namely, as recognizing that the skeptic's quest for certainty draws attention to the absence of such certainty in our own world relations. Hölderlin recognizes that human knowledge is finite, but does not give up on the possibilities of subjective orientation altogether: he proceeds to consider the possibilities for human subjectivity's understanding of itself in the absence of such knowledge in terms of the subject/world relation and along the Kantian lines of the modalities of necessity, possibility, and reality.

In "Being and Judgment," Hölderlin thus offers an epistemological reading of the problem of human dividedness, the problem I explained as the particularly post-Kantian appearance of skeptical worries about human mindedness. He does so, moreover, in precisely the terms of active opposition and unification I elaborated above as central to his philosophical and poetological thought. Self-consciousness is possible only in the division of the I from itself ("But how is self-consciousness possible? By opposing me to myself, separating me from myself").[56] That division,

---

52. The Munich edition applies the editorial title "Seyn, Urtheil, Modalität" (MA 2:49–50). Adler and Louth translate "Being Judgment Possibility." I omit "Modality" or "Possibility" from the title because the modalities are not presented as italicized definitions or subject headings as "Judgment" and "Being" are.
53. Violetta Waibel, "Kant, Fichte, Schelling," in *"Hölderlin-Handbuch: Leben—Werk—Wirkung*, ed. Johann Kreuzer (Stuttgart: Metzler Verlag, 2002), 90–106.
54. The Fichte critique and Hölderlin's resources for arriving at it have been discussed extensively and helpfully in the scholarship; see esp. Frank, "Hölderlins philosophische Grundlagen," 176.
55. Hölderlin, *Essays and Letters*, 231.
56. Ibid.

however, does not (must not) preclude the subject's recognition of itself in itself, at least to some extent ("but notwithstanding this separation recognizing myself in the opposition as one and the same. But to what extent the same?").[57] These two problems open up the questions of finitude in Hölderlin's oeuvre and establish the terms in which he will investigate them. "Being as such" is an example of indivisible unification (*Vereinigung*),[58] and the subject's identity sentence ("I am I"/"Ich bin ich") performs the kind of active opposition (*Entgegen-setzung*, "placing or positing *against*") that appears repeatedly in Hölderlin's poetological texts. Perhaps as a result of its brevity, the text does not enter into the obsessive delineation of further steps or the proliferation of terms that characterizes so much of Hölderlin's writing; he uses the term "intellectual intuition" (*intellectuale Anschauung*) as the capacity that can provide access to the Absolute Being, but does not explain how that capacity works nor how (or where) it ought to be cultivated, thus avoiding the anxious prescriptions for poetic production that will appear in later texts.[59]

Hölderlin takes up this line of inquiry in drafts for a set of letters on aesthetics, philosophy, poetry, and religion.[60] The letters expand the problem of human diremption and seek its resolution in aesthetics, using, once again, the structures of opposition and unification or continuity. Hölderlin discusses the agenda for his project in a personal letter:

> In the philosophical letters I want to find the principle that will explain to my satisfaction the divisions in which we think and exist, but which is also capable of making the conflict disappear, the conflict between the subject and the object, between our selves and the world, and between reason and revelation,—theoretically, through intellectual intuition, without our practical reason having to intervene. To do this we need an aesthetic sense.[61]

Significantly, "conflict" (*Widerstreit*) appears in the singular, despite the list of oppositions, indicating that Hölderlin reads these conflicts as instantiations of a single condition of dividedness. Even as he rejects the Kantian solution of an appeal

---

57. Ibid.
58. "*Being*—expresses the connection of subject and object. Where subject and object are absolutely, not only partly, united, namely so united that no division can be executed without damaging the essence of that which is to be separated, there and nowhere else can one speak of a *being as such*" (Hölderlin, *Essays and Letters*, 231).
59. It should be noted briefly here that intellectual intuition was the locus of much of the idealist debate on reuniting the subject and/or accessing the absolute (again, in idealism these are one and the same goal; see Henrich, *Der Grund im Bewußtsein*). Kant claimed it was possible only in divine consciousness; Fichte, Reinhold, and Jacobi all attempt in various ways to show that intellectual intuition could be possessed by human subjects. See also Frank, "Hölderlins philosophische Grundlagen"; and Waibel, "Kant, Fichte, Schelling."
60. "I shall call my philosophical letters *New Letters on the Aesthetic Education of Man*. And in them I will go on from philosophy to poetry and religion" (Hölderlin to Niethammer, 24 February 1796, in Hölderlin, *Essays and Letters*, 68).
61. Hölderlin, *Essays and Letters*, 68.

to practical reason to link freedom and necessity, Hölderlin postulates the need for an aesthetic sense or meaning, which he begins to investigate in the arenas of poetry and religion.[62]

The project of elucidating poetry's tasks and capabilities prompts the introduction of Hölderlin's correlative to unification: what he calls continuity or connection (*Zusammenhang*). Hölderlin argues that human subjects know, rationally/theoretically, that they live in a "higher, more than mechanical *connection*" (*Zusammenhang*)[63] with an absolute or infinite, and that this relation supersedes physical causality. But this *Zusammenhang* cannot be experienced in real (particular, singular), rather than ideal (rational, universal), life. The task of poetry, for Hölderlin inherently religious, is to make this connection felt in its infinite qualities *and* in its concrete presence in real or actual life (*das wirkliche Leben*), linking ideal and real, mind and world, in aesthetic production.

In explicating that task, Hölderlin makes specific reference to the historico-literary category of myth, and to the genres of the lyric, the dramatic, and the epic.[64] Consequently, problems diagnosed as epistemological in "Being and Judgment" now take part in religious, aesthetic, and specifically literary projects. In a further passage, Hölderlin links the problem of standing in relation to a divine absolute to the problem of sharing that relation with other members of a human community, thus returning to the political dimension of seeking subjective orientation in an unsponsored world.[65] He also initiates the tic of self-qualification and proliferation of terms that will come to haunt his texts. These features place a substantial strain on the language of Hölderlin's text: although the first sentence of the text[66] asks a difficult but linguistically straightforward question (Why must human subjects make themselves an image or representation of their relations to their world?), it obscures the question by inserting numerous qualifying clauses between the beginning and the end of the question.[67] Furthermore, Hölderlin connects each of his poetological terms with each other, deriving the genres of the

---

62. It is already clear at this juncture that although Hölderlin works within post-Kantian vocabulary and problems, he decisively rejects the Kantian aesthetic principle of disinterestedness and autonomy of artistic production.

63. Hölderlin, *Essays and Letters*, 235.

64. Ibid., 238–40.

65. Successfully brought into human life, this continuity will be felt such that "everyone celebrates his own higher life and all celebrate a common higher life, the celebration of life, in a mythical way" (Hölderlin, *Essays and Letters*, 239).

66. The text has been transmitted as a series of manuscript pages with great thematic consistency but without a clear order; although neither the Munich edition nor Adler and Louth list it first, the page that begins "You ask me . . ." (Du fragst mich . . .) is the only one in which the beginning of a sentence and the beginning of a manuscript page coincide.

67. The sentence thus reads: "You ask me why—even if man, according to his nature, rises above need and thus finds himself in a more manifold and more intimate relation to his world, even if, as *far* as he rises above physical and moral need, he always lives a higher human life, so that there is a higher, more than mechanical *connection*, a higher *fate* between him and his world, even if really this higher connection is most holy to him, since in it he feels himself and his world, and everything he possesses

lyric-mythic, the historic-mythic, and the epic-mythic, each of which functions on levels of plot (content) and presentation. Perhaps unsurprisingly, the letters were never finished, in part because Hölderlin was unable to elucidate a place for all the terms in his system.[68]

What began as an explanation of the need for poetry thus becomes an attempt to derive terms and conditions that, should they be fulfilled, would guarantee poetry's success. Even when Hölderlin begins with a project that does not fall under the contradiction I read as guiding his texts—he never claims that the *need* for poetry cannot be stated discursively—the texts slide into the language of process and technique. The letters spend far more time on the different permutations of myth than they do on the potential for shared religious and moral life; the yearning for responsive attunement to the world, to other subjects, and to the divine disappears into poetological microelements that Hölderlin is unable to link to his satisfaction.

In the summer of 1799, Hölderlin began soliciting contributions for a literary journal. A letter to his publisher describes the journal's project—in the terms of opposition and unification I argue are characteristic of Hölderlin's engagement with problems of finitude—as "the union and reconciliation of theory with life, of art and taste with genius, of the heart with the understanding, of the real with the ideal."[69] Hölderlin here adds further content to the generalized condition of dividedness presented in "Being and Judgment" and expanded in the letters. These themes are continued in literary-critical and poetological texts intended for inclusion in the journal.[70] In a series of seven maxims, Hölderlin theorizes the poetological import of the dynamic temporality of poetic works for the first time. He argues that a poet "must accustom himself not to wish to achieve the whole that he intends in the

---

and is, as being united—why he has to *represent* the connection between himself and his world, why he has to form an idea or an image of his fate, which, strictly speaking, can neither really be thought, nor is available to the senses?" (Hölderlin, *Essays and Letters*, 235). Adler and Louth keep much of Hölderlin's nested syntax, but some of it is combed out in translation. The original reads: "Du fragst mich, wenn auch die Menschen, ihrer Natur nach, sich über die Noth erheben, und so in einer mannigfaltigern und innigeren Beziehung mit ihrer Welt sich befinden, wenn sie auch, in wie *weit* sie über die (physische und moralische) Nothdurft sich erheben, immer ein menschlich höheres Leben leben, (in einem mehr als mechanischen *Zusammenhange*, daß ein höheres *Geschik* zwischen ihnen und ihrer Welt sei) wenn auch wirklich dieser höhere Zusammenhang ihnen ihr heiligstes sei, weil sie in ihm sich selbst und ihre Welt, und alles, was sie haben und seien, vereiniget fühlen, warum sie sich den Zusammenhang zwischen sich und ihrer Welt gerade *vorstellen*, warum sie sich eine Idee oder ein Bild machen müssen von ihrem Geschik, das sich genau betrachtet weder recht denken ließe noch auch vor den Sinnen liege?" (MA 2:53).

68. Hölderlin offers only "hints for the continuation" (Hölderlin, *Essays and Letters*, 238), and the remark in the discussion of genres that "the lyrical-mythical is yet to be determined" (239).

69. Hölderlin to Johann Friedrich Steinkopf, 18 June 1799, in Hölderlin, *Essays and Letters*, 142.

70. In this grouping I am including "The Standpoint from Which We Should Consider Antiquity" (Hölderlin, *Essays and Letters*, 246–47); "Seven Maxims" (ibid., 240–43); "I Am Pleased . . ." ("On Achilles [I]," ibid., 249); "But Most of All I Love . . ." ("On Achilles [II]," ibid., 250–51); "A Word on the *Iliad*" (ibid., 252–53); and "On the Different Modes of Poetic Composition" (ibid., 254–57). The originals are to be found as "Der Gesichtspunct aus dem wir das Altertum anzusehen haben" (MA 2:62–64); "Frankfurter Aphorismen" (MA 2:57–61); "Am meisten aber lieb' ich . . ." (MA 2:64–65); "Ein Wort über die *Iliade*" (MA 2:66–67); and "Über die verschiedenen Arten, zu dichten" (MA 2:67–71).

individual moments, and to suffer that which is momentarily incomplete; his desire must be, that he surpasses himself from one moment to the next, *to the degree and in the manner that the object demands it*, until finally [he attains the main tone of the whole]."[71] This is a recognition (on the thematic level) that poetry cannot be assured from the outset, and that poetic success does not follow a formula known in advance, but rather involves responsiveness, waiting, or even "suffering." Instead, the poet must "bear the momentarily incomplete," allowing the moments of a poem to succeed each other from one to the next in ways appropriate to the content ("in the manner that the object demands it") rather than determined in advance by a poetological or philosophical system. Hölderlin will later attempt to systematize the self-superseding of a poem from moment to moment using genre and character designations; the tension between self-identity and boundary transgression will become a major principle in his depictions of poetry as working to construct subjectivity.

In the maxims, the concept of a progression from moment to moment that eventually yields a unifying "main tone" (*Hauptton*) works in conjunction with the ideas of unification (of disparate moments) and of opposition, as each moment stands in contrast to the previous and subsequent moments. Hölderlin describes the opposition of individual moments using the names of literary genres (epic, lyric, dramatic) to characterize affective modes (naive, ideal, and historic, respectively) appearing within single works. Several sketches on Homer's *Iliad* work out some of the characteristics of each tone, but falter on the conflict between assigning tones to individual characters and the effort to read a primary tone out of an entire work.[72] The treatment of Homer also leads Hölderlin to differentiate emphatically between ancient and modern poetry, linking character types to epochs in history.[73]

Here, then, Hölderlin begins the systematization that he will eventually burden with an impossible proliferation of terms and clarifications. He also ties the poetic potential elucidated in the maxims back to the stakes of subjectivity that were barred from discursive language in "Being and Judgment." Moreover, even in the relatively colloquial style he adopts for the journal, he is unable to complete any of the texts except the aphorisms; he considers only one of the several character types in any detail, making repeated marginal notes calling for further steps (e.g., "Examples presented

---

71. Hölderlin, *Essays and Letters*, 241. For an analysis of this text similar to mine but with specific reference to German idealism, see Richard Eldridge, "'To Bear the Momentarily Incomplete': Subject Development and Expression in Hegel and Hölderlin," special issue, *Graduate Faculty Philosophy Journal* 27, no. 2 (2006): 141–58.

72. So, for example, in the sketch "On the Different Modes of Poetic Composition" (Hölderlin, *Essays and Letters*, 254–57), Hölderlin describes Achilles as ideal, but the *Iliad* as epic, and cannot balance the different characters and tendencies in poetic works to explain their existence as organically whole artworks.

73. See "The Standpoint from Which We Should Consider Antiquity," and the remark in "On the Different Modes of Poetic Composition" that "everyone has his qualities and at the same time his own faults" and the character we most wish to have present in "great [upheavals]" is the naive or epic character, who lives simply and "wholly in the present" (Hölderlin, *Essays and Letters*, 254–55).

in a lively manner" and "Expand").[74] Both the acknowledgment of human finitude and the anxiety to overcome it, then, remain constant in Hölderlin's theoretical writings as their scope widens from epistemology to religion to poetry to genre and history.

Hölderlin links the problems of divided subjectivity and its struggle to overcome human finitude most directly to his considerations of genre, epoch, and character in his attempts to write a tragedy on the death of Empedocles.[75] When the drafts run into difficulties, he turns to poetological explorations in an effort to overcome the problems of contingency that beset the literary work. In doing so, he projects his philosophically inflected poetic techniques into the constitution of the subject: the poetic problem of unification within a dynamic whole that changes over time becomes a problem for historical subjects (or, better, becomes once again a problem for human subjects, given the difficulties of self-identity in self-consciousness raised in "Being and Judgment"). Hölderlin takes the themes of opposition and unification and analyzes them within a single character (Empedocles) and within a historical era. Whereas in the journal sketches Hölderlin discussed the poetic enterprise of allowing momentary incompleteness to persist on the way to an aesthetic whole, in the "Ground of the *Empedocles*" he presents Empedocles as a figure whose desire to unite opposed character modes by himself within himself eventually proves fatal.[76] Empedocles becomes the "victim of his time"[77] rather than a poet or a hero because of the extremity of opposition present in his era: "The fate of his time, the [violent extremes in which he grew up,] . . . demanded a *sacrifice*."[78] The sacrificial victim unites the extremes of his age within himself, but such unity is fleeting and individual, and the victim or sacrifice perishes in his efforts to extend it. Such temporary unity and subsequent sacrifice appear "more or less with all tragic persons, who in their characters . . . are all more or less attempts to resolve the problem[s] of fate."[79] This structure, however, presents a problem for the plot of the tragedy, which also remained unfinished: if Empedocles's suicide is the inevitable result of his character's opposition to his era, he has every reason at any time for throwing himself into Mount Etna, and the actual act becomes contingent.[80]

---

74. Hölderlin, *Essays and Letters*, 246.
75. Hölderlin seems not to distinguish between tragedy and *Trauerspiel*, usually describing the *Empedocles* project as the latter. However, he discusses the project at length under the rubric of an analysis of *die tragische Ode* (the tragic ode).
76. Empedocles might also be seen as an instantiation (and condemnation) of the solipsism of the Fichtean "I am I" (Ich bin Ich). One cannot, for Hölderlin, secure human cognition of or relation to the absolute in a single subject, no matter how self-assured.
77. Hölderlin, *Essays and Letters*, 265.
78. Ibid.
79. Ibid., 265. Adler and Louth translate "problem of fate" in the singular, while the original is unambiguously plural: "*die* Probleme des Schicksals" (MA 1:873).
80. See Constantine, *Friedrich Hölderlin*, chap. 7. Hölderlin worried explicitly about the entry of contingency into tragic plot in a letter to Neuffer of 3 July 1799. He explains that "tragic subjects are made to proceed . . . with all possible sparing of accidentals" to "a whole that is full of powerful, meaningful parts" (Hölderlin, *Essays and Letters*, 146).

Hölderlin applies the idea of fatal *Auflösung* (resolution or dissolution) of dissonances in individuality to the progress of history in a sketch beginning "The declining fatherland..." (*Das untergehende Vaterland...*), written on a page of the last *Empedocles* draft.[81] The theme of the ending and beginning of opposing moments, previously the finitude of moments in a poem, now extends all the way to the periodic dissolution of entire historical epochs. But whereas the aphorisms presented the poetic process as a patient progression lacking assurances of final completion or success, now the process of history appears as a series of catastrophes whose losses *must* necessarily be recouped into a new era.[82] It is the role of "the free imitation of art," specifically tragedy, to render the catastrophe a "terrible but divine dream."[83] Tragedy enumerates the loss of old worlds in the formation of new orders; the creation of a work of art from the experience of catastrophe renders that catastrophe part of a narrative of progress. This narrative enables "union of the gap... which sets in between the new and the past."[84] Poetic work (here, tragedy) no longer preserves contrasts within unity; rather, in a move that would elide the problems of finitude opened but not answered by skeptical questioning, tragedy must smooth over any gap between human cognition of historical experience and an absolute or infinite cognition that can perceive historical tragedy as a seamless narrative progression.[85] Moreover, Hölderlin calls for a third stage of reflection of the ideal and the historical into each other, but does not work it out, drawing a line under an incomplete sentence and noting: "After these oppositions, the tragic union of the characters; and after this the opposition of the charters to the reciprocal and vice versa. After these, the tragic union of both."[86] In "The declining fatherland," then, anxiety over finitude, expressed as a need for wholeness, exceeds metatextual symptoms and appears in the thematic content on the level of individual subjects and entire historical epochs.

In his final attempt to treat poetological questions in abstraction of literary texts,[87] a draft convolution typically titled "When the poet is once in command of

---

81. Hölderlin, *Essays and Letters*, 271; MA 2:72.
82. This dissolution allows a new world to emerge, and every decline (*Untergang*) initiates a new beginning (see Hölderlin, *Essays and Letters*, 272–73).
83. Hölderlin, *Essays and Letters*, 272.
84. Ibid.
85. This "smoothing out" is what Eric Santner describes as "narrative vigilance" in *Friedrich Hölderlin: Narrative Vigilance and the Poetic Imagination* (New Brunswick, NJ: Rutgers University Press, 1986). Santner also provides the most succinct explanation of Hegel's absence in this project, despite the Hegelian designation of the phenomenology as *der sich selbst vollbringende Skeptizismus* (self-completing skepticism). For all the tragedies of death and rebirth in the *Phenomenology of Spirit*, the philosopher-observer "is initiated in the ways of the dialectic and thus knows that these various tragic breakdowns are inscribed in a grand Comedy of Homecoming and Recognition" (Santner, 40) The two sketches on tragedy are Hölderlin's most Hegelian texts (a fact perhaps explained by the proximity of the two thinkers at the time, as Hölderlin found Hegel a house tutor position in Frankfurt).
86. Hölderlin, *Essays and Letters*, 275.
87. The style of the text (it lacks the direct addresses and the fictionalized letter gestures that appear in the journal plan texts and the philosophical letters) and the sketched charts of poetic tones following it suggest that it was not intended for publication but was, like the *Empedocles* texts, an attempt to work through compositional difficulties. Hölderlin did write further poetological reflections as part of/in relation to his translations of Sophocles and Pindar.

the spirit . . ." (Wenn der Dichter einmal des Geistes mächtig ist . . .) and written in 1800. Hölderlin offers his most extended formulation of the processes of opposition and unification that make up poetry's project.[88] This draft, followed by several tables of permutations of genre designations (which Hölderlin here calls "tones") mapped onto components of poetic work, undermines efforts to designate a single genre or tone as paradigmatic or primary.[89] Instead, I track the six features I read as involved in problems of human finitude through several key moments of the text in order to understand its interweaving of the concerns that accrue to Hölderlin's investigations of human mindedness and poetic production.

In the interaction of these features, the text epitomizes Hölderlin's struggles to elucidate the tasks and possibilities of poetry and the anxiety that adheres to these struggles. My analyses of these features outline Hölderlin's picture of the tasks and problems of poetry while reinforcing the distinction between theoretical content and poetic language that forbids the direct application of his poetological schemata to his poetry. The themes of unity or continuity, active opposition, and dynamic temporality structure a contrast that drives much of the text: that between constancy (or identity) and change (or difference). These poles constitute an opposition that must be either harmonized or temporally suspended. Moreover, the smaller-scale oppositions that occur in the text (between kinds of content for a poem, for example, or between content, form, and what Hölderlin will call *Geist*, usually translated as "mind" or "spirit") all unfold in the temporal framework of the opposition between constancy and change. The textual symptoms indicating the presence of anxiety are also fully manifested here. Hölderlin calls for a further step repeatedly; perhaps the central experience of reading the text is one of having struggled through an extended series of unifications, only to arrive at a remark like "and when all this has been accomplished, still there is another stage." Further, the sheer number of terms and qualifications render the text extraordinarily difficult to read, and like so much of Hölderlin's theoretical work, it remained incomplete.

The first sentence presents two guiding oppositions, each of which will reappear throughout the text. The first opposition reiterates a version of the skeptical

---

88. Norbert von Hellingrath, who first published the sketch in his 1916 edition, titled it "Die Verfahrungsweise des poëtischen Geistes" (The Poetic Spirit's Mode of Proceeding), which felicitously conveys the draft's emphasis on temporality and processuality.

89. That numerous illustrious readers have failed to agree on either a central tone or an order of tones for any given poem suggests that this is not the most fruitful approach. For example, Karlheinz Stierle and Dieter Henrich argue for the lyric/ideal tone as central, Gerhard Kurz and Werner Hamacher for the tragic, and Peter Szondi and Eric Santner for the epic. See Karlheinz Stierle, "Die Identität des Gedichts—Hölderlin als Paradigma," in *Poetik und Hermeneutik* 8 (1979): 505–52; Dieter Henrich, *Der Gang des Andenkens: Beobachtungen und Gedanken zu Hölderlins Gedicht* (Stuttgart: Klett-Cotta, 1986); Kurz, *Mittelbarkeit und Vereinigung*; Werner Hamacher, "Parusie, Mauern: Mittelbarkeit und Zeitlichkeit, später Hölderlin," *Hölderlin Jahrbuch* 34 (2004/5): 93–142; Santner, *Narrative Vigilance*; and Peter Szondi, "'Überwindung des Klassizismus': Der Brief an Böhlendorff von 4. Dezember 1801," in *Hölderlin-Studien: Mit einem Traktat über philologische Erkenntnis* (Frankfurt a.M.: Insel Verlag, 1970), 85–104.

question of the fit between mind and world: Hölderlin worries about the integration of *Geist* and *Stoff*, where *Geist* suggests both mind/spirit in the idealist sense and the poetic topos of inspiration, while *Stoff* indicates content and is subsequently linked to the resistance to ideality of real life.[90] Hölderlin's second overarching opposition, the dichotomy between constancy and change or variation, continues the principle of reciprocity or interaction (*Wechselwirkung*) that he adapted from Fichte and Schiller, as well as the problems of identity and dynamic wholeness from his considerations of subjectivity and history. The integration of these four elements (*Geist*, *Stoff*, constancy/identity, and variation/difference) is Hölderlin's criterion for poetic success: stripped of its elaborate qualifications and correlative statements, the initial sentence reads: "When the poet is once in command of the spirit . . . then everything depends for him on the receptivity of the subject-matter to the idealic import and to the idealic form."[91] The sentence strays, however, into an attempt to clarify every condition for being *des Geistes mächtig* before reaching its conclusion three pages and eleven conditional *Wenn* clauses later:

> When the poet is once in command of the spirit, when he has felt and appropriated the common soul, that is common to all and peculiar to each, has held it fast, assured himself of it, when further he is certain of the free movement, the harmonious alternation and onward striving, with which the spirit tends to reproduce itself in itself and in others, certain of the beautiful *progressus* planned in the ideal of the spirit and its poetic deductive mode, when he has understood that a necessary conflict arises between the most original demand of the spirit, which aims at the community and united simultaneity of all parts, and between the other demand, that commands it to depart from itself and reproduce itself in itself and in others in a beautiful progress and alternation, when this conflict always holds him fast and draws him on, on the way to realization . . .[92]

---

90. On account of the peculiar connotations of *Geist* and the potential material meaning of *Stoff*, I use both terms in German throughout. Adler and Louth translate these terms as "spirit" and "subject-matter."

91. Hölderlin, *Essays and Letters*, 277–79.

92. Ibid., 277. Here, again, the grammatical necessities of translation in fact make the sentence easier to understand in translation than in the original, which reads: "Wenn der Dichter einmal des Geistes mächtig ist, wenn er [der Dichter] die gemeinschaftliche Seele, die allem gemein und jedem eigen ist, gefühlt und sich zugeeignet, sie [die Seele] vestgehalten, sich ihrer versichert hat, wenn er ferner der freien Bewegung, des harmonischen Wechsels und Fortstrebens, worinn der Geist sich in sich selber und in andern zu reproduciren geneigt ist, wenn er des schönen im Ideale des Geistes vorgezeichneten Progresses und seiner [des Progresses] poëtischen Folgerungsweise gewiß ist, wenn er eingesehen hat, daß ein nothwendiger Widerstreit entstehe zwischen der ursprünglichsten Forderung des Geistes, die auf Gemeinschaft und einiges Zugleichseyn aller Theile geht, und zwischen der anderen Forderung, welche ihm [Geist] gebietet, aus sich heraus zu gehen, und in einem schönen Fortschritt und Wechsel sich in sich selbst und in anderen zu reproduciren, wenn dieser Widerstreit ihn [den Dichter] immer vesthält und fortzieht, auf dem Wege zur Ausführung . . ." (MA 2:77; the bracketed clarifications of the referents of pronouns are mine).

The strain on language is immediately apparent: Hölderlin's appositions make it difficult to tell which agents perform which actions; each qualification has several subordinate conditions. Finally, the clauses presented here represent only the first stage in a progression from the apprehension of the poetic spirit that Hölderlin then continues in the subsequent clauses' explication of poetic execution. Hölderlin adds complications to the most originary demands (*ursprünglichste Forderungen*) of the poetic spirit. He asserts that each tendency or drive only becomes palpable by a conflict with its opposite. Conversely, the variation demanded by the second drive or demand can be felt only in contrast to the unity of what Hölderlin calls *sinnliche Form* (sensory form). By the end of the eighth clause, then, Hölderlin has deployed the substantive terms "form" and "content" (*Gehalt*) and qualified them with the adjectives "ideal," "material," "sensuous," and "spiritual."[93] Any term (made up of the combination of one adjective and one noun) that remains constant will be opposed to the variation of another; the opposition between any two terms is made up for by the complementarity of another two.

The three features of unification or continuity, opposition, and dynamization continue to structure the process depicted. Unification appears in the original demand or tendency of the poetic spirit as well as in the several elements that remain constant throughout the poetic process. Opposition occurs in the second drive to variation or differentiation and in the varying elements of the poetic execution. Moreover, there is an implicit opposition for the poet to traverse in the contrast between the concrete or actual and the ideal: although Hölderlin does not say so directly, the use of terms like "material" and "sensual" indicates that in the course of poetic execution, *Geist* moves out of the sheerly ideal realm into the concrete or actual. Finally, both opposition and unification appear on a structural level in the dynamic conflict between (and eventual harmony of) constancy and change that unfolds across the temporal space of the poem. Hölderlin gives here the most detailed version of the work he has been ascribing to poetry: the temporal unfolding of a poem offers the possibility for the unification or continuity of oppositions that do not disappear but can nonetheless be felt as an aesthetic whole.

But the sentence itself seems to strive, against Hölderlin's own precepts, to complete this work. The extensive correlatives that appear between the first and last clauses try *themselves* to overcome the opposition between content and spirit by elaborating every step of the process for their interrelation. The sheer difficulty of following the sentence is an effect of the text's proliferation of terms and conditions. While Hölderlin does not explicitly call for further steps, he repeatedly introduces clauses with the word *ferner* (further, furthermore), indicating that he sees the clause as yet another step to be taken. And while the sentence is (somewhat miraculously) grammatically complete, the sequence it lays out is so detailed that the remainder of

---

93. Hölderlin, *Essays and Letters*, 277–79.

the essay is unable to explicate most of its components in any detail: some disappear, others seem to change their referents throughout the piece, whose only gestured-at explications, footnotes, and repeated remarks that only the first stage of a process has occurred render its eventual incompleteness inevitable as Hölderlin once more tries to theorize the poetic process that he himself has denied to discursive presentation.

Rather than attempting to follow Hölderlin's (incomplete) explication of the terms in the first sentence, I will turn to perhaps the most striking instance of the active opposition of the poetic process: what Hölderlin calls the *Grund des Gedichts*, the ground, foundation, or even reason of (or for) the poem. After attempting to recreate the integration of *Geist* and *Stoff* in the first sentence, Hölderlin considers different kinds of material or content,[94] and then acknowledges the difficulty of making *Stoff* receptive to the poetic spirit.[95] Each poem begins from an initial conflict between *Stoff* and *Geist*, which Hölderlin claims must prove to be a necessary stage en route to the mutual completion of each by the other. In order to effect the transition from conflict to complementarity, Hölderlin deploys a new term, the "ground of the poem"; he also uses *Begründung* (foundation or even reason for existing). The primary characteristic of this ground is that it is self-oppositional: "It is characterized by the fact that it is everywhere opposed to itself."[96] Hölderlin locates the ground of the poem "between the expression (the representation) and the free idealic treatment,"[97] terms that point to the real or concrete execution in the content of the poem and to the (ideal, spiritual) *Geist* that must infuse both content and form, respectively. His description of the grounding or foundation (*Begründung*) as "the spiritually sensuous, the formally material,"[98] presents it as a figure of mediation between *Geist* (as spirit or mind) and the material, sensuous external world as they are worked together in poetic presentation.

Hölderlin makes this term extremely important for poetic success, as is perhaps clear in its designation as the ground or foundation, or even poem's purpose or cause. As such, it gives the poem "its seriousness, its firmness, its truth,"[99] and prevents it from falling into mannerism or empty virtuosity. And the unifying work of the ground of the poem occurs within the process of a poem's unfolding, in keeping with Hölderlin's conception of poetic temporality. The individual moments of the

---

94. These seem to correspond to the characters or tones he discussed in the earlier essays and will incorporate into poetological schemata. *Stoff* can be "a series of events, or views, or realities," "a series of endeavours, ideas, thoughts, or passions," or "a series of fantasies, possibilities." The first corresponds to the naive or epic tone, the second to the heroic or tragic, the third to the ideal or lyric (Hölderlin, *Essays and Letters*, 279).

95. "The poet is all too easily led astray by his subject, in that the latter, being taken out of its context in the living world, resists poetic limitation, in that it does not wish to serve as a mere vehicle for the spirit" (Hölderlin, *Essays and Letters*, 280).

96. Hölderlin, *Essays and Letters*, 281.

97. Ibid., 280.

98. Ibid., 281.

99. Ibid., 280.

poem's content oppose each other and the variation of the poetic spirit, and these oppositions occur as each moment proceeds into the next, eventually arriving at the aesthetic whole of a complete poem. But—perhaps due to the immensely high stakes for poetic unification and thus success attached to it—the *Grund* as an overarching term of mediation eventually collapses into a single stage of a greater reflective process. Hölderlin divides it into a "subjective" and an "objective ground" and proceeds to elaborate their roles and characteristics.[100] Here, as so often, a further step is necessary; moreover, that step prompts an additional proliferation of terms as a seemingly unifying term shifts to one side of an opposition to make room for a further reflective level, and the text succumbs to skeptical anxiety.

The theme of active opposition embodied in the ground of the poem reappears as a constitutive component of subjective and poetic identity in Hölderlin's presentation of what he calls the poetic I (*das poetische Ich*). The notion of a poetic subject links the questions of aesthetic wholeness and divided subjectivity that Hölderlin treated in his earlier texts to the poetic procedures he worked out throughout his career and develops in great detail here. Hölderlin introduces the poetic subject in a call for a further opposition in the progress of the poetic spirit to overcome its oscillation between wholeness and seriality. Here he makes explicit the analogy between the problems of wholeness for the subject and the problems of wholeness or completion for poetry: because the poetic spirit cannot simultaneously conceive of itself as self-identical and divided, it must place itself in relation to something outside itself in order to investigate the unity of those states. As Hölderlin has argued since his first theoretical sketches, the structure of divided identity or unified difference is precisely that of the human subject. The proper object in which the poetic spirit can grasp the overarching unity in its internal division is the poetic I. Hölderlin thus outlines a process of mutual completion on the part of the poetic subject and the poetic spirit.

The themes of unification or continuity, opposition, and dynamic temporality characterize the poetic subject as they do the poetic spirit: like the poetic spirit, the subject cannot think itself as simultaneously united and divided. Either it recognizes its own divisions (*Entgegensetzungen*), in which case the unity of its identity is illusory,[101] or it recognizes its own unity, in which case it is divided from the world and incapable of recognizing itself in its own past or future acts. In that case, it is not self-identical across time, and so its identity is once more an illusion. Instead, the subject must freely choose an object to which it can oppose itself in an act of harmonic opposition. The act of harmonic opposition permits the subject to perform the reflection necessary for comprehending an object as both cohesive and self-divided upon an external object before projecting them back into himself.[102]

---

100. Ibid., 282.
101. Ibid., 285.
102. "Just because he [the human subject] is not so intimately connected with this sphere, he can abstract from it and from himself, insofar as he is posited in it, and can reflect upon himself" (Hölderlin, *Essays and Letters*, 291).

Only in this act of free self-opposition and reflection can the subject understand itself as a being that encompasses both a state of indivisible, unreflected unity and reflective, rational self-consciousness in a subjectivity that persists across time. This self-understanding[103] is what Hölderlin calls the destiny or disposition of the human (*Bestimmung des Menschen*), and it can be reached only via poetic production.

The necessary relation between the poetic spirit and the poetic subject and the ability of the poetic subject to reach its destiny in poetic production also motivate Hölderlin's insistence on the necessity of individual and particular aesthetic production. He explicitly equates the progression of the subject to the progression of poetry before insisting that the poet's individual experience of the realization of his destiny gives rise to his poetic language. That language must be specifically his own in order to complete the linking of world, subject, and absolute in a successful work. If the poet uses language external to his subjective experience (i.e., if he tries to imitate another poet), the organic connection between the poetic *Geist*, the grounding of the *Geist* in *Stoff*, and the expression of their unification in a poetic work cannot occur.[104]

Hölderlin's final theoretical text, then, insists that the unification of the poles of human subjectivity that could make palpable the fit between self-conscious minds and the external world occurs only in poetic production.[105] He adds specific attention to the individual and communal use of language in which the poetic spirit and poetic subjectivity reflect into, enable, and complete one another. Both the arguments about the necessity of specific poetic production for the experience of aesthetic or subjective wholeness (a wholeness that does not overcome finitude but does point beyond itself) and the difficulty that results from the textual features indicating skeptical anxiety forbid the application of Hölderlin's theoretical texts directly to his poetic work. These texts do, however, elucidate the stakes for poetic production: any understanding by a human subject of itself as striving for something more than an individual pursuit of advantage must come in poetic activity, and that poetic activity must emerge out of particularized individual experience. In the next chapter, I will use the criteria for successful poetry loosely developed here as a general—but crucially, not directly prescriptive—framework for reading Hölderlin's late poetry. The themes of unification or continuity of oppositions across the space of a poem are complicated by their appearances in poetic works, but Hölderlin's poems work toward what his theoretical texts, by their own lights, cannot: a felt understanding of what it means to be subjects that are both aware of ourselves as limited, finite beings and alive to the world outside our limitations.

---

103. The German word Hölderlin uses is *Erkenntnis*, which denotes both cognition and recognition (MA 2:92–93).

104. Hölderlin, *Essays and Letters*, 294–96.

105. Although Hölderlin does produce analytical texts about the writing of poetry after 1800, he does so only in conjunction with completed works by other authors.

Friedrich Hölderlin, "Blödigkeit," "Das Nächste Beste," "Andenken"

Blödigkeit[1]

Sind denn dir nicht bekannt viele Lebendigen?
    Geht auf Wahrem dein Fuß nicht, wie auf Teppichen?
        Drum, mein Genius! tritt nur
            Baar in's Leben, und sorge nicht!   [4]

Was geschiehet, es sei alles gelegen dir!
    Sei zur Freude gereimt, oder was könnte denn
        Dich belaidigen, Herz, was
            Da begegnen, wohin du sollst?   [8]

Denn, seit Himmlischen gleich Menschen, ein einsam Wild
    Und die Himmlischen selbst führet, der Einkehr zu,
        Der Gesang und der Fürsten
            Chor, nach Arten, so waren auch   [12]

---

1. Friedrich Hölderlin, *Sämtliche Werke und Briefe*, ed. Michael Knaupp (Munich: Hanser Verlag, 1992), 1:443–44 (hereafter MA, followed by volume number and page number); cited by line number in chapter 3.

Wir, die Zungen des Volks gerne bei Lebenden,
    Wo sich vieles gesellt, freudig und jedem gleich,
        Jedem offen, so ist ja
            Unser Vater, des Himmels Gott, [16]

Der den denkenden Tag Armen und Reichen gönnt,
    Der, zur Wende der Zeit, uns die Entschlafenden
        Aufgerichtet an goldnen
            Gängelbanden, wie Kinder, hält. [20]

Gut auch sind und geschikt einem zu etwas wir,
    Wenn wir kommen, mit Kunst, und von den Himmlischen
        Einen bringen. Doch selber
            Bringen schikliche Hände wir. [24]

Timidness[2]

Of the living are not many well-known to you?
    On the truth don't your feet walk as [on carpets]?
        Boldly, therefore, my genius,
            Step right into the thick of life! [4]

All that happens there be welcome, a boon to you!
    Be disposed to feel joy, or is there anything
        That could harm you there, heart, that
            Could affront you, where you must go? [8]

For since gods grew like men, lonely as woodland beasts,
    And since, [according to kinds], song and the princely choir
        Brought the Heavenly in person
            Back to earth, so we too, the tongues [12]

Of the people, have liked living men's company,
    Where all kinds are conjoined, equal and open to
        Everyone, full of joy—for
            So our Father is, Heaven's God, [16]

Who to rich men and poor offers the thinking day,
    At the turning of Time holds us, the sleepy ones,
        Upright still with his golden
            Leading-strings, as one holds a child. [20]

---

2. Friedrich Hölderlin, *Poems and Fragments*, trans. Michael Hamburger, 4th ed. (London: Anvil Press Poetry, 2004), 265; cited by line number in chapter 3; modifications in brackets.

Someone, some way, we too serve, are of use, are sent
  When we come, with our art, and of the heavenly powers
    Bring one with us. But fitting,
      Skilful hands we ourselves provide. [24]

Das Nächste Beste[3]

    offen die Fenster des Himmels
Und freigelassen der Nachtgeist
Der himmelstürmende, der hat unser Land
Beschwäzet, mit Sprachen viel, unbändigen, und
[5]   Den Schutt gewälzet
Bis diese Stunde.
Doch kommt das, was ich will,
Wenn
Drum wie die Staaren
[10] Mit Freudengeschrei, wenn auf Gasgogne, Orten, wo viel Gärten sind,
Wenn im Olivenland, und
In liebenswürdiger Fremde,
Springbrunnen an grasbewachsnen Wegen
Die Bäum unwissend in der Wüste
[15] Die Sonne sticht,
Und das Herz der Erde thuet
Sich auf, wo um
Den Hügel von Eichen
Aus brennendem Lande
[20] Die Ströme und wo
Des Sonntags unter Tänzen
Gastfreundlich die Schwellen sind,
An blüthenbekränzten Straßen, stillegehend.
Sie spüren nemlich die Heimath,
[25] Wenn grad   aus falbem Stein,
Die Wasser silbern rieseln
Und heilig Grün sich zeigt
Auf feuchter Wiese der Charente,
Die klugen Sinne pflegend.   wenn aber
[30] Die Luft sich bahnt,
Und ihnen machet waker

---

3. MA 1:420–23; cited by line number in chapter 3.

Scharfwehend die Augen der Nordost, fliegen sie auf,
Und Ek um Eke
Das Liebere gewahrend
[35] Denn immer halten die sich genau an das Nächste,
Sehn sie die heiligen Wälder und die Flamme, blühendduftend
Des Wachstums und die Wolken des Gesanges fern und athmen Othem
Der Gesänge. Menschlich ist
Das Erkentniß. Aber die Himmlischen
[40] Auch haben solches mit sich, und des Morgens beobachten
Die Stunden und des Abends die Vögel. Himmlischen auch
Gehöret also solches. Wolan nun. Sonst in Zeiten
Des Geheimnisses hätt ich, als von Natur, gesagt,
Sie kommen, in Deutschland. Jezt aber, weil, wie die See
[45] Die Erd ist und die Länder, Männern gleich, die nicht
Vorüber gehen können, einander, untereinander
Sich schelten fast, so sag ich. Abendlich wohlgeschmiedet
Vom Oberlande biegt sich das Gebirg, wo auf hoher Wiese
    die Wälder sind wohl an
Der bairischen Ebne. Nemlich Gebirg
[50] Geht weit und streket, hinter Amberg sich und
Fränkischen Hügeln. Berühmt ist dieses. Umsonst nicht hat
Seitwärts gebogen Einer von Bergen der Jugend
Das Gebirg, und gerichtet das Gebirg
Heimatlich. Wildniß nemlich sind ihm die Alpen und
[55] Das Gebirg, das theilet die Tale und die Länge lang
Geht über die Erd. Dort aber rauschen, über spizem Winkel
Frohlokende Bäume. Gut ist, das gesezt ist. Aber Eines
Das ficht uns an Anhang, der bringt uns fast um heiligen Geist Barbaren
Auch leben, wo allein herrschet Sonne
[60] Und Mond. Gott aber hält uns, wenn zu sehn ist einer, der wolle
Umkehren mein Vaterland.

[P. 74 in upper margin: "Zwei Bretter und zwei
    Brettchen *apoll envers terre*]
Gehn mags nun. Fast, unrein. Bei Ilion aber auch
Das Licht der Adler. Aber in der Mitte
Der Himmel der Gesänge. Neben aber
[65] Am Ufer zornige Greise, der Entscheidung nemlich; die alle
Drei unser sind.

Das Tagwerk aber bleibt,
Der Erde Vergessenheit,

                    Wahrheit schenkt aber dazu
[70]   Den Athmenden
                    Der ewige Vater.

[P. 75 "Vom Abgrund nemlich" Marginal note: Die *apriorität* des Individuellen über das Ganze]
                    und kehr' in Hahnenschrei
                    Den Augenblik des Triumphs
                    Werber!   keine Polaken sind wir
                    Vom Abgrund nemlich haben
[5]   Wir angefangen und gegangen
                    Der Gelehrten halb
                    Μα τον ορκον[4] in Zweifel und Ärgerniß,
                    Denn sinnlicher sind Menschen
                    In dem Brand
[10]   Der Wüste
                    Lichttrunken und der Thiergeist ruhet
                    Mit ihnen. Bald aber wird, wie ein Hund, umgehn
                    In der Hizze meine Stimme auf den Gassen der Gärten
                    In denen wohnen Menschen
[15]   In Frankreich
                    [   ][5]
                    Frankfurt aber, neues zu sagen, nach der Gestalt, die
                    Abdruk ist der Natur,
[20]   Des Menschen nemlich, ist der Nabel
                    Dieser Erde. Diese Zeit auch
                    Ist Zeit, und deutschen Schmelzes.
                    Ein wilder Hügel aber stehet über dem Abhang
                    Meiner Gärten. Kirschenbäume. Scharfer Othem aber wehet
[25]   Um die Löcher des Felses. Allda bin ich
                    Alles miteinander. Wunderbar
                    Aber über Quellen beuget schlank
                    Ein Nußbaum sich und Beere, wie Korall
                    Hängen an dem Strauche über Röhren von Holz,

---

    4. "By the oath"; see Dieter Burdorf, *Hölderlins späte Gedichtfragmente: "Unendlicher Deutung voll"* (Stuttgart: Metzler Verlag, 1993), 360.
    5. Here the Munich edition incorporates text from a separate column from the left margin into the main text; I have omitted that text to preserve the startling lexical coherence between *Frank*reich and *Frank*furt in Hölderlin's manuscript.

76   *Lyric Orientations*

[30[6]] Aber schwer geht neben Bergen der Frohe weg   ]
         Aus denen. Rechts liegt aber der Forst.
         Ursprünglich aus Korn, nun aber zu gestehen, bevestigter Gesang von
                   Blumen als
         Neue Bildung aus der Stadt.
         Bis zu Schmerzen aber der Nase steigt
[35]   Citronengeruch auf und von dem Öl aus der Provence und wo
                   Dankbarkeit
         Und Natürlichkeit mir die Gasgognischen Lande
         Gegeben. Erzogen aber, noch zu sehen, hat mich
         Die Rappierlust [und des Festtags gebraten Fleisch
[40]   Der Tisch und braune Trauben, braune][7]
                   und mich leset o
         Ihr Blüthen von Deutschland, o mein Herz wird
         Untrügbarer Krystall an dem
         Das Licht sich prüfet
[45]   Vor   Deutschland

[The Nearest the Best/] What Is Nearest[8]

         open the windows of heaven
         And the night spirit [let] loose
         The heaven-stormer, who has persuaded our land
         With many unruly languages and
[5]   Has rolled his rubble
         Up to this hour.
         But what I want will come,
         When
         Therefore like the starlings
[10]   With shouts of joy, when in Gascony, places, where many gardens are,
         When in [the] olive land, and
         In lovely foreign lands,
         Fountains on paths overgrown with grass
         The unknowing trees in the desert

---

6. At this point the Munich edition skips from 25 to 35 in its line numbering; my numbering diverges hereafter rather than preserving the error.

7. The following lines are omitted in the Munich edition but are clearly integrated—as much as any of the text fragments in this section are—in the manuscript. See chapter 3, figure 2.

8. Friedrich Hölderlin, *Selected Poems of Friedrich Hölderlin*, trans. Maxine Chernoff and Paul Hoover (Richmond, CA: Omnidawn, 2008) 370–75; cited by line number in chapter 3; modifications in brackets.

[15] Stung by the sun
      And the heart of [the] earth
      Opens itself, where
      Around the hill of oaks
      From a burning land
[20] The streams and where
      On Sundays among dances
      The thresholds are hospitable to guests
      On streets strung with garlands, quietly swaying.
      For indeed they sense home,
[25] When straight   from pale yellow stone
      The waters ripple silver
      And holy green appears

      On a damp meadow of the Charente,

      Tending the clever senses.   but when
[30] The air prepares a way for itself
      And the North Wind, blowing sharply,
      Makes their eyes wide-awake, they fly off,
      And corner to corner
      Becoming aware of what is more dear,
[35] For they are always guided by exactly what is nearest,
      They see the holy forest and the flames of growth
      Blossoming fragrantly and the clouds of song far away
      And breathe the breath of songs. It's human
      To have perceptions. But the heavenly
[40] Also have something like that in them, and in the mornings they watch
      The hours and at evening the birds. To the heavenly
      This also pertains. [Very well, then.] But at those times
      [Of mystery I should, as though from nature, have said]
      "They are coming in Germany."
[45] But now, because the earth is like the sea,
      And the countries are like men,
      Who cannot pass one another,
      But scold each other, so I say, [well-forged, nocturnally,]
      The mountain range bends in the highlands,
[50] Where in pastures the forests overlook
      The Bavarian plain. For mountain ranges go far and stretch beyond
      Amberg and the Franconian hills. These are famous. Not for nothing
      Someone bent the mountain of youth sideways
      And turned it to face toward home.

78   *Lyric Orientations*

[55]   For the Alps are wilderness to him and
       The mountain range that divides the valley and stretches full-length
       Over the earth. But there [rustle over craggy peaks
       Joyful trees. Good is that which is solidly affixed.
       That contests our annexation, it robs us almost of the holy spirit   Barbarians
[60]   also live, where alone the sun rules
       And the moon. But God preserves us, when one is to be seen who will
       Overturn my fatherland.⁹]

   Let it run now. Nearly impure, [   ] But near Ilion
   There was also the light of eagles. But in the middle
[65]   The heaven of songs. But nearby,
   [Scornful] old men on the shore of decision, all three
   Of which are ours.

   [But the daily work remains
   Of the earth's forgottenness
[70]   Truth unto the mortal
   Gives, however
   The eternal father.]

[P. 75 Marginal note: "The apriority of the individual over the whole"]
       [and turn at the cocks' crow
           The moment of triumph

       Supplicants!   no Polacks are we]

       [10] We began of course at the abyss

       And have gone forth like lions
[5]   [through the learned
       Μα τον ορκον¹¹] In doubt and anger,
       For men are more sensual
       In the heat
[10]   Of deserts
       Drunk with light, and the spirit of animals

---

9. At this point the English editions (Chernoff and Hoover as well as Hamburger) follow the Stuttgart edition with some additions from the Frankfurt edition; no translations as yet have been based on the Munich edition, and therefore the translation of lines 57–62 is my own.

10. Chernoff and Hoover translate this section separately under the editorial title "Beginning at the Abyss." Hölderlin, *Selected Poems of Friedrich Hölderlin*, trans. Chernoff and Hoover, 392–95; cited by line number in chapter 3.

11. "By the oath." See note 4 above.

>   Lies down with them. But soon, like a dog
>   My voice will wander in the heat
>   Through the garden paths
> [15]   In which people live
>   In France.
>   [   ]
>   Frankfurt, rather, for to speak of nature
> [20]   Is to take its shape, human nature, I mean
>   [Navel] of this earth, our time
>   Is also time, and of German making.
>   An overgrown hill hangs above
>   My gardens. Cherry trees. But a sharp breath
> [25]   Blows through the holes in stone. And there I am []
>   All things at once. A wonderful
>   Nut tree bends over
>   The well springs and   itself. Berries like coral
>   Hang on the bush above the wooden downspout
> [30]   Which they used to make of corn,
>   But now,
>   Quite frankly, it sings most forcefully of flowers,
>   As news from town, where the smell of lemons
>   And oil from Provence rises almost painfully
> [35]   To the nose, [this thankfulness
>   And naturalness the region of Gascony
>   has given me.] Still to be seen,
>   What tamed and nourished me,
>   A love of the skewer and holiday roast,
> [40]   The table and brown grapes, so ripe
>   and gather me [o]
>   [You flowers of Germany], o my heart is turning
>   Into the truest crystal, in which
>   The light [tests itself]
>
> [45]   when   Germany

Andenken[12]

Der Nordost wehet,
Der liebste unter den Winden

---

12. MA 1:473–75; cited by line number in chapter 3; modifications in brackets.

Mir, weil er feurigen Geist
Und gute Fahrt verheißet den Schiffern.
Geh aber nun und grüße
Die schöne Garonne,
Und die Gärten von Bourdeaux
Dort, wo am scharfen Ufer
Hingehet der Steg und in den Strom
Tief fällt der Bach, darüber aber
Hinschauet ein edel Paar
Von Eichen und Silberpappeln; [12]

Noch denket das mir wohl und wie
Die breiten Gipfel neiget
Der Ulmwald, über die Mühl',
Im Hofe aber wächset ein Feigenbaum.
An Feiertagen gehn
Die braunen Frauen daselbst
Auf seidnen Boden,
Zur Märzenzeit,
Wenn gleich ist Nacht und Tag,
Und über langsamen Stegen,
Von goldenen Träumen schwer,
Einwiegende Lüfte ziehen. [24]

Es reiche aber,
Des dunkeln Lichtes voll,
Mir einer den duftenden Becher,
Damit ich ruhen möge; denn süß
Wär' unter Schatten der Schlummer.
Nicht ist es gut,
Seellos von sterblichen
Gedanken zu seyn. Doch gut
Ist ein Gespräch und zu sagen
Des Herzens Meinung, zu hören viel
Von Tagen der Lieb',
Und Thaten, welche geschehen. [36]

Wo aber sind die Freunde? Bellarmin
Mit dem Gefährten? Mancher
Trägt Scheue, an die Quelle zu gehn;
Es beginnet nemlich der Reichtum
Im Meere. Sie,
Wie Mahler, bringen zusammen

Das Schöne der Erd' und verschmähn
Den geflügelten Krieg nicht, und
Zu wohnen einsam, jahrlang, unter
Dem entlaubten Mast, wo nicht die Nacht durchglänzen
Die Feiertage der Stadt,
Und Saitenspiel und eingeborener Tanz nicht. [48]

Nun aber sind zu Indiern
Die Männer gegangen,
Dort an der luftigen Spiz'
An Traubenbergen, wo herab
Die Dordogne kommt,
Und zusammen mit der prächt'gen
Garonne meerbreit
Ausgehet der Strom. Es nehmet aber
Und giebt Gedächtniß die See,
Und die Lieb' auch heftet fleißig die Augen,
Was bleibet aber, stiften die Dichter. [59]

Remembrance[13]

The north-easterly blows,
Of winds the dearest to me
Because a fiery spirit
And happy voyage it promises mariners.
But go now, go and greet
The beautiful Garonne
And the gardens of Bordeaux,
To where on the rugged bank
The path runs and into the river
Deep falls the brook, but above them
A noble pair of oaks
And white poplars looks out; [12]

Still well I remember this, and how
The elm wood with its great leafy tops
Inclines, towards the mill,
But in the courtyard a fig tree grows.
On holidays there too
The brown women walk

---

13. Hölderlin, *Poems and Fragments*, trans. Hamburger, 577–79; cited by line number in chapter 3.

On silken ground,
In the month of March,
When night and day are equal
And over slow footpaths,
Heavy with golden dreams,
Lulling breezes drift.   [24]

But someone pass me
The fragrant cup
Full of the dark light,
So that I may rest now; for sweet
It would be to drowse amid shadows.
It is not good
To be soulless
With mortal thoughts. But good
Is converse, and to speak
The heart's [meaning], to hear many tales
About the days of love
And deeds that have occurred.   [36]

But where are the friends? Where Bellarmine
And his companion? [Some]
[Are] shy of going to the source;
For wealth begins in
The sea. And they,
Like painters, bring together
The beautiful things of the earth
And do not disdain winged war, and
To live in solitude for years, beneath the
Defoliate mast, where through the night do not gleam
The city's holidays
Nor music of strings, nor indigenous dancing.   [48]

But now to Indians
Those men have gone,
There on the airy peak
On grape-covered hills, where down
The Dordogne comes
And together with the glorious
Garonne as wide as the sea

The current sweeps out. But it is the sea
That takes and gives remembrance,
And love no less keeps eyes attentively fixed,
But what is lasting the poets provide. [59]

3

CALLS FOR COMMUNION

Hölderlin's Late Poetry

In chapter 2, I read Hölderlin's theoretical or poetological texts as struggling both thematically and metatextually with the dissatisfactions of subjectivity, a struggle I used the horizon of skepticism in the broad sense elaborated by Stanley Cavell to characterize as the subject's "argument . . . with itself (over its finitude)."[1] Because Hölderlin works within the historical paradigm of post-Kantian German philosophy, particularly idealism, he addresses problems of finitude in terms of unification: of the subject, of mind and world, of reason and freedom. Hölderlin contends (as I showed in the previous chapter) that philosophy undertakes to *solve* the problem of unification once and for all, performing the shift from metaphysical finitude to intellectual lack that I analyzed as skeptical.[2] Hölderlin likewise understands that the quest for certain *knowledge* necessarily fails. He succumbs, however, to the anxiety over finitude that drives such efforts in his theorizations, even as he

---

1. Stanley Cavell, *In Quest of the Ordinary: Lines of Skepticism and Romanticism* (Chicago: University of Chicago Press, 1988), 5.
2. Of course, not everything that we would today call philosophy operates according to this logic; as I discussed in the previous chapter, precisely at the moment Hölderlin is making this genre distinction between poetry and philosophy, Jena romanticism is experimenting with nonsystematic styles of philosophical or theoretical writing; later writers such as Nietzsche or Kierkegaard also come to mind. I discuss the overlaps and significant disagreements between Hölderlin and Jena romanticism in the section "Hölderlin's Context and His cultural Critique" in chapter 2.

sees unification not as a problem to be solved but as a task to be undertaken in poetry, repeatedly and without advance assurances of success. This paradox, I argued, shifts the relation between poetry and theory or poetology.

The question of the relation between poetry and theory becomes particularly acute in the period of Hölderlin's work that I treat in this chapter—namely, the years between his return from Bordeaux in 1802 and his institutionalization in 1806. Hölderlin had returned to his mother's house in Nürtingen in poor health, and his condition was likely worsened by learning of Susette Gontard's death in 1802. He remained in Nürtingen until 1804, when he moved at Sinclair's instigation to Homburg to work as court librarian until 1806; during these years, reports have him working diligently—causing both his mother and friend further concern for his health—but he did not write any abstract meditations on the purpose or techniques of poetry.

Moreover, it is possible to identify, at least in general terms, a shift in poetry in these years. Hölderlin's poetry can be loosely divided into five periods, although with significant overlaps: first, poems from his school years in Maulbronn and especially Tübingen (1786–93); then, works (including poems but also most of the poetological texts, as well as the novel *Hyperion* and the attempts at the *Empedocles* tragedy) written as he was winning his way to poetic and philosophical maturity (1794–1800); third, a period of formal mastery and cohesion, producing the long-form elegies and other poems (1800–1802); fourth, the period from 1802 to 1806 under consideration here, which exhibits a simultaneous expansion and concretion of Hölderlin's poetic world; and finally, the poetry written after his mental collapse in 1806, which contracts to a limited set of images and forms.[3]

Particularly compared with the years immediately prior, the poems from the period between 1802 and 1806 that I consider in this chapter exhibit a wide range of forms: Hölderlin increasingly experiments with poems in irregular or free rhythms

---

3. This is only a loose division; the boundaries are not absolute. Winfried Kudszus has argued for an incorporation of Hölderlin's "latest" (post-collapse) work into the main corpus of his poetic writings, based on stylistic features (see Kudszus, *Sprachverlust und Sinnwandel: Zur späten und spätesten Lyrik Hölderlins* [Stuttgart: Metzler Verlag, 1969]). Although I recognize some similarities and occasional overlaps between periods, I by and large share David Constantine's view of the matter: "Since 1826 Hölderlin's editors and the accompanying scholars have designated more and more of his work as fit for general consumption. Now there is nothing, not one legible word in the whole corpus of his writings, which any serious reader would dismiss as of no consequence.... There are two critical attitudes which, I think, need combatting. One is Bertaux's: that Hölderlin, perhaps like Rimbaud, fell silent of his own accord and isolated himself in silence. The other is Sattler's: that in the Tübingen poems Hölderlin worked through, in reverse, all the forms and phases of the first half of his creative life, to finish, Sattler says, 'im schimmernden *Wohllaut* der letzten Gedichte, in wiedererlangter Kindheit [in the shimmering euphony of the last poems, in a childhood reattained].' Neither of these theories seems to me to make any sense whatsoever, and both, I think, do Hölderlin serious injustice. To say that a writer who (as is well known) fought with all his resources against mental collapse fell silent deliberately, seems to me merely insulting, and a hypothesis deriving from the falsest romanticism. And likewise to pretend that the rhyming quatrains signed by Scardanelli are in any sense, moral or aesthetic, a culmination" (David Constantine, *Friedrich Hölderlin* [Oxford: Clarendon Press, 1988], 306).

while also continuing to write in some of the meters he adapted from ancient Greek poetry. The spheres of reference for his poetry change, too: from references to southwest Germany (Hölderlin's native soil) and ancient Greece they expand to France, the Near East, the Vatican, Poland, and the Americas; figures in the poems now include not only gods and demigods (Dionysus, Christ, Heracles) but specific historical figures (Columbus, potentially the Marquis de Lafayette, and a character from *Hyperion*, Bellarmin). While these changes result in a poetry of exceptional vividness,[4] they also present considerable difficulties as regards cohesion or occasionally even coherence.[5]

It might seem, therefore, that Hölderlin has abandoned his poetics of unification and moved on to an atomized, fragmentary, and particularized poetic world. And if we look in this poetry for unequivocal instances of the three particular tones—the lyric, the epic, and the dramatic—that Hölderlin attempts to map out in his earlier poetologies, or if we attempt to identify the specific poetic moments of each one, we will indeed be forced to conclude that the earlier poetology has been abandoned. But if we understand this kind of prescriptive, one-to-one relation between poetry and theory to be prohibited by the paradox I read as resulting from Hölderlin's anxiety over finitude, then it becomes clear that *what* Hölderlin's poetry strives for remains consistent, even as *how* his poetry undertakes its tasks changes after 1802. Indeed, the simultaneous expansion and concretion of the poetry from this period represent not a departure but an ever more rigorous attempt to fulfill the tasks of Hölderlin's earlier poetologies, and it is for this reason that I concentrate on it here. These works represent the culmination of Hölderlin's career-long struggle to create world orientations in language out of a divided subjectivity;[6] the rigor with which he pursues this program also brings it to the brink of failure.

---

4. See, e.g., Annette Hornbacher, "Wie ein Hund: Zum 'mythischen Vortrag' in Hölderlins Entwurf 'Das Nächste Beste,'" *Hölderlin Jahrbuch* 31 (1998/99): 227; Rolf Zuberbühler, *Hölderlins Erneuerung der Sprache aus ihren etymologischen Ursprüngen* (Berlin: Erich Schmidt Verlag, 1969), 20; and Gerhard Kurz, "Vaterländischer Gesang," in *Interpretationen: Gedichte von Friedrich Hölderlin*, ed. Gerhard Kurz (Stuttgart: Reclam, 1996), 166–85.

5. This concretion, combined with the frequently fragmentary character of Hölderlin's late work and his psychological breakdown, has resulted in readings of Hölderlin as a protomodernist shattered subject working with an aesthetic program of fragmentation. See, e.g., Werner Hamacher, "Parusie, Mauern: Mittelbarkeit und Zeitlichkeit, später Hölderlin," *Hölderlin Jahrbuch* 34 (2004/5): 93–143; Roland Reuss, *"Die eigene Rede des anderen": Hölderlins "Andenken" und "Mnemosyne"* (Frankfurt a.M.: Stroemfeld/Roter Stern, 1990); and Götz E. Hübner, "Nach Port-au-Prince: 'Andenken' als Hölderlins geschichtspoetologisches Vermächtnis," *Le Pauvre Holterling* 9 (2003): 43–54. This approach is both anachronistic and overly influenced by the biographical; while many of Hölderlin's drafts are fragmentary and unfinished, they posit and work toward a finished state indicated by the format of many of the manuscripts.

6. I am not arguing that only this subsection of Hölderlin's poetry may be read as striving to create lyric orientations that inhabit finitude; quite the contrary, throughout his career Hölderlin sees poetry as partaking in projects of cultural reform that involve—even if Hölderlin himself had not yet worked this out in detail—an engagement with the finitude of human subjectivity.

And his poetic tasks remain exceptionally ambitious. First, Hölderlin argues that successful poetry should create harmony between people (*Menschenharmonie*). Second, it is for Hölderlin only through poetic activity that the subject reaches its purpose or destiny (*Bestimmung*) as a self-divided and yet continuous entity. Third, in his view poetic representation enables human subjects to feel as well as deduce their place in a higher continuity between nature and the divine, and it unites subjects in a community that endeavors to overcome the limitations and isolation of its era. Finally, and perhaps the most difficult, all of this work (each of these tasks) must be accepted and attempted anew each time in each poem, since Hölderlin's acknowledgment of human finitude establishes that its success cannot be assured at the outset. And even if an authorial sense of success in achieving poetic closure occurs, because Hölderlin's poetic goals demand awaiting responsiveness from others (readers, hearers), even finished poetic work cannot fully banish anxiety, since there is no assurance that the poet's words will find any response (and indeed, a great part of Hölderlin's oeuvre did not in his lifetime).

As indicated by the distinction between theoretical and poetic language, as well as Hölderlin's poetic temporality in his command to the poet to "suffer that which is momentarily incomplete,"[7] poetic achievement for Hölderlin centrally involves experiences of waiting or responsiveness on several levels. The poet must be responsive to the world in its finitude, particularity, and separation from the subject, and to the finitude of particulars and their separation from and opposition to each other. He must likewise create a space for, rather than forcing, responsiveness from other minds or a larger community, as evidenced in Hölderlin's political stakes for poetry, in his adapting his poetic programs to his culture, and in his repeated use of figures of individual or cultural communication such as travel, letters, song, or conversation (*Gespräch*). And finally, the poetic rather than discursive or philosophical nature of poems involves openness or responsiveness to the reader: unlike idealism, in which the reader simply has to accept (and—less easily—comprehend) an entire system in which each part is supposed to follow from the first principles, a poem does not control every relation from its beginning to its end. Instead, the writing poet and the reading reader hold together each poem's (occasionally disparate or challenging) images, create temporal continuity between beginning and end, and are free to find, test, and accept or reject the orientations in language and to the world that suggest themselves as they orient their attentiveness to the poem. Hölderlin's thematizations of responsiveness and waiting reveal his recognition that lyric orientations cannot be successfully established once and for all, even as the desire that grounds the search for certainty bespeaks a fundamental human desire. In response he neither forces a coercive community nor gives up altogether on the possibility of shared attunement in our finite and fallible orientations.

---

7. Friedrich Hölderlin, *Essays and Letters*, ed. and trans. Jeremy Adler and Charlie Louth (New York: Penguin, 2009), 241.

Without a view of language that takes language and world as mutually influential in a form of life, it becomes difficult if not impossible to see how Hölderlin can ask poetry to undertake the unifying and orienting tasks he assigns to it.[8] But if human subjects learn language and the world together, along the lines of community, then the achievement of cohesion or unity within the linguistic working through of a poem poses the possibility of a radically new world orientation—for Hölderlin, unified oppositions, continuous communities, and dynamically changing but coherent worlds. This is precisely the project of revivifying culture through language (in Thoreau's terms) or the "convening on the social contract" (in Bernstein's) that I elaborated as a response to finitude that seeks acknowledgment rather than knowledge, inhabitation rather than overcoming, orientation rather than systematization.[9] Moreover, the increased concretion and particularity of the works from the years between 1802 and 1806 locate this acknowledgment ever more persistently in a finite and earthly ordinary, one whose fitness for subjectivity must constantly be rediscovered in the face of encroaching rationalism, national conflict, and modern isolation. To understand Hölderlin's poetic striving toward these goals I turn to the themes derived from but never fully realized in his poetological or theoretical texts as taking up the problems of finitude—namely, unification/continuity (*Zusammenhang*), opposition (*Entgegensetzung*), and dynamic temporality, as they develop and modulate in poetic form. These themes appear in his late poetry on both thematic and structural or formal levels (which become quite difficult to distinguish from one another) as the poems offer and explore various particular modes of inhabiting finitude.

Simply put, according to Hölderlin the completion of a poem is the creation of cohesion between the oppositions of discrete (thus opposed to one another) moments or images within the dynamic temporality that develops between the beginning and end of the poem. This process is perhaps easier to understand on the level of semantic content (rather than form or structure): poetic portrayals of active opposition occur in presentations of particular groups, landscapes, cultures, animals, and images, which often appear as separate or isolated from one another; themes of continuity, connection, or unification are portrayed through images of physical connection; the progress of a poem elaborates the dynamic temporality in which opposition and unification converge. Formally or structurally, dynamic poetic temporality relies on the opposition between individual moments and an entire work that Hölderlin elaborates, but necessarily (and by his

---

8. Therefore, readers who subscribe to a view of language as working only on itself because it fails to refer perfectly to the world will tend also to subscribe to the view that Hölderlin's late poetry is a poetry of fragmentation, failure, and loss that abandons his earlier poetics. This approach risks erasing the immense struggle for cohesion apparent—as I show below—even in Hölderlin's unfinished drafts.

9. See the section "Skepticism and/in the Ordinary" in chapter 1.

own lights) cannot execute, first in his journal sketches and later at great length in the overarching opposition between constancy and change in "When once the poet . . ." On a macro level of form, then, unification of or cohesion between oppositions occurs in the formal incorporation of different themes, images, or moments of a poem into an aesthetic whole; on a micro level, poetic form may separate groups or images via line breaks, or it may interrupt and isolate the cohesion of syntax via enjambment or fragmentation; that syntax itself may isolate particulars in paratactic constructions that render the relationships between them unclear.

The three poems I consider in this chapter take different approaches toward the problems of finitude, and consequently the features of continuity, opposition, and dynamic temporality appear in them in different ways. They thus offer a reasonably comprehensive picture of the most complete unfolding of problems of finitude in Hölderlin's work in his most ambitious period, and may consequently be deemed representative for this period of his oeuvre. "Blödigkeit" (Timidness), the first poem I treat, participates in the program of Hölderlin's "*Nachtgesänge*,"[10] as they foreground the lack of communal connectedness or continuity and allow isolation to persist as a preliminary call for union; "Blödkigkeit" in particular states a paradoxical call for poetic confidence based only on the lack of any assurances that could justify such confidence. The second poem I treat is a long-form draft fragment, "Das Nächste Beste" ("Whatever Is Nearest" or, more literally, "The Nearest the Best"), which seeks to integrate maximal sensory particularity into a large-scale poetic narrative; its self-imposed program of prioritizing the individual over the whole on the way to aesthetic cohesion eventually fails, leaving the poem a draft and reiterating that poetic unity and all it seeks to accomplish carry no guarantees of success. Finally, "Andenken" (Remembrance), perhaps Hölderlin's best-known work from this period, unfolds a startling number of finite oppositions that are held together by the work's strict thematic and formal symmetry; both the poem's midpoint and its final lines call for the kind of responsiveness from and to others that I read as central to Hölderlin's poetic inhabitations of finitude that yearns to exceed itself. In all three cases, I derive the terms of unification or continuity, opposition, and dynamic temporality from the images and forms of the poem being treated, unfolding them via careful description of the work before demonstrating its participation in Hölderlin's ambitious goals for poetry.[11]

---

10. *Nachtgesänge* is usually translated as "night songs." See, e.g., Friedrich Hölderlin, *Selected Poems and Fragments*, trans. Michael Hamburger (London: Penguin, 1994); and Hölderlin, *Selected Poems of Friedrich Hölderlin*, trans. Maxine Chernoff and Paul Hoover (Richmond, CA: Omnidawn, 2008); since the term is a neologism of Hölderlin's, I use the German *Nachtgesänge* throughout.

11. The three poems are provided in the original German with English translations directly preceding this chapter. Line numbers cited in the discussion of the poems in this chapter correspond to the German text and translations there provided.

"Blödigkeit" (Timidness)

"Blödigkeit" is one of the so-called *Nachtgesänge* written in 1803; the title (or genre designation) comes from a letter Hölderlin wrote to his publisher, Friedrich Wilmans, describing the poems being submitted; Wilmans then applied the term to the group of poems he published in 1805. In the letter, Hölderlin hints at a program for the poems (a set of nine short poems including asclepiadic and alcaic odes and poems in free rhythms[12]) as poetry written specifically for his era, understood as one in which limitation and isolation form the grounds of a call for community. The program Hölderlin hints at in his letter suggests a stance of deliberate participation in the limitations of modern culture: "I am in the middle of going through a few [*Nachtgesänge*] for your almanac. . . . It is a joy to sacrifice oneself to the reader and to enter with him into the narrow limits of our still child-like culture."[13] The ideas of boundedness ("narrow limits") and the tentativeness or timidity that might be described as childlike accurately describe both the themes and the material presentation of "Blödigkeit," as I show below; conversely, "timidity" describes the programmatic stance of the *Nachtgesänge* as a whole, in which poetic work seeks to show the isolated particulars (groups, objects, cultures) of the external world as calling forth and awaiting a community of responsiveness that has not yet arrived. Hölderlin thus acknowledges both the isolation and separation of the world as he finds it and the impossibility of undoing such isolation (and thus overcoming human finitude) once and for all.

I suggest that "Blödigkeit" and the *Nachtgesänge* as a group accept the uncertain task of creating unsponsored continuity between opposed or isolated groups, states, or objects. In doing so, the ode in particular and the *Nachtgesänge* together offer one set of responses—shaped by the features of opposition, continuity, and dynamic temporality—to the problems of finite subjectivity struggling to make sense of its own experience that I read as paradigmatic both for Hölderlin and for acknowledgment of human finitude. Poem and program undertake this task in the presentation of radically opposed states that are both held apart and mediated by poetic form, as, for example, in "Hälfte des Lebens" (Half of Life) or in the portrayal of unmediated cultural and temporal separation undermined by zeugmatic syntax in "Lebensalter" (Ages of Life). In my readings of Hölderlin's poetological texts in chapter 2, I showed his linking of poetic activity and human subjectivity to be his response to the post-Kantian form of problems of human finitude and world orientation. The striving of poetic activity toward a future unreachable cohesion between the components of the world both acknowledges the separateness that

---

12. Especially since it is unclear whether the poems were published in the order Hölderlin intended, I avoid the term "cycle" in referring to them. On the ordering of the poems, in particular the placement of the three in free rhythms together at the end, see Wolfram Groddeck, "*Lebensalter*," in Kurz, *Interpretationen*, 153–65.

13. Hölderlin, *Essays and Letters*, 217; MA 2:927.

motivates such striving and, in the successful instantiations and formal manifestations of both separateness and continuity of the *Nachtgesänge*, reminds an isolated modern culture that there is a unification still to be yearned for.

"Blödigkeit," the only asclepiadic ode in the *Nachtgesänge*, is in fact a heavily revised version of an earlier ode entitled "Dichtermuth" (usually translated as "The Poet's Courage"). While "Blödigkeit" seems to narrate a progression from assertive fearfulness to modest confidence, it also holds open a tension between uncertainty and destiny, skill and hesitation. The poem begins with an address, apparently from the poet to himself, then continues this address over two strophes and three rhetorical questions (in lines 1–2 and 5–8); it seems to answer those questions (or rather justify their implied answers) over the third through fifth strophes. Finally (lines 21–24), it appears to offer a concluding declaration about a group (in the first-person plural), presumably poets, that contributes its own skill to the task of aesthetic mediation between the isolated or opposing orders, including heavenly and earthly, as well as human, animal, and divine.

Because of its status as a revised version of an earlier poem, "Blödigkeit" also returns to the question of the shift in Hölderlin's poetic strategies that I raised at the opening of this chapter. Here, too, I argue that the later draft is more particular and concrete; moreover, it addresses explicitly the challenges to cohesion posed by this increased concretion and links them to the poetic task of the *Nachtgesänge* in calling attention to the divisions and isolation of Hölderlin's contemporary culture.[14] Diction changes between the two poems show that, in general, the transition from first to last versions changes descriptions of simply present affinities to expressions of cognitive work (e.g., the first line changes from "Isn't everything alive already in your blood?" to "Of the living are not many well-known to you?"—from blood

---

14. Walter Benjamin usefully points out key differences between "Blödigkeit" and its earlier versions in his 1916 interpretation of "Dichtermuth" and "Blödigkeit." Walter Benjamin, "Two Poems by Friedrich Hölderlin: 'The Poet's Courage' and 'Timidity,'" in *Walter Benjamin: Selected Writings*, ed. Marcus Bullock and Michael W. Jennings (Cambridge, MA: Belknap Press of Harvard University Press, 1996), 1:18–36. With a normative valence that I accept, Benjamin differentiates between what he calls myth or the mythical (*Mythos, das Mythische*) and the mythological (*das Mythologische*). Benjamin understands the mythological as a poem's inclusion of elements from the cultural reservoir of mythologemes; the mythic refers to the intensity and indissolubility of the relations between elements within a poem, that is, to precisely the intensive connectedness between disparate or even opposing elements that I characterize using Hölderlin's vocabulary of *Zusammenhang*. Wolfram Groddeck sees this conception of myth as evidence that Benjamin did read some of Hölderlin's theoretical texts, which he could have accessed in Böhm's 1911 edition. Groddeck also points out a slippage in Benjamin's use of the term "mythic" from an unequivocally positive to a destructive concept even within the Hölderlin essay, one that he explains will ramify further in Benjamin's later essay on Goethe's *Wahlverwandschaften*. See Wolfram Groddeck, "Ästhetischer Kommentar: Anmerkungen zu Walter Benjamins Hölderlinlektüre," *Le Pauvre Holterling* 1 (1976): 20. "Dichtermuth" is, Benjamin argues, "mythological"; in "Blödigkeit," by contrast, all of the elements in the poem are fully and intensively woven into one another, making it (for Benjamin) "mythic." Benjamin elegantly points out the transition in the poems in miniature in the change of the title: *Dichtermuth* is a compound neologism of Hölderlin's, forced by necessity and derived from a false relation to the people; *Blödigkeit*, by contrast, is a word in general usage (Benjamin, "Two Poems," 24).

relation to knowledge or familiarity; the heavenly father grants "the thinking day," no longer "the joyful day" [line 17], etc.).[15] Regardless of the precise terms in which the poem's opening questions are posed (affective or cognitive, passive or active), the apparent stating of the program that justifies the poet's assurance introduces the most radical departure between versions (lines 9–20).[16]

In both versions, the third and fourth strophes present the grounds for the poet's potential achievement of continuity or cohesion between opposed or separate groups; the two strophes accomplish this presentation, however, in radically different ways. The syntax differs greatly between the two versions: in "Dichtermuth," the inversions and interjections are less prominent than those in the corresponding lines in "Blödigkeit," in which two direct objects (the heavenly and humans, *Himmlischen* and *Menschen*) are designated as alike (*gleich*) in their similarity to *ein einsam Wild* (lonely as woodland beasts, 9). The subject of the sentences, *der Gesang* (song), does not appear until the third line of the strophe, and a description of the activity of *Gesang* precedes the naming of its agent: *Gesang* leads both humans and heavenly beings toward *Einkehr* (return or refuge).[17] "Blödigkeit" uses syntax that makes the terms of comparison between the heavenly and the earthly unclear; the insistence on

---

15. Jochen Schmidt, *Hölderlins später Widerruf in den Oden "Chiron," "Blödigkeit" und "Ganymed"* (Tübingen: Max Niemeyer Verlag, 1978), 113. As should be obvious from my reading Hölderlin's late work using terms from (though not direct application of) his poetological texts, I disagree with Schmidt's main claim that Hölderlin's revisions of earlier texts represent a full-scale recantation (*Widerruf*) of his earlier poetics.

16. After this crucial point, "Dichtermuth" has an extra strophe, and the poems end very differently. "Dichtermuth" makes the setting sun an image of the death of the sun god, and requires submission to transience modeled by the god of mortals, culminating in praise of beautiful death.

17. See Robert André, "Hölderlins Auf-Gabe und die Ode *Blödigkeit*," in *Das Denken der Sprache und die Performanz des Literarischen um 1800*, ed. Stephen Jaeger and Stefan Willer (Würzburg: Königshausen und Neumann, 2000), 63. Benjamin describes the weaving together of these groups or elements in "Blödigkeit" as "an infinite chain of series (*Reihen*)" (Benjamin, "Two Poems," 25). The idea of a row or series helps level the seemingly hierarchical relation of heavenly and earthly beings that appears in the poem (lines 9–12, 16–20, and 22–24). By using the term *Reihe* or "series," Benjamin makes a useful analogy between Hölderlin's poetic composition and the musical strategies of serialism, contemporaneous with the essay, in which the use of a twelve-tone compositional row avoids the teleological organizational structures of Western tonal harmony but does so without insisting on either sameness or unorganized multiplicity. For a discussion of Benjamin's *Reihe* as the negation of vertical hierarchies of organization, see Giovanni Scimonello, "Benjamin, Adorno und Hölderlin: Interpretation der Ode 'Dichtermuth/Blödigkeit,'" in *In Bildern Denken: Studien zur gesellschaftskritischen Funktion der Literatur*, ed. Giovanni Scimonello and Ralph Szukala (Bielefeld: Aithesis Verlag, 2008), 11–32. Scimonello also points out that Adorno takes this description of the poem and attempts to formulate a discussion of Hölderlin's late style in general in the parataxis essay (25–26). I would contend that there is nothing in the concept of parataxis, understood as next-to-ness, that means it must take on the fragmentary and rupturing connotations Adorno assigns to it in the essay, and so my adoption of the term does not conflict with my discussion of *Zusammenhang* or continuity in Hölderlin's late works. I am not, of course, suggesting any kind of influence or direct relation whatsoever between twelve-tone composition and Hölderlin; rather, Benjamin's analogy is a helpful heuristic for imagining what he, and by extension Hölderlin, could mean by nonhierarchical organization leading to intensive interpenetration of elements. I demonstrate below that the principle of organized, noncontingent proximity, an instantiation of the theme of *Zusammenhang* or continuity, structures both the form and the thematic material in the ode "Blödigkeit."

Arten ("kinds" or even "species," line 12) differentiates orders of beings, from animal to human to divine. The fourth strophe of "Blödigkeit," then, amounts to a paradox: the heavenly and humans are asserted to be alike (*gleich*) precisely insofar as they are different according to kinds (*nach Arten*).[18] Moreover, the two versions present different temporalities: in "Dichtermuth," the grounds for the poet's confidence rest on the history of poetry: ever since mortals have sung, poets' songs have brought joy to the hearts of men. In "Blödigkeit," by contrast, it remains ambiguous whether the "turning of Time" (18), in which song will lead both humans and gods toward *Einkehr*,[19] has passed, occurs in the moment of the poem's speaking, or is yet to come.

The ambiguity of both syntax and temporality complicates the poem's statement of its own task and the grounds for the poet's confidence (in lines 9–16): particularly if the crucial moment in which each of the orders is led toward homecoming has not yet arrived, the role of song (*Gesang*) in securing continuity between opposed orders that would found the poet's confidence is fundamentally unclear. In a circularity that at once seems to trap the poet in uncertainty and to tighten the relations between gods, animals, and men (which should counteract that uncertainty), the poem posits its own task or program as justification for the risk of undertaking that task. This circular self-grounding seems to explain the change in the poem's title from "Dichtermuth" to "Blödigkeit": given that the poem's assurances are grounded only in its self-risking task, timidity would be the natural standpoint from which to confront the undertaking of writing poetry.

And yet "Blödigkeit" ends with a cautious statement of poetic talent or ability, emphasizing the contribution of mortal poets to their task of bringing the heavenly (22–24). It does so, moreover, in a way that reiterates the separateness of gods and men and the role of the human poet in creating a continuity between them: the poets bring skillful, suitable, or fitting hands to their poetic task:

> Doch selber
> Bringen schikliche Hände wir.
>
> (23–24)

Hölderlin repeats the verb *bringen*, describing both what it is the poetic task to bring ("of the heavenly powers . . . one," 22, 23) and what poets themselves bring to the task ("skillful hands," 24). *Schicklichkeit* (with connotations of propriety, seemliness, and expediency) and *Geschicktheit* (adroitness, deftness, skill) bespeak an aptness or ability (in keeping with the insistence on contribution *nach Arten*, according to one's kind, in the fourth strophe) that contrasts with the modesty and uncertainty attaching to the concept of timidity. The poem thus instantiates

---

18. André, "Hölderlins Auf-Gabe," 64.
19. *Einkehr* is further related to *Wende* ("turning"; in line 18, "turning of time") by way of *kehren*, "to turn."

an ambiguity, tension, or openness between opposing semantic fields: the terms *Schicklichkeit* and *Geschicktheit* are semantically aligned with the contemporaneous rhetoric of perfectibility, but the poem also emphasizes the deficiency in presence of mind and confidence that are attached to *Blödigkeit*.[20]

The poem thus presents its own program as one of being ungrounded or unsponsored; it does so via tensions between confidence and timidity on both semantic and formal levels. Line 2 of the poem provides its own figure or image for the formal (both spatial and temporal) organizing capacities of poetic work. This poetic work, for which the poets' hands are later described as *schicklich* (skillful), reiterates the presence of the poets at the turning of time—the word carries connotations of being in the right place at the right time, able to take action. Further, the sense of *place* spatializes poetic capabilities, taking up the idea of *Ge*legen*heit* ("opportunity, occasion, or chance," but containing *legen*, the word for "to place or lay something down," 5) and the curious simile "On the truth don't your feet walk as [on carpets]?" (2). Hölderlin's figure of the carpet indicates the organization of truth (*Wahres*) into an aesthetic rather than systematic or hierarchical schema; "weaving" or "patterning" might be understood as a figure for what poetry can do that, according to Hölderlin, philosophy or theory cannot.[21] The unification or connection of oppositions I have read as occurring across the temporal unfolding of a poem occurs in the space of the simile; the physicality of the foot that steps onto true things (*Wahrem*) as on carpets underscores the concreteness of the figure of continuity even as the form of the ode temporalizes the idea of patterned organization and repetition.

But this creation of continuity or cohesion in the space and time of the poem is undermined by tensions within the poem's form and by the circularity in its self-describing narrative; these tensions are held open by both form and program. Particularly in the three verses I examined in detail, the structure of the asclepiadic ode is overrun by the poem's syntax:[22] repeated enjambment causes phrases to spill

---

20. On the historical semantics of *Blödigkeit* (timidity, timidness), see Georg Stanitzek, *Blödigkeit: Beschreibungen des Individuums im 18. Jahrhundert* (Tübingen: Niemeyer, 1989), 272.

21. Benjamin points to the patterned carpet as related to the principle of the arabesque as a visual representation of an infinity filled with particulars. See Benjamin, "Two Poems," 28; and Beatrice Hanssen: "Just as the Oriental ornament was consumed in and by the absolute, so the early Romantics' idea of a progressive *Universalpoesie*, Benjamin implied, held out the promise of an infinite process of completion or consummation (*Erfüllung*). . . . Yet he refused to read this endless expanse of infinitude as the reign of a syncopating, empty, mechanical time. Instead, the distance between the present and the as yet inaccessible future for him unmistakably carried messianic overtones, pointing to the however distant, yet possible return of plenitude" (Beatrice Hanssen, "'Dichtermuth' and 'Blödigkeit': Two Poems by Hölderlin Interpreted by Walter Benjamin," *MLN* 112, no. 5 [1997]: 794).

22. Hans Jürgen Scheuer points this out as well. In doing so, however, he reaches considerably outside Hölderlin and appeals to Horace's description of such forms as *disiecti membra poetae*, "the limbs of the mutilated poet," thus linking it to the earlier versions' depictions of rivers, temporal flow, and the death of the poet as a trope of poetic vulnerability centered around the mutilated body of Orpheus. Since "Blödigkeit" is the version with the most extreme enjambment and also the version that discards the stoic ending with the death of the poet, this seems to me a misguided application of a genuinely helpful insight. See Scheuer, "Verlagerung des Mythos in die Struktur: Hölderlins Bearbeitung des Orpheus-Todes in der Odenfolge 'Muth des Dichters'—'Dichtermuth'—'Blödigkeit,'" *Jahrbuch der deutschen Schillergesellschaft* 45 (2001): 271–72.

over from lines into strophes, and in fact, strophes 3 to 5 are made up of a single sentence. The questions that open the poem are not answered; their being asked suggests that the questions themselves are in response to uncertainty on the part of the speaker. And the third strophe, which looks like an answer to those questions, is in fact not an assurance that the connectedness the poem asks for in the first strophe exists or is achievable. Instead, the poem's assurances are grounded only on a statement of its own program: the attempted cohesion between opposed and isolated groups that will nevertheless maintain their individual identities. The poem is thus caught between the confident placing of its regular form (which it describes in the simile of the carpet or tapestry) and its disruptive syntax, a further opposition whose poles belong together in the aesthetic whole of the poem. Semantically, timidity is *both* one pole of the programmatic ambiguity between timidity and aptness *and* the response to their conflict; it is the proper stance of a poet confining himself to the narrow limits of his culture, in which the problems of human finitude are held open.

"Blödigkeit" thus enacts (crucially, it does not simply state) the difficulty of attaining any world orientation that incorporates the finitude of the human subject and of separate particulars or kinds (*Arten*) within the kind of cohesion Hölderlin strives for in his theoretical texts; here, this cohesion is sought by the linking of oppositions within the dynamic temporality of poetic form and syntax. Hölderlin's use of form and syntax to challenge and balance each other, and his portrayal of specific figures whose relations of equality and specificity offer an unattained yet yearned-for image of belonging, together address the problems of finitude he grapples with across his career, using resources specific to poetry.[23] In the tensions between its form and its syntax and in its paradoxical call for equality according to kinds the poem stakes its own wholeness on such cohesion without advance assurances that it can be attained—indeed, the program of the *Nachtgesänge* and the poems themselves imply that the separateness of orders in fact may not be overcome. The poem thus demonstrates that the only possible grounding for continuity is the attempting of its creation—that is, the writing of poetry that takes as its task the creation of continuity between separate and opposed orders across the temporal space of a poem. The separation of different orders or kinds is not elided; instead, precisely that separation and the attempt at cohesion across poetic form serve as a preliminary call for union.

"Das Nächste Beste" (Whatever Is Nearest)

"Das Nächste Beste" reverses the approach to subjective finitude and the ensuing problems of world orientation taken by "Blödigkeit" and the *Nachtgesänge* in

---

23. Of course, poetry does not, as it were, do *everything*: the very shift to particularity and formal shaping deprives the poem of the assured universality and theoretical certainty desired in Hölderlin's theoretical texts and in systematic philosophy more generally; but then, this is precisely the anxious drive toward totality that produces the paradox of Hölderlin's theoretical texts and converts metaphysical finitude to an intellectual lack; that is to say, the drive toward assurances that by his own lights Hölderlin's poetry must do without.

general even as it continues to investigate those problems in formal and thematic treatments of unification/continuity, opposition, and dynamic temporality. Here, these problems appear in terms of the problems of the relation between part (or particular) and whole (or absolute). This relation is one instance of the opposition between unified cohesion and differentiated particularity that Hölderlin takes up in "When once the poet . . ." as the struggle for dynamic wholeness shared by subjectivity and poetry.[24] The poem's approach to this problem is stated explicitly in a marginal note on the third page of the draft: "Die *apriorität* des Individuellen über das Ganze" (The apriority of the individual over the whole). Like the title (in English, "The Nearest the Best"), the note seems to attribute primacy to the individual, particular or near, even suggesting that such wholeness or continuity between the particular and the absolute (between the nearest and the best) is possible only through an intensity of attention to the particular. This problem, task, or program is both thematic and formal, and unfolds within precisely the kind of dynamic temporality I read out of Hölderlin's theoretical texts. There Hölderlin explains that the varieties of active opposition I have been tracking throughout his work arise not only between each moment and its successor and predecessor but also between the identity of each individual moment and the flux of moments on the way to a whole. "Das Nächste Beste" presents at least one successful figure of how achievement of orientation to the near, next, or nearest contributes to and even creates a continuous goal or destination, one that is linked explicitly to poetic production.

But while the poem's themes and images seem to suggest a necessary relation between orientation to the particular and achievement of totality or integration, the poem's form calls this possibility into question. The problem of wholeness turns out to be symptomatic for the draft, given that it remained a disparate collection of notes, images, and longer stretches of text (in free rhythms). These fragments occupy four pages (73–76) in the so-called Homburg Folio, a notebook of finished or nearly finished poems, edited versions of earlier poems, and draft sketches.[25] The draft can be broken into two main sections,[26] but the continuation of thematic material between sections suggests that the second is not an entirely new fragment but rather a new treatment of the same or intimately related topics.[27] Because of the state of the draft, it is neither possible nor productive to incorporate every element of it into a single interpretation. Instead, I contrast the opening scene of chaos and discontinuity with Hölderlin's main figures of continuity and then follow the poem

---

24. See the section "Hölderlin's Theoretical Oeuvre" in chapter 2.
25. See Dieter Burdorf, *Hölderlins späte Gedichtfragmente: "Unendlicher Deutung voll"* (Stuttgart: Metzler Verlag, 1993), 52.
26. Sometimes separated under editorial titles as "Das Nächste Beste" (Whatever Is Nearest") and "Vom Abgrund nemlich" (From the Abyss of Course), respectively.
27. Dieter Burdorf, "Der Text als Landschaft: Eine topographische Lektüre der Seiten 73–76 des Homburger Folioheftes," in *Neue Wege zu Hölderlin*, ed. Uwe Beyer (Würzburg: Königshausen und Neumann, 1994), 139.

into its images of remarkable sensory and particular intensity that nonetheless remain punctual, fulfilling the project of the apriority of the individual at the cost of aesthetic wholeness.

The poem's opening characterizes the historical moment of its writing vividly, as it describes and then criticizes the chaos (both atmospheric and linguistic) of its era into which a new event seems to erupt:

> offen die Fenster des Himmels
> Und freigelassen der Nachtgeist
>
> (1–2)

The "night spirit" (*Nachtgeist*) recalls the cultural separation and disorganization of the *Nachtgesänge*, suggesting its role as a figure of disruption or discontinuity. In a grammatical underscoring of the scene's chaos, the ambiguity of the genitive makes it unclear whether the windows are open *to* the heavens—so also vulnerable to the night spirit—or the windows *of* the heavens might be open, releasing the night spirit. In this ambiguity, the poem anticipates the physical and dynamic continuity between heaven and earth that will motivate aesthetic production later in the poem, but here dynamism and energy appear threatening: the connection between heaven and earth releases an elemental force that storms the earth. The next clause further emphasizes the disorder of the opening scene:

> Der himmelstürmende, der hat unser Land
> Beschwäzet, mit Sprachen viel, unbändigen, und
> Den Schutt gewälzet
>
> (3–5)

It portrays Babel-like confusion: a multiplicity of languages blurs into befuddling palaver. Hölderlin lists several adjectives over *unbändigen* (unruly), including *unfriedlichen* (unpeaceful), *unendlichen* (unending), and *undichtrischen* (unpoetic). The adjectives, though not equivalent, collectively condemn chaotic multiplicity as opposed to boundedness, peace, and poetry, thus conveying a multifaceted rejection of unorganized numerousness. (And Hölderlin seems to have been more decided on the stress/meter of the adjective than its content: all are stressed on the middle syllable, and he alters *undichterischen* to *undichtrischen* so that it remains four rather than five syllables.) Here, Hölderlin's critique of unbound language is illuminated by the draft situation; the draft's chaos and confusion mirror the linguistic multiplicity and perplexity it portrays as symptomatic of its era.

The subsequent clause reiterates the condemnation and highlights the arrival of a turning point or new event, with potentially political consequences: the *Nachtgeist* has stirred aimlessly through rubble until the present time. In his placement of the break between the fifth and sixth lines, Hölderlin reiterates the breaking in of the event that began the poem on a formal level:

> Den Schutt gewälzet
> Bis diese Stunde.
>
> (5–6)

Moreover, this event has national, political, and/or geographical implications, indicated by "our land." Hölderlin depicts the consequences of a nonpoetic era for the multiple particulars that drive his program: without the binding effects of poetic speech, countries are divided, things are rubble, and language is babble. Any merging or linking of orders that would place disparate objects, words, and verses into sense-making continuity with each other (rather than heaped-up multiplicity) requires the interruption of history.

After the opening scene of chaos and discontinuity, Hölderlin introduces what will be a central figure in the poem and its primary vehicle for the portrayal of connectedness or continuity: starlings. They become an effective poetic subject for his thematizations of connections between the orders of gods, animals, and humans. The starlings in particular are introduced in the ninth and tenth lines:

> Drum wie die Staaren
> Mit Freudengeschrei
>
> (9–10)

As birds, the starlings function as figures that blur the boundaries between animals, humans, and gods: they are animals, but move within the ethereal realm of the gods in a physical topos of continuity. Their physical movement also creates a geographical continuity via their migratory route, as they trace the southwestern to northeastern European axis present in many of Hölderlin's late works. They take flight, goaded by traces of their home, just as the landscape seems to be its most hospitable:

> Sie spüren nemlich die Heimath,
> Wenn grad   aus falbem Stein,
> Die Wasser silbern rieseln
> Und heilig Grün sich zeigt
> Auf feuchter Wiese der Charente
>
> (24–28)

Air and wind give the final impetus for the starlings' departure, underscoring their belonging to the ethereal world as well as the animal world:

> wenn aber
> Die Luft sich bahnt,
> Und ihnen machet waker
> Scharfwehend die Augen der Nordost, fliegen sie auf
>
> (29–32)

Wind—itself a fluid but physical connection between geographically disparate locations—blowing from the migratory destination perhaps recalls the starlings to their aerial element and seems to initiate their sudden taking flight.

The peculiar nature of the starlings' flight justifies their role as figures of continuity that can create a harmonious community; moreover, Hölderlin uses a poetic description of that flight to introduce the theme of *Gesang*, aesthetic production enabled by the felt and enacted relation between the near/particular and the divine/absolute. Appropriately, his depiction of the starlings' flight reintroduces the title's theme of "das Nächste":

> Und Ek um Eke
> Das Liebere gewahrend
> Denn *immer halten die sich genau an das Nächste*
>
> (33–35; my emphasis)

The line's description of the starlings' orientation to the particular (*das Nächste*) is, as it happens, accurate, and the ornithological background helps explain the role of the starlings in the poem: starlings, unlike most other migratory birds, fly oriented to each other and to the alterations of the landscape beneath them rather than only toward the migratory goal.[28] This orientation to the particular motivates the poem's appeal to flight as a figure of poetic cohesion: unwavering focus on the nearest landscape simultaneously leads toward a distant goal or a whole journey (or, I would want to say, poem). Moreover, their orientation toward particular features that nonetheless leads toward a goal does *not* produce chaotic individuals moving randomly in multiple directions.[29] This program for aesthetic production presents, here in poetic form, Hölderlin's remarks that while subjective orientation to the absolute can produce consciousness of duty, it cannot ground harmony either within the subject or between subjects.[30] For that, an aesthetic community grounded in particularity—here represented by the starlings—is required.

---

28. Burdorf, *Hölderlins späte Gedichtfragmente*, 124. Whether or not Hölderlin knew that ornithology confirmed this behavior, he had ample opportunity to observe starlings as he walked the first section of their migratory route—the route described in the poem—from Bordeaux to Nürtingen in the summer of 1801. The starlings' flocking behavior (called murmuration) is visually striking, enough so that it is still occasionally reported on—with photographs—in contemporary media.

29. Burdorf, *Hölderlins späte Gedichtfragmente*, 124.

30. See letter to Carl Gock, 1 January 1799, in Hölderlin, *Essays and Letters*, 123.

And indeed, the starlings offer a vision of orientation to the particular that enables an overarching trajectory and a cohesive community. Furthermore, it is this community based on the particular from which poetry or *Gesang* (song) emerges.[31] Here, *Nächste* as neighbor (in German, *der Nächste*) is hinted at beneath the grammatical meaning; the term *Nächste* seems initially to refer to the neighboring bird. While the article *das* denies this reading, the suggestion of the importance of the relations between individuals in a poetic space remains. Furthermore, the poem follows the prescription it derives from the starlings in its attention to the particular landscape of the South of France through which Hölderlin walked returning from Bordeaux to Nürtingen in 1802: it describes sun, rivers, trees, and inhabitants of the landscape (11–23), basing its orientation to particulars on individual perception and personal memory.

Just as Hölderlin's perceptions and memories make up the poem's images, the poem itself thematizes poetic production based on the starlings' orientation to the particular:

Sehn sie die heiligen Wälder und die Flamme, blühendduftend
Des Wachstums und die Wolken des Gesangs fern und athmen Othem
Der Gesänge.

(36–38)

In a masterful progression from the flight of the starlings, by way of what (initially) seem to be merely the objects they see, Hölderlin raises the gaze of the starlings and the attention of the reader from the forest floor to the leaves to the rising perfume of flowers called forth by the sun to the clouds.[32] The starlings breathe clouds that do not contain but are, themselves, song (the description never ceases to make imagistic sense: birds do fly through clouds, and would breathe them). This song emerges out of the rapid and yet full connectedness of the earthly to the heavenly as enacted in the poem in the flight of the starlings.

At this point, then, the era of chaos and multiplicity depicted in the opening sentence seems to have been overcome, as particulars are organized into a pattern

---

31. Gerhard Kurz points out that the word *Freudengeschrei* (shouts of joy) links the draft to Hölderlin's description of the *Frohlokken vaterländischer Gesang* (Adler and Louth translate—unjustifiably—"the high and pure rejoicing of poems on our times"; Hölderlin, *Essays and Letters*, 217. There is no indication that Hölderlin thinks he or anyone in his era has successfully written such poetry. A better translation would be "rejoicing of patriotic or fatherlandic song.") The term *Frohlokken* (rejoicing) in the Luther Bible translation refers to explicitly vocally expressed joy. Conversely, the shrieking of the starlings seems to render them unfit for the melodiousness implied by *Gesang*; perhaps precisely the fact that they seem less effortless and beautiful in their singing makes them an appropriate figure for modern poetic production.

32. I have made "flame" far too benign in glossing it as plumes of rising scents; throughout the draft there is a sense of sunlight being threatening or too intense. Hölderlin may have derived the image from watching the starlings: in flight, a swarm of starlings looks like clouds or plumes of smoke, indicating the (imagined) presence of "flames" beneath them.

of flight or song. Having used his depiction of the starlings' migration to show that they have privileged access to *Gesang* by virtue of their form of life, Hölderlin links their perceptions in flight to human perception or recognition: "Menschlich ist / Das Erkenntniß" (38–39; "It's human / To have perceptions"). Although the translation interprets the line as a general remark about having perceptions in the plural, Hölderlin uses the singular, thus suggesting the additional possibility that *this* perception, that is, of the starlings' flight, is observed by humans. Moreover, Hölderlin places the human specifically between gods (the heavenly) and birds as he qualifies the human location of this recognition:

> Aber die Himmlischen
> Auch haben solches mit sich
>
> (39–40)

Not only does the song through which the starlings move serve as an aesthetic mediation between gods, animals, and men; the gods also seem to share attributes of human perception. Gods, animals, and humans are placed in their proper relation by way of the poetic portrayal of the migration of individuals (starlings) focused on the particular (in the landscape) who nevertheless form a community and take part in an overarching trajectory.

This depiction seems more hierarchical than that in "Blödigkeit," for example—first animals, then humans in the middle, and then gods in heaven—but precisely the physical form of connectivity Hölderlin derives from the starlings' flight undermines these clear distinctions: seen by humans, starlings are animals that move in the sphere of the heavenly. Hölderlin's depiction of an animal's physical process—the migration of birds—allows him to move fluidly between the life forms he presents in his derivations of the poetic project of song in a nonabstracted version of continuity (*Zusammenhang*).[33] Like "Blödigkeit," "Das Nächste Beste" thematizes and struggles with the unification of opposed orders or groups, but whereas the former posits the absence of connection between gods, animals, and humans as a preliminary call for union, "Das Nächste Beste" uses depictions of physical movement to effect poetic jointure of orders, if only for the moment of the poem.

While the starlings seem to offer the possibility of at least a tenuous version of this continuity between opposed groups and orders, unified within aesthetic production, the comparison of human nations to a divided earth that immediately follows the description of their flight makes clear that such merging cannot guarantee universal wholeness or cohesion, and the subsequent images of the poem undergo

---

33. Again, poetry's ability to fill in the abstract idea of connection (*Zusammenhang*) with specific content whose attributes change or deepen the notion of continuity is Hölderlin's reason for turning to poetry rather than to the abstractions of theory or philosophy.

the chaotic fracturing the poem's opening portrays.[34] In what appears to be an effort to secure the poem's connection between its particular descriptions and a divine or absolute, Hölderlin shifts abruptly at the bottom of the poem's second page (page 74 in the notebook) from (particular) landscape description to a link between human work and an eternal father:

> Das Tagwerk aber bleibt,
> Der Erde Vergessenheit,
> Wahrheit schenkt aber dazu
> Den Athmenden
> Der ewige Vater.
>
> (68–72)

Several factors, however, render this connection ambivalent or uncertain. "The eternal father" is nominative, and as such the source of the gift to *Den Athmenden* (literally, "the breathing ones"; here presumably, "mortals") The gift, *Wahrheit* (truth), locates the iterative *Tagwerk* (daily work) in relation to the eternal father, setting it between the material being of the earth and the heavenly father. But the precipitousness with which the connection is made departs radically from the specificity and particularity of the earlier images (for example, the description of the starlings' flight occupies thirty lines; the connection to the heavenly father only five). Likewise, the physical tropes of connectedness (represented earlier by depictions of migration and by dynamic verbs and adjectives) disappear. The particularity demanded by the poem's title and internal program drops out as the draft merely asserts a relation to "the eternal father." Hölderlin's uncertainty about that relation emerges as he tries out the words three times, in three different places, in the draft (see fig. 1). This leap to the divine, then, interrupts and undermines the particularized continuity appearing in the earlier moments of the draft. Hölderlin seems to attempt to assure poetic success by imposing a posited end point distinct from the previous images and strategies of the poem.

The uncertainty of this attempt appears to motivate the abandonment of the first version of the draft's material and to prompt a shift in strategy on the next page (page 75 in the notebook). And indeed, the page opens with the remark I cited at the outset of my reading: "Die *apriorität* des Individuellen über das Ganze" (The apriority of the individual over the whole). Appropriately, it exhibits a remarkable

---

34. The lines seem to imply that before, in some other time, merely the image of the starlings would have been enough, whereas now something additional is required: "Sonst in Zeiten / Des Geheimnisses hätt ich, als von Natur, gesagt, / Sie kommen, in Deutschland. Jezt aber, weil, wie die See / Die Erd ist und die Länder, Männern gleich, die nicht / Vorüber gehen können, einander, untereinander / Sich schelten fast, so sag ich." (42–47; "But at those times / [Of mystery I should, as though from nature, have said,] 'They are coming in Germany.' / But now, because the earth is like the sea, / And the countries are like men, / Who cannot pass one another, / But scold each other, so I say.")

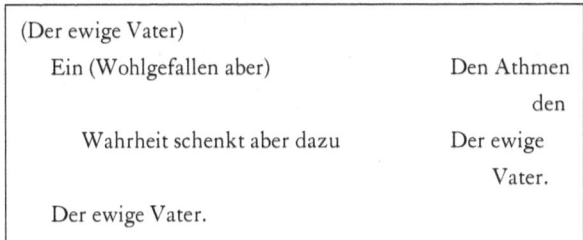

Figure 1. Der ewige Vater/The eternal father. From FHA Suppl. III Beil., 100.

intensity of sensory description as the themes of continuity, dynamic vertical movement, revolution, landscapes, and geographic particularity recur in more stubbornly terrestrial form. The poem's second beginning, like its first, depicts a moment of decision and departure:

> Vom Abgrund nemlich haben
> Wir angefangen und gegangen
>
> (4–5)

Here, however, those departing are a poetic "we," not the unspecified and ethereal figure of the night spirit. And in contrast to the first version's figure of poetry, the starlings, the second attempt presents an entirely earthly animal:

> Bald aber wird, wie ein Hund, umgehn
> In der Hizze meine Stimme auf den Gassen der Gärten
> In denen wohnen Menschen
> In Frankreich
>
> (12–15)

The locus of the comparison between a subjective (potentially poetic voice) and a dog is somewhat opaque; if the dog is understood not as a watchdog or domesticated but as feral or semidomesticated, it might function as a figure of betweenness, standing for animality and the wild or uncultivated in the middle of culture.[35] A figure of liminality, then, replaces the figure of ethereal mediation; the aesthetic notion of song (*Gesang*) does not appear at this stage in the draft; moreover, the potential for community in the starlings' flight and the mediation between orders that followed on the mention of song are absent here. Instead, Hölderlin compares a (first-person possessive) poetic voice to an (animal) figure both within and outside

---

35. Hornbacher, "Wie ein Hund," 230–31.

culture whose reception within that culture is uncertain and whose connection to the divine has disappeared.

Hölderlin further underscores the terrestrial sphere of the second part of the draft by introducing specific (and *written*) geographical names that replace the aerial trajectory completed by the starlings:

> In denen wohnen Menschen
> In Frankreich.
>
> Frankfurt aber
>
> (15–17)

The text moves along the same axis as before, from southwest to northeast, but here the aerial tracing of the trajectory in the birds' flight is replaced by a material/lexical jointure. Instead of a flight pattern, the written names of the two locations instantiate the geographical shift along purely lexical lines, from Frank*reich* (France) to Frank*furt*. The connective work performed earlier by an avian figure suspended between terrestrial and ethereal moves inside the text of the poem itself. The connection between the two locations is created only by way of what Hölderlin calls solid letters that both bind the two places together and differentiate them.[36] Hölderlin's device foregrounds the necessarily double character of language as both referential and material, but the shift feels abrupt and oddly specific.[37]

This specificity gives rise to several sets of extraordinarily vivid imagery, whose precision fails to coalesce into any series, group, or process (physical or narrative); the draft's attempts to fulfill the program of the primacy of the individual over

---

36. Hölderlin's command to attend to *die veste Buchstabe* (the solid letter; "Patmos," first version, line 225; MA 1:453) is well known; less so a letter in which he dwells on the pleasing solidity (*Veste*) of the raw printing of his Sophocles translations: "I almost preferred the raw print, probably because in this typography the traits which mark the solid aspect of the letters [*welche an den Buchstaben das Veste anzeigen*] hold their own so well in relation to the modifying traits, and this was even more noticeable in the raw print than in the filed or polished version" (Hölderlin to Friedrich Wilmans, 2 April 1804, in Hölderlin, *Essays and Letters*, 219; MA 2:929).

37. Frankfurt also appears in one of the more mystifying metaphors in the poem. The metaphor combines classical Greek imagery with landscape figures and potentially biographical or political significances: "Frankfurt aber, neues zu sagen, nach der Gestalt, die / Abdruk ist der Natur / Des Menschen nemlich, ist der Nabel / Dieser Erde." (18–21; "Frankfurt, rather, to speak of nature / Is to take its shape, human nature, I mean / [Navel] of this earth.") Hölderlin interweaves human and natural forms to the extent that they become extremely difficult to unravel. He concretizes the layering of landscapes and bodies in a single point, Frankfurt as the earth's navel—a metaphor usually applied to the oracle at Delphi. Given that Frankfurt is where Hölderlin met and fell in love with Susette Gontard, and where she died, this is perhaps the reason for an otherwise unremarkable European city's affiliation with the holy site of Apollo. It has also been argued that the metaphor derived from contemporary visual culture: Bennholdt-Thomsen and Guzzoni have uncovered maps of Europe in which the continent was a woman with Germany as stomach, although they could not determine that there was such a map in any library Hölderlin used. See Anke Bennholdt-Thomsen and Alfredo Guzzoni, *Analecta Hölderliana I: Zur Hermetik des Spätwerks* (Würzburg: Königshausen und Neumann, 1999).

the whole founders on the sheer vividness and multiplicity of sensory particulars. After the abrupt shift from Frank*reich* to Frank*furt* the poem juxtaposes the image of berries on branches over a spring with an evocation of the South of France.[38] In the lines

> Bis zu Schmerzen aber der Nase steigt
> Citronengeruch auf und von dem Oel aus der Provence
>
> (34–35)

the sensory (olfactory) presence of southern France seems to erupt into southwestern Germany, perhaps an eruption of the speaker's memory into his present. The juxtaposed images are not mediated or explained by any statement of memory, however, or by any connective figure; instead, the draft shuttles back and forth between France ("the region of Gascony," 34) and Germany once more as images of grapes and meat (perhaps the material version of Hölderlin's earlier feasts or festivals as figures of community), God and *Schicksal* (fate, destiny), and light refracted through a crystal heart are scattered across the page (see fig. 2). At the end of the draft, then, the vivid sensory particularity of the images—themselves in keeping with Hölderlin's demand for the "apriority of the individual"—precludes the production of a poetic whole. The poem's images are juxtaposed against one another without mediation; the poem's form does not hold together the disparate moments or images to create an aesthetic whole—indeed, as the image shows, the poem's form is overrun by single images on unconnected lines.

But the struggle to attain continuity or cohesion in "Das Nächste Beste" is not exclusively a problem of linking singular and potentially opposing moments, nor is it merely a matter of abstract oppositions subsumed in theoretical syntheses. Concerns about or portrayals of continuity, unification, cohesion, or connectedness also occur on imagistic, thematic, and structural levels. These movements represent the kind of *Zusammenhang* (cohesion or continuity) I read out of Hölderlin's theoretical texts, imbued with particular or individual content enabled by poetic rather than theoretical language. As is evident in the depictions of starlings, landscapes, and cultures, Hölderlin dwells on images of particular landscapes, and animals along with their activities of opening, flowing, dancing,

---

38. "Ein wilder Hügel aber stehet über dem Abhang / Meiner Gärten. Kirschenbäume. Scharfer Othem aber wehet / Um die Löcher des Felses. Allda bin ich / Alles miteinander. Wunderbar / Aber über Quellen beuget schlank / Ein Nußbaum sich und Beere, wie Korall / Hängen an dem Strauche über Röhren von Holz." (23–29; "An overgrown hill hangs above / My gardens. Cherry trees. But a sharp breath / Blows through the holes in stone. And there I am / All things at once. A wonderful / Nut tree bends over / The well springs and itself. Berries like coral / Hang on the bush above the wooden downspout.") The spring is linked, as it will be in "Andenken," to an intense coalescence of potentiality in the line "Allda bin ich / Alles miteinander" (25–26; "And there I am / All things at once").

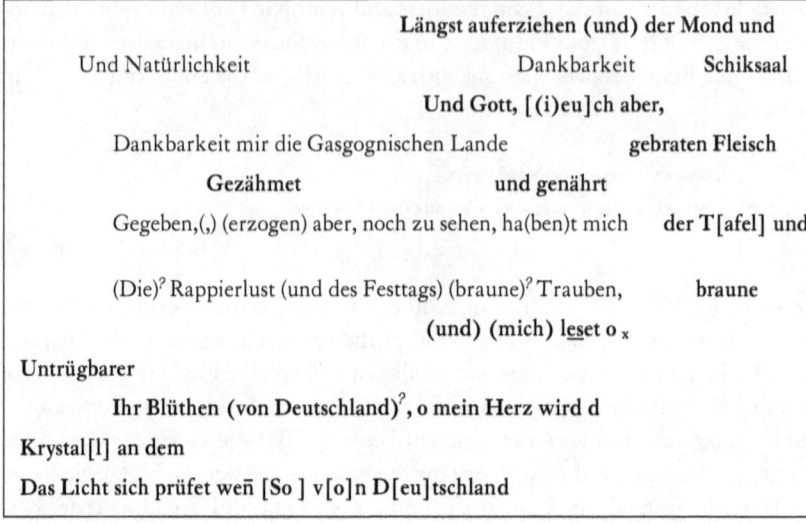

Figure 2. Image scattering. From FHA Suppl. III Beil., 100.

going, flying, bending, and so on. As a theme, continuity between or unification of oppositions occurs in portrayals of, for example, the unification of differences, traversal of geographical or cultural spaces, and liminal or boundary sites such as thresholds or coastlines. As a structure, this connectedness appears in Hölderlin's blending of the poem's different themes into one another as opposed or disparate orders merge throughout the poem. Gods, humans, and animals are mentioned in rapid succession; generalized descriptions of sweeping geographical scope blend with precise descriptions of single landscapes as distant locations collapse into each other; landscapes merge with anatomy; beginning and ending combine as the time of the poem's writing takes up the dynamic temporality that shapes it on a thematic level.

These structural, thematic, and imagistic versions of cohesion exemplify Hölderlin's experiments with lyric poetry as a mode of world orientation that does not elide individual particularity in the search for an absolute and permanent orientation, but rather struggles to use poetic language to link finite elements into a cohesive whole. The draft explicitly casts the tension between atomized opposition and continuity as a problem of part/whole relations; in doing so, it reveals the ways in which continuity emerges not merely as a thematic concept but as a formal principle striven for but not achieved in a draft of the magnitude of "Das Nächste Beste." And the draft is in some sense a performance of the worries the *Nachtgesänge* in general and "Blödigkeit" in particular express: the grounding of continuity and community on poetic activity that has nothing but itself to assure cohesion may always fail.

"Andenken" (Remembrance)

Like "Blödigkeit" and "Das Nächste Beste," "Andenken" poses several problems for interpretation. In particular, it seems to integrate personal memories from Hölderlin's time as a house tutor in Bordeaux with universalizing and normative statements about poetry's tasks without any explanation of their relation. The poem thus forces the question of how individualized and subjective experience might or might not fit with statements about what is "good" and "not good" (in the third strophe) and apparent maxims for poetic production such as the final line of the poem: "Was bleibet aber, stiften die Dichter" (59; "But what is lasting the poets provide"). Interpretations of these seemingly universal statements, however, remain curiously bifurcated. One line of interpretation reads the poem as a successful coalescence of personal memory into timeless poetic maxim.[39] The other, conversely, interprets it as a lament for the failure of language and expressivity, marked throughout by death and absence.[40] This bifurcation is the second problem posed for interpreters standing at the end of a long tradition of twentieth-century scholarship: what, in the poem itself, has led readers to disagree in this way? And finally, perhaps because of the interrelation between personal memory and universal maxim, the poem has almost invariably been read as programmatic, thematizing the role of the poet and poetry in relation to other forms of life. In particular, the poem is often read as presenting the task of poets in contrast to an intersubjective vision of love and a heroic or active depiction of seafaring.

At least some of these perplexities are accounted for by understanding "Andenken" as taking a third approach to the holding open of the problems of finitude, with which Hölderlin is engaged from early in his career. Within the poem, precisely the kinds of oppositional structures in which finite particulars balance one another are held together within a strictly symmetrical form. The integration of personal memory and seemingly universal maxim bespeaks the desire to transcend individual finitude without abandoning the particular and is itself an overarching opposition subsumed within the dynamic temporality of the poem's form. And the bifurcation of interpretations may derive from the oppositional nature of the images, as readers attend either to the images of cohesion and unity or to those of finitude and absence that are woven together across the poem. Finally, understanding the oppositional structures that characterize Hölderlin's work as themselves always

---

39. Its proponents include, for all their differences, Martin Heidegger (*Erläuterungen zu Hölderlins Dichtung* [Frankfurt a.M.: Vittorio Klostermann, 1951]), Dieter Henrich (*The Course of Remembrance and Other Essays on Hölderlin* [Stanford, CA: Stanford University Press, 1997]), and Hans-Georg Gadamer ("Anmerkung zu Hölderlins 'Andenken,'" in Beyer, *Neue Wege zu Hölderlin*, 143–52).

40. Advanced most directly by Reuss, *Hölderlins "Andenken" und "Mnemosyne"*; and Cyrus Hamlin, "Die Poetik des Gedächtnisses: Aus einem Gespräch über Hölderlins 'Andenken,'" *Hölderlin Jahrbuch* 24 (1984/85): 119–38; and in line with Adorno's reading of Hölderlin's oeuvre as a whole; see Theodor Adorno, "Parataxis: Zur späten Lyrik Hölderlins," in *Gesammelte Schriften in 20 Bänden* (Frankfurt a.M.: Suhrkamp, 2003), 11:447–94.

already seeking unification enables a reading of the poem's task that does not suggest that poets supersede love and seafaring in producing lasting works, but rather requests and waits for responsiveness or *Gespräch* (conversation) with others, even when none may be forthcoming.

Even at the level of thematic summary the poem's form emerges as an instantiation of the cohesion of oppositions within a dynamic temporality. An overarching opposition between the first two and the last two strophes creates thematic and formal symmetry around the midpoint of the third strophe. The first two strophes depict an idyllic landscape (in which natural and cultural features merge in tropes like gardens and woods) as the place of social ritual (*Feiertage*, "holidays"); that ritual is, moreover, loosely gendered feminine: *braunen Frauen* (brown women, 18) are the human figures located in the landscape. The final two strophes, in contrast, begin with an acknowledgment of absence in the question "Wo aber sind die Freunde?" (37; "But where are the friends?") and describe a (male-gendered) life of seafaring, war, and deprivation. This overarching opposition is complicated, however, by the introduction of smaller-scale oppositions between strophes 1 and 2, 4 and 5, and within individual verses and even lines. So, for example, the second strophe differentiates itself from the first in that it portrays its own speech as memory, suggesting that the plenitude of the strophe's images is past, not (as it appears in the first strophe) present; conversely, the fifth strophe's thematization of departure returns to the description of the Bordelaise landscape and figures of mariners that opened the poem, thus differentiating itself from the fourth strophe even as it links itself to the first.

Within its place in the oppositional structures of the entire poem, the first strophe unfolds thematic oppositions and figures of continuity (see fig. 3). It introduces four main figurations of opposition, many of which will recur throughout the poem: between the speaker and the mariners (3–4), between the sea and the land (8), between the river and the brook (9, 10), and between oaks and poplars (12). Its first image, however, presents a physical instantiation of connection or continuity: the northeast wind draws a physical (atmospheric) connection between disparate geographical locations and between the poetic voice and a separate group, "mariners," who are introduced in the fourth line. Hölderlin makes use of the inherently double nature of wind designations: the wind blows *from* the northeast and *to* the south and west, in this case creating a trajectory that extends from Germany to Bordeaux to the New World and joining the significant locations of the poem in a single continuity.[41] In doing so, it introduces the marine theme that will appear throughout and, in its granting of

---

41. Hölderlin revises "India" to "Indians" in the last verse, making the line dual-directional, but Bordeaux was primarily a port for transatlantic trade. See Jean-Pierre Lefebvre, "Auch die Stege sind Holzwege," *Hölderlin Jahrbuch* 26 (1988/89): 202–23. Nonetheless, the potential eastward directionality remains: the northeast wind was called the Grego or Greek wind in Bordeaux, and *Indiern* could refer to the inhabitants of eastern as well as western India.

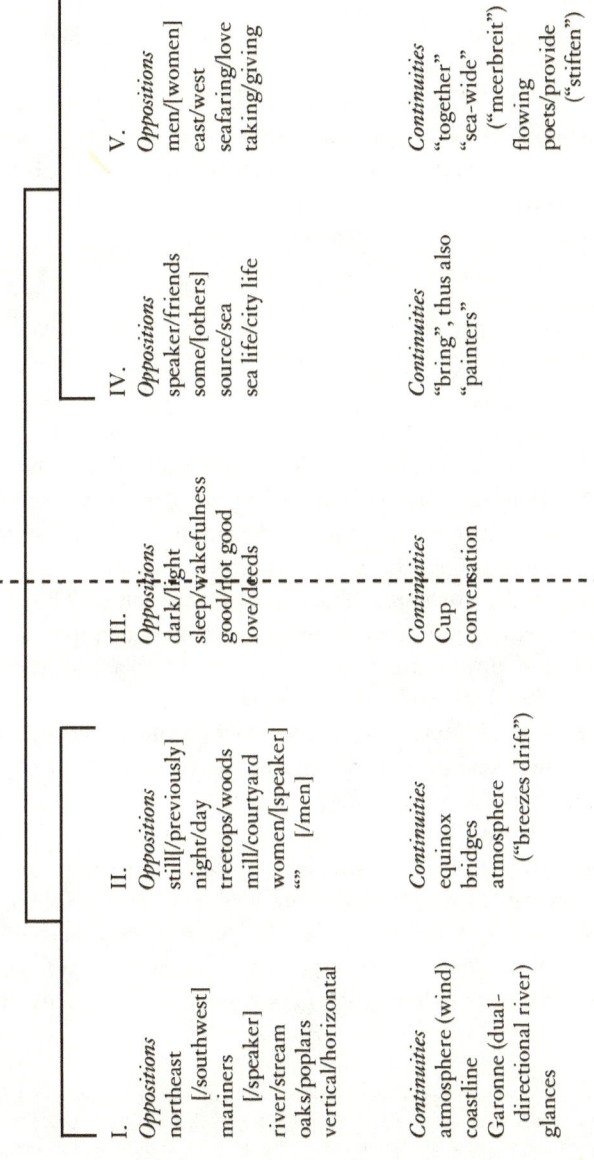

Figure 3. Map of oppositions in "Andenken."

> feurigen Geist
> Und gute Fahrt
>
> (3–4)

to the mariners, functionalizes the poetic topos of inspiration to a geographical (or better, meteorological) movement and a connection—by way of the communicative greeting—between the poet and the mariners.[42]

The first strophe is likewise characterized by extensive use of the modal particle *aber* in figures of both opposition and continuity, particularly in images that balance stasis against vertical and horizontal movement, themselves opposed to structural forms of connectedness or continuity. The northeast wind also links the speaker to the surrounding landscape in the command

> Geh aber nun und grüße
> Die schöne Garonne
>
> (5–6)

The command uses *aber* (but, though) to direct the link between each of the poem's components, introducing the idyllic description of Bordeaux that closes the strophe. This description involves repeated figures of horizontal and vertical movement and stasis (again using *aber* in a context of mediated opposition rather than direct contradiction). Thus the opposition between sea and land is blurred by the city's location on the coastline, itself a figure of betweenness. The gardens, too, reflect the city's status as a cultural site intimately bound to its natural landscape in a portrayal of continuity via semantic content.[43] And the spatially opposed trees and bodies of water are both held apart and linked by repeated horizontal and vertical motion and stasis: the brook falls (vertical, moving) into the flowing river (horizontal, moving); the steep banks (vertical, static) are crossed by the bridges (horizontal, static),[44] over which stretch the glances (horizontal, moving in the verb hin*schauen*, "to look *out*") of trees (vertical, static).

In counterpoint to the first strophe, the second begins by characterizing its speech as memory, "Noch denket das mir wohl" (13; "Still well I remember this"). In doing so, the line differentiates the first two strophes; it also underscores the importance of individual memory in poetic practice. Furthermore, the second strophe extends the first strophe's figures of opposition and continuity (thus linking as

---

42. See Thomas Poiss, *Momente der Einheit: Interpretationen zu Pindars Epinikion und Hölderlins "Andenken"* (Vienna: Österreichische Akademie der Wissenschaften, 1993), 200.
43. Henrich cites several contemporaneous descriptions of the city as a cultural site blessed by nature (Henrich, *Course of Remembrance*, 172–77).
44. For *Steg* as "bridge," and not *Steig* (path) or even *Bürgersteig* (pavement/sidewalk) as per Henrich, see Jean-Pierre Lefebvre, "Abschied von Andenken: Erörtern heißt hier verortern," *Hölderlin Jahrbuch* 35 (2006/7): 227–51.

well as opposing the two strophes). The verbs and adjectives of the second line of the second strophe take up the first strophe's vertical and horizontal instantiations of physical continuity in the stretching and bending (underscored by the repeated *ei* sounds in *breite* [broad] and *neiget* [bends]) of the (natural) elm tree inclining to the (cultural) mill and courtyard, enclosing a (natural) fig tree (that repeats the *ei* sound) and is, furthermore, both linked with and opposed to the elm by the particle *aber*. While the strophe references the opposed times of night and day, it immediately undoes that opposition as the equinox joins them:

> Zur Märzenzeit,
> Wenn gleich ist Nacht und Tag
>
> (20–21)

In the equinox, the trajectory of the sun seems to be suspended in equivalence by the word *gleich*. The double-directional wind in the first line, too, is suspended by the end of the second strophe as *einwiegende Lüfte* (lulling breezes, 24) flow over *langsamen Stegen* (slow footpaths or bridges, 22), themselves a figure of connectedness between the two sides of streams or rivers. And finally, the women introduced in line 18 stand in contrast to the speaker (the designation *braun* seems to mark them as ethnically other as well) and to the mariners of the first and fifth strophes. The structure of balanced, suspended, and merging oppositions I traced on the level of thematic summary, then, also enters into the individual images and lines of the poem.

The second group of two strophes (the fourth and fifth) stands in contrast to the first two strophes even as it continues the presentations of internal and overarching oppositions that characterized the first two-strophe grouping. In particular, distinctions or oppositions emerge between social groups and individuals, with letters presented as a potential figure of continuity or connection as communication. The fourth strophe begins with the awareness of absence:

> Wo aber sind die Freunde? Bellarmin
> Mit dem Gefährten?
>
> (37–38)

The question reveals the speaker's isolation and opposes him to the group *Freunde*. But the figure of Bellarmin introduces the possibility of attenuated communicative exchange: in Hölderlin's novel *Hyperion*, Bellarmin is the recipient of Hyperion's letters. Letters mediate between presence and absence: their arrival is supposed to elide the distance between reader and writer, but their being written insists on the need for a material vessel for communicative exchange. They might thus serve as a medial figuration of the kind of continuity that I have been reading throughout; the poem, however, does not insist on this connection, as it makes no explicit reference to letters or writing. Instead, a new group, or perhaps subset of the previous groups, emerges in the designation *Mancher* (some, 38). The group is vague enough that it could encompass mariners, who fear to go to the source where poets do not, or vice versa; some poets and some mariners could be opposed to others, who do or do not shy away from the source, and so on. In every case, the group's *Scheue* (shyness, 39) problematizes its relation to a source or spring (line 39); the spring itself seems to stand in an oppositional relation to the sea (line 41; perhaps also to the rivers in strophes 1 and 5).

The scene at the end of the fourth strophe stands in sharp contrast to the end of the second, supporting the poem's thematic symmetry of oppositions: the earlier visions of communal celebration oppose the fourth stanza's absence of holiday ritual, even as those rituals are present to and as memory; tropes of movement, this time not horizontal or vertical but dual-directional, also contribute to the final strophe's oppositional themes and structures. The memory of these rituals (down to the repetition of *Feiertage*, "holidays," 47) in their absence initiates the poem's transition to the beginning of the fifth strophe, which seems to answer the questions posed earlier (lines 37 and 38). Even the apparent answer to the question "But where are the friends?" (37) contains the oppositions that have characterized virtually every image and structure of the poem. Hölderlin altered

> Nun aber sind zu Indiern
> Die Männer gegangen
>
> (49–50)

from *zu Indien* (to India) in the draft manuscript, thus changing the line's direction from unequivocally eastern (to India) to eastern or western and enclosing the opposition between east and west in a single word: *Indiern* can refer to the inhabitants of the East or West Indies.[45]

Tropes of movement combine with the themes of landscape descriptions and of bodies of water that appeared in all of the previous strophes, completing the weaving together of oppositions within this theme. The western movement extends the motion of the poem's opening; its movement toward the sinking sun and out past the *Abendland* (land of the evening/the West) connotes the ending that the poem attributes to the rivers that flow into the sea. The adjective *meerbreit* (wide as the sea, 55) collapses the river/sea distinction derived from the structural parallel between the first and fourth strophes; further, *ausgehet* (sweeps out, 56) can refer both

---

45. Columbus, a mariner who sailed west to go east, also occupied Hölderlin's attention; see the late draft "Kolomb." The consequences of Columbus's journey and the history of colonialism almost unavoidably contaminate this image, but Hölderlin emphasizes the potential for cultural renewal by contact with the foreign or strange over the prospect of foreign wealth or national (economic) enrichment.

to end and to origin.[46] Between the Indies and the flowing of the river into the sea Hölderlin places topographical details of the Bordelaise landscape that repeat the vertical and horizontal dynamism of the previous strophes. Vertical movement, in the elevation of the *luftigen Spitz* (airy peak, 51),[47] in the height of the vineyards,[48] and especially by way of the strong downward motion of *herab* (down, 52), broadens into the horizontal movement of the joined rivers flowing into the sea. In the figure of joined rivers merging with the sea (lines 52–56), the poem creates a dynamic horizontal and vertical flow from which Hölderlin can then develop the most directly stated double movement of the poem:

> Es nehmet aber
> Und giebt Gedächtniß die See
>
> (56–57)

The image makes intuitive visual sense: the tides of the sea take and give; seafarers depart and return. But the memory that it takes and gives both continues and complicates the metaphysical connotations of bodies of water that inhere around source and sea in the fourth strophe. The distinction between source and sea, beginning and ending, dissolves completely in the linking of love, seafaring, and memory.

Most readings postulate love and the sea as alike in being portrayed as inconstant in relation to memory;[49] poets supersede love and seafaring because poets are able to create work that persists beyond the particulars it subsumes.[50] Contra this reading, I contend that the mediated oppositions within the poem insist on a more complicated relation between love, seafaring, and poetry, as opposed to but dependent upon each other. Both love and seafaring are finite; they invoke both presence and absence or loss; both involve encounters with and waiting for responsiveness from others. I have been arguing throughout that Hölderlin's understanding of poetry that unfolds within but yearns beyond human finitude takes up such stances of waiting and responsiveness. Moreover, Hölderlin's weaving together of opposing and ending yet continuous moments across the temporality of a poem precludes the subsumption of

---

46. Poiss, *Momente der Einheit*, 210.
47. The *luftigen Spitz* recalls the wind of the first strophe and the *breiten Gipfel* (broad peaks) of the second.
48. The vineyards link the fifth strophe to the cup of wine in the third.
49. See, e.g., Poiss, *Momente der Einheit*, 211–12; and Henrich, *Course of Remembrance*, 208–9.
50. Several readers further identify the three terms ("sea," "love," and "poets") with the three tones of "When once the poet . . ." as heroic/tragic, naive/epic, and ideal/lyric, respectively; they contend that the poem's ending reveals the lyric tone as paramount. See, e.g., Poiss, *Momente der Einheit*; Jochen Schmidt, *Hölderlins letzte Hymnen: "Andenken" und "Mnemosyne"* (Tübingen: Max Niemeyer Verlag, 1970); and Michael Franz, "Hölderlins Gedicht 'Andenken,'" in *Friedrich Hölderlin*, special issue, *Text + Kritik*, ed. Heinz Ludwig Arnold and Andreas Döhler (Munich: e:t+k, 1996), 195–212. As I argued in chapter 2, this reading is inconsistent with the insistence on continuity and change, merging and difference, in Hölderlin's poetology.

two elements by the third, as does his use of *und* (and) as well as the complicated role played by the modal particle *aber* (but, though) throughout the poem. The unique import of his poetics derives from its presentation of the self-transgressive nature of every individual moment (in each tone) that joins into a whole only across the progress of a poetic work. "Andenken" is exemplary in its creation of particular oppositions not subsumed but sustained and held together by the poem's continuous form.

The third strophe, at the poem's midpoint, offers the highest concentration of balanced oppositions and thus at once the greatest challenge to continuity or cohesion and the most appropriate place for its instantiation. In the first image of the strophe, the oppositional structure coalesces into a single, oxymoronic phrase:

Es reiche aber,
Des dunkeln Lichtes voll
Mir einer den duftenden Becher

(25–27)

Dark light echoes the suspended time of the equinox (described in line 21 as the equality between night and day) and expands into a multiplicity of significances. It refers to Bordeaux wine;[51] wine links the cup to the Eucharist (a ritual that anticipated loss and was repeated to transubstantiate absence to presence); dark light is a Neoplatonic formula for God; the divinity in the image might also be pre-Christian, as it recalls Hölderlin's doubly constituted Dionysian tropes. These structural, imagistic, and allegorical levels flow into the liquid of the wine itself, which links each of them to the semantics of fluidity whose oppositions (brook/river/sea/source) shape the poem. Finally, the effects of wine as both intoxicating and soporific create a further internal opposition and begin the contrast between the idyllic tropes of the first strophes and representations of absence and death in the last two.[52]

The third strophe's abrupt contrasts further begin to unfold a notion of the kind of poetic activity proposed by the final line, one that requires communication with the finitude of subjective lives as expressed in both love and seafaring. The paradoxical image of "dark light" introduces the most striking opposition in the poem, between *gut* and *nicht gut* ("good" and "not good"), as well as an anticipation of the final triad of love, seafaring, and poetry. Slumber *unter Schatten* can describe sleep in the shade, but shades refer also to the souls of the dead, and the proliferation of *s* and *g* sounds (*Schatten, Schlummer, gut, sterblichen Gedanken, gut, Gespräch* [shadows, slumber, good, mortal thoughts, good, conversation]) hints at the loss of Hölderlin's steadfastly preserved love, Susette Gontard.[53] The opposition between

---

51. Henrich, *Course of Remembrance*, 158.
52. See Poiss, *Momente der Einheit*, 204.
53. For a brief treatment of Hölderlin's biography, see the section "Hölderlin's Context and His Cultural Critique" in chapter 2.

Nicht ist es gut and *Doch gut / Ist* ("It is not good," 30; and "But good / Is," 32–33) contrasts the poem's rejection of mortal thoughts—thoughts of death, but also the thoughts of mortals, that is, finite, human thought—with an anticipation of the final triad (sea, love, poets). Love appears directly, and the *Thaten, welche geschehen* (And deeds that have occurred, 36) recall (and anticipate) the active seeking of the mariners; the communicative exchange of *Gespräch* (conversation, "converse") hints at the weaving of experience into poetic activity. Hölderlin uses *doch* rather than *aber* to create a strong opposition between mortal thoughts—with the potentially infinite expansions of love, poetry, and seafaring. With the use of the additive conjunction *und*, the relation between the three emerges: without love and without deeds, there can *be* no *Gespräch*.

The poets' activity (*stiften*) in the final line thus requires the vivid attention to the particulars of lived life that Hölderlin explicates as a poetological principle in "When once the poet . . ." and works out in unfinished and inverse versions in "Das Nächste Beste" and "Blödigkeit." In "Andenken," he achieves a fully integrated, continuous, and cohesive presentation of finite particulars that does not fall into an *Atomenreihe* (series of atoms) of images. This achievement, understood in the terms of Hölderlin's poetology that I read as accepting the task of keeping the arguments of human finitude open, takes place within the dynamic unfolding the poem's form: oppositions stretch from images within lines to contrasting lines to balanced verses around the center of fluid imagery that holds together not only those oppositions but their resonances within itself. The image of dark light does not elide the opposing forces of the poem any more than acknowledgment of finitude overcomes the delimitedness of the human subject. Just as the placing of human subjectivity between nature and freedom is a continuing, ungrounded process, the "missing" final line of the poem (the final strophe has only eleven lines, in contrast to the other strophes' twelve) prompts the reader to return to the beginning, filling in the space with the *Andenken* that is the poem itself.

These three poems, then, offer three different but related modes of world orientation that acknowledge both the striving of the human subject for unities that would take it beyond isolated individuality and also the impossibility of certainty in attaining such unification. "Blödigkeit" unfolds a poetic program of tentative confidence, in which the poet's task of weaving together the opposing and disparate orders of gods, humans, and animals in order to reach past the finitude of individual subjects is vouchsafed by nothing other than the undertaking of that task. Hölderlin portrays both the possibility and the difficulty of this poetic program in its blending of formal regularity with paradoxical semantics and paratactic syntax. The lack of insistence or certainty in poetic work underscores that the instantiation of poetic cohesion or community must be risked anew each time in poetic labor in an era in which previous modes of ensuring that community no longer fit or work (that is, the era of the *Nachtgesänge*). In this era, loss and absence, as part of portrayals of cultural separation and limitation, form the grounds of a preliminary call for union.

"Das Nächste Beste" opens with a portrayal of this discontinuous epoch, characterized by disorganization and linguistic confusion, against and within which the poem struggles to create continuity between particular and extraordinarily vivid images and objects on thematic and formal levels. Hölderlin gives an extended depiction of starlings as a figure of orientation to the particular that enables a harmonious continuity between the orders of gods, animals, and human beings; this continuity is the basis of a *Gesang* (song; perhaps a figure for aesthetic production more generally) that is constantly under threat both from the chaos of the opening scene and from the poem's own program of the priority of the individual over the whole. This program ultimately yields an intensity of sensory description that precludes the attainment of a poetic whole, as the poem remains a draft fragment, thus reinforcing that there can be no advance assurances (of the kind Hölderlin's theoretical texts so anxiously seek) in poetic attempts to form communities that acknowledge both subjective separation and the desire to reach beyond it.

Finally, "Andenken" balances, mediates, and weaves together an exceptional number of oppositions within poetic form, creating a thoroughly textured poetic space with strict thematic and formal symmetry. These oppositions, ranging from the temporal (between present speech and memory) to social (between men and women, between communal groups, and between countries) and geographical (between sea and source, between rivers and the sea, and between east and west), are connected not only in the poem's form but in its syntax (via the extensive use of the modal particle *aber*) and in its semantics, via tropes of movement, and in two figures of communication, namely, letters and conversation or *Gespräch*. Each of these figures offers tenuous connections, unfolded within poetic activity, for the complicated relation between the poem's final components: love, seafaring, and poetry. These images of poetry in dialogue with the finite elements of lived life (those who journey in the world and those who love in it, being human, necessarily come to an end) emphasize once again the element of waiting for responsiveness that Hölderlin calls for in poetic production. Poetry, unlike philosophy, poetology, or poetic theory (at least as Hölderlin conceives each), cannot and must not seek to spell out every element of the unifications it calls for in advance. This active waiting for what is outside certainty, whether in the world or in the other, is what I describe as acknowledgment, in which the only slight hope for community within our isolation comes from the capacity to seek and wait for something that answers us.

I have traced these poetic orientations using the themes and structures of continuity, opposition, and dynamic temporality not as a schema into which Hölderlin's poetry must fit, but rather to show, using Hölderlin's own terms, how the vivid, particular, and occasionally extremely difficult language of his late poetry participates in the formation of world orientations that undertake the unification he calls for but cannot achieve in his poetological texts. Doing so shows how these unifications not only participate in a post-Kantian search for the grounds of self-consciousness but also undertake a larger project of seeking world orientation in language. That is, understanding Hölderlin as engaged with the difficulties of acknowledging and inhabiting human finitude links Hölderlin's poetry to a conception of language use in which language has the power to reach between subject and world, as we "learn language and the world together." Conversely, Hölderlin's particular and poetic treatments of the struggles of finitude provide images of community, yearning, and communication despite isolation or separateness that I could only outline abstractly in the discussions of language and finitude I derived from Cavell. Over a century later, Rainer Maria Rilke works within a drastically different historical moment and poetological horizon. But he, too, turns to lyric poetry as taking up the interlocking problems of mind, language, and world, self and other, calling for the same kind of attention and responsiveness that I have traced in Hölderlin—that is, for acknowledgment.

4

Malevolent Intimacies

Rilke and Skeptical Vulnerability

The problems of finitude do not look the same at every moment; no more do the social, political, poetic, psychological, and philosophical landscapes of Hölderlin and Rilke. There are, further, several asymmetries in the way I approach Hölderlin and Rilke and in the way each poet approaches finitude. First, as I address below in my sketch of Rilke's biographical context, there is a one-way intertextual relationship between them: Rilke makes direct reference to Hölderlin as a poetic predecessor. Second, Rilke, unlike Hölderlin, does not write abstract poetologies that consider what poetry or poets in general ought to do. Instead, he repeatedly stages the question—in letters, prose texts, and some of his poems—of how *he*, in his era and in the face of the historical, social, and political as well as literary problems it poses, can write poetry. (Nevertheless, I hope to have shown in chapter 2 that even Hölderlin's most abstract and calculated poetologies are also alive to the anxiety surrounding the question of how he can write.)

Finally, Rilke has a different relation from Hölderlin to the discursive considerations of finitude of his era. For Rilke as for Hölderlin, the problems of finitude I elaborated using skepticism in a broad sense become problems of how to write poetry. In contrast to Hölderlin, however, Rilke is not directly engaged with the contemporaneous epistemological explicators of these problems—predominantly psychologists in the empiricist tradition[1]—in the way that Hölderlin took part in the initiating discussions of post-Kantian German philosophy, deriving many of the terms of his considerations of finite subjectivity from that discourse. That is, Rilke does not read and critique Ernst Mach, for example, the way Hölderlin read and critiqued Fichte; nor does he take up directly technical-psychological vocabulary. Instead, Rilke reads, observes, and analyzes authors and artists influenced by empiricist psychology (most prominently Walter Pater and Hugo von Hofmannsthal);[2] more than that, however, he brings to his considerations of all artists and authors his own questions of how art is, can be, or should be made. He shares these concerns with many of the overlapping, contending, and emerging movements in literature and the visual arts at the end of the nineteenth and the outset of the twentieth century without subscribing to any single movement or school.[3]

Since the texts I read here as documenting Rilke's treatment of problems of finitude are not, unlike Hölderlin's, theoretical poetologies that attempt to work through compositional quandaries, it is neither possible nor desirable to derive internal criteria for the achievement of poetry from his prose works. Instead, I identify several thematic clusters in his prose texts that cast finitude as a problem for human subjects, one that appears directly on an emotional or psychological level. I argue that Rilke's 1910 novel, *The Notebooks of Malte Laurids Brigge* (*Die Aufzeichnungen des Malte Laurids Brigge*), registers the fear and danger inherent in the uncertainty of finitude—nothing assures in advance that the objects of the world or the others we acknowledge will not be threatening or destructive. Rilke never denies the fear and anxiety that appear in his novel, but in later texts he places them in relation to a freedom of attention and responsiveness that are enabled by a hopeful relation to the body and a categorical rejection of (especially Christian) *Jenseits-Denken*, or thinking (of) the beyond. For Rilke, moreover, the possibility of a productive rather than fearful responsiveness cannot be determined in advance. Rather—as for Hölderlin—the fit, continuity, resonance, or coherence between finite subjectivity and what is outside it has to be worked out over and over again.[4]

---

1. See Judith Ryan, *The Vanishing Subject: Early Psychology and Literary Modernism* (Chicago: University of Chicago Press, 1991), 2–5.

2. Ibid., 57–58.

3. "Although he was in the thick of conversations about aesthetic principles and practices, Rilke never became an exclusive disciple of any particular school. His poetry belongs to none of the movements that rapidly followed one another in the development of twentieth-century modernism. Even when Rilke was in a culturally central location, as was certainly the case in Paris, he took up a position on the margins, preferring to remain unaffiliated" (Judith Ryan, *Rilke, Modernism and Poetic Tradition* [Cambridge: Cambridge University Press, 1999], 16).

4. This is the project that Cavell uncovers as that of American transcendentalism, as part of a response to Kant, the project of elaborating the existence of the world in its separateness from but also responsiveness to me. See the section "Skepticism and/in the Ordinary" in chapter 1; and Stanley Cavell, *The Senses of Walden—An Expanded Edition* (Chicago: University of Chicago Press, 1992), 107–8 and 146.

Rilke's Epoch and Influences: Problems of Finitude around 1900

René Karl Wilhelm Johann Josef Maria Rilke was born in Prague in 1875 to a middle-class family in the city's German-speaking minority.[5] Like the Holy Roman Empire of the German Nation at Hölderlin's birth, the Austro-Hungarian Empire in 1875 was an increasingly unstable amalgamation of states held together in an imperial framework; Hapsburg Austria-Hungary was marked, however, by far greater linguistic, racial, and cultural heterogeneity.[6] (This heterogeneity is perhaps one reason nationhood plays almost no role in Rilke's poetry, either as a chauvinistic or utopian-communal framework.[7]) After attending a number of schools in Bohemia between 1882 and 1895, he began studies in art history, history of literature, and philosophy at Carl Ferdinand University in 1895, then moved to Munich in 1896 and enrolled in the university there, this time officially studying philosophy but also pursuing interests in "renaissance art, aesthetics, and Darwinism."[8]

In Munich he met Lou Andreas-Salomé, who was to remain an influence on Rilke for the rest of his life.[9] He lived in varying degrees of proximity to and intimacy with her for the next three years, accompanying her on a trip to Russia and through her meeting numerous important figures of fin-de-siècle European life, among them Stefan George, Hugo von Hofmannsthal, and Georg Simmel. Through the painter Heinrich Vogeler, Rilke was invited in 1900 to live at the artists' colony in Worpswede, Germany.[10] There he met the sculptor Clara Westhoff, whom he married in April 1901; in 1902 they separated, and Rilke moved to Paris to write a monograph on Auguste Rodin.[11] Rodin's influence on Rilke was enormous; the city of Paris was equally overwhelming. Combining both with his ongoing quest for self-definition as a writer, Rilke made Paris his center of operations for the next nine years while leading a peripatetic life that took him from Paris to the South of France to Spain, Italy, and Egypt.[12] Although many of these locations appear directly or indirectly in his poetry, the castle of Princess Marie von Thurn and

---

5. Donald Prater, *A Ringing Glass: The Life of Rainer Maria Rilke* (Oxford: Clarendon Press, 1986), 1. For an account of the increasing marginalization of the German-speaking community in Prague in the latter half of the nineteenth century, see George C. Schoolfield, *The Young Rilke and His Time* (Rochester, NY: Camden House, 2009), 4–6.

6. Prater, *Ringing Glass*, 1.

7. Another is certainly his observation of the destructive effects of nationalism during the First World War, as I discuss below.

8. Prater, *Ringing Glass*, 27.

9. Ibid., 36ff.

10. His move to Worpswede for a long-term stay was arranged at least in part by Lou Andreas-Salomé when Rilke resisted his demotion to a brotherly or pupil-like role (Prater, *Ringing Glass*, 67).

11. Prater, *Ringing Glass*, 88.

12. Prater covers these moves in exhausting detail, to the point where the year he discusses sometimes disappears under the month-to-month moves his subject undertook. The clearest outline he gives is in his table of contents, as the chapter titles are organized by date and location. Thus "Paris, Rome, and Sweden 1902–1905" and "France, Italy, and North Africa 1905–1911" show how unsettled Rilke was during those years.

Taxis-Hohenlohe stands out for having given its name, Duino, to Rilke's *Elegies*. Rilke subsequently described the *Elegies* as begun in 1911 and interrupted by the catastrophe of the First World War, but his letters from the years between 1908 and 1914 indicate that even before the war he felt himself mired in a creative crisis surrounding the writing and completion of *The Notebooks of Malte Laurids Brigge*.[13]

The outbreak of the war in 1914 found Rilke in Munich and stranded him in German territory for its duration. And during a brief period of enthusiasm, in which he described himself as swept up in the communal excitement, Rilke turned to Hölderlin. He heard Norbert von Hellingrath, editor of a new Hölderlin edition, lecture on the earlier poet,[14] whom they also discussed privately.[15] Under the combined influence of the war and his self-described "Hölderlin experience," Rilke wrote five *Cantos* (*Gesänge*) on the flyleaf of his copy of Hellingrath's edition.[16] Rilke's access to Hölderlin was thus mediated entirely by Hellingrath, whose edition performed the valuable service of rehabilitating Hölderlin's late work but also inscribed the poet into the mythology of the "poet-seer" promulgated by Stefan George.[17] Hellingrath paid detailed attention to the form of Hölderlin's late poetry, with its inversions, Greek meters, and enjambed syntax;[18] Rilke imitates this style in the *Cantos* and uses some aspects of it into his late works, and in this respect he is genuinely close to Hölderlin. But his approach to Hölderlin as a poet of national chauvinism derives from Hellingrath, not Hölderlin himself,[19] and Rilke's

---

13. Ryan groups this series of struggles under the unifying rubric of "Writing Troubles" (Ryan, *Rilke, Modernism*, 98–155).

14. Hellingrath's aunt, Elsa Bruckmann, founded the organization Kriegshilfe für geistige Berufe (War Aid for the Intellectual Professions) in Munich, where Hellingrath gave two lectures on Hölderlin while waiting to be called up. Rilke missed the first, "Hölderlin und die Deutschen" (Hölderlin and the Germans), but heard the second, "Hölderlins Wahnsinn" (Hölderlin's Madness). Bruckmann also organized lectures by Alfred Schuler, a student of Bachofen whose analyses of ancient Rome and Orphic mysticism Rilke heard with enthusiasm. See Rainer Maria Rilke, *Rainer Maria Rilke-Norbert von Hellingrath: Briefe und Dokumente*, ed. Klaus E. Bohnenkamp (Göttingen: Wallstein Verlag, 2008), 133.

15. Hellingrath's diary notes for 17 October 1913: "With Rilke in the English Gardens: Greco—Cezanne—despair—isolation—world of the arts—Stefan George—Hölderlin" (Rilke, *Rilke-Hellingrath*, 73; my translation).

16. Rilke, *Rilke-Hellingrath*, 105.

17. For a discussion of the commonalities and differences between Hellingrath's reception of Hölderlin and that of the larger George circle, see Christoph Jamme, "'Rufer des neuen Gottes': Zur Remythisierung Hölderlins im Georgekreis und ihren Heideggerianischen Folgen," in *Hölderlin in der Moderne: Kolloquium für Dieter Henrich zum 85. Geburtstag*, ed. Friedrich Vollhardt (Berlin: Erich Schmidt Verlag, 2014), 80–92.

18. Jamme, "'Rufer des neuen Gottes,'" 85–86.

19. Ryan attempts to rehabilitate the hymns, claiming that they are not an enthusiastic welcome of a violent "war God" but rather were "constructed as an attack on the notion that war might revive a flagging sense of national identity and restore lost cultural vigor"; she accurately remarks that "the rhythms, vocabulary, syntax, and imagery of Hölderlin's late hymns pervade the *Cantos*," but what "scheme" of Hölderlin's she believes Rilke "reinterprets" when he says that "the god of war has emerged only because we have too long ignored the goals of peace" she never says. Ryan thus accepts without question the version of Hölderlin presented by Hellingrath and George when she says that Hölderlin's contemporaries "saw in him a precursor of a cultural rebirth still to come" (Ryan, *Rilke, Modernism*, 148–49). It was, rather, *Rilke's* contemporaries who thought of Hölderlin this way, and Rilke shared their view, as I explain above.

letters make clear that part of Hölderlin's attraction for him was precisely the impact of Hölderlin's work on contemporary thinkers.[20] Both because of Rilke's highly filtered and idiosyncratic reading of Hölderlin and because my concern is not to argue comparatively about the two poets, but rather to treat both as exemplary of ways in which the powers of lyric poetry can be world orienting, I do not treat the *Cantos* in this book.[21]

Hellingrath, who began to have doubts about the war not long after Rilke,[22] died on the front on 14 December 1914. Rilke himself was called up in January 1916 and spent three weeks in barracks near Hütteldorf, after which he was transferred to the War Archive in Munich, where he helped produce propaganda from January to June 1916, when he was demobilized.[23] After the war he continued seeking conditions that would enable him to write, contemplating a move to Berlin or a return to Paris. He left for a lecture tour of Switzerland in June 1919, planning to return, but he settled in Switzerland and remained there (though not without travel) until he died of acute myelogenous leukemia on 29 December 1926.[24] His will, made a few months earlier, contains two provisions of note for considerations of his stance toward finitude. First, he urgently requested that "any priestly assistance that might be pressed upon me" be "kept away" from him, even if he were to lose his mental faculties: any go-between would be an insult and an impediment "to the movement of my soul, toward

---

20. Thus he writes to Hellingrath's aunt, Caroline Cantacuzène: "Es ist ergreifend zu sehen, wie ein Einsamer, in jenem entschiedensten Sinn in dem Hölderlin es war, an einem solchen Herzen wie Norberts, zum Erzieher, zum Theilnehmer, zum steten Mitwerker werden kann, so ganz hereingeneigt, so ganz eingezogen, so innig mitwohnend—und das aus den Fernen seiner unfasslichen Ewigkeit." (Rilke, *Rilke-Hellingrath*, 141–43; my translation: It is moving to see how a solitary person, in the decided sense in which Hölderlin was, becomes an educator, a participant, a co-operator in a heart like Norbert's, so completely drawn in, so central—and that from the distance of his ungraspable eternity.) Terms like "participant," "co-operator," and "drawn in" take on a sinister ring in light of the Nazi co-opting of Hölderlin to their nationalistic and racist discourse; a discourse in whose furtherance Hellingrath's extended family (especially the Bruckmanns) played no insignificant role. See, e.g., Fabrice d'Almeida, *High Society in the Third Reich* (Cambridge: Polity Press, 2008), 19 and 26–28; and David Clay Large, *Where Ghosts Walked: Munich's Road to the Third Reich* (New York: Norton, 1997), 29, 151–52, and 214.

21. See the section "Orphic Implications: The Place of the *Sonnets to Orpheus* in Rilke's Late Work" in chapter 5 for a differentiation of the *Sonnets to Orpheus*, my main focus there, from earlier and contemporaneous works of Rilke's.

22. Rilke, *Rilke-Hellingrath*, 127.

23. Prater, *Ringing Glass*, 273–75. In Prater's telling, Rilke objected even to the easy life in the archive and was demobilized as unfit thanks to the interventions of his friends: "Literature enjoyed high standing in the Austro-Hungarian Empire, and whatever faults the authorities may have shown in their prosecution of the war, they had at least taken care to enlist their literary men in the service where they could be best employed, namely propaganda for the sustaining of morale" (274). Ryan paints a more flattering picture: "For a brief moment, the outbreak of the war seems to inspire the poet to become a mouthpiece for his nation. But the agonies of war overwhelm him and increase his despair. The mundane clerical duties Rilke performed while in the army, turning disastrous battles into official reports of victorious engagements, were extremely disturbing to him" (Ryan, *Rilke, Modernism*, 99).

24. Prater, *Ringing Glass*, 405.

the Open."²⁵ Second, he authorized the publication of his letters, remarking that "from certain years on, I was accustomed occasionally to direct a part of the creativity of my nature into letters."²⁶ The letters, which he often used as a sort of springboard to poetic productivity, raise again and again the questions of how to write and how to live in what Rilke identified as an era of belatedness and catastrophe.²⁷

For Rilke, then, as for Hölderlin, the problems of finitude become questions of how to write. In order to trace Rilke's struggles with these questions, I track the conflict in his oeuvre between two contemporaneous models of poetic production: the model of inspiration (whether from a divine, angelic, or unspecified source) he identified in much of the poetic tradition and taken up by the symbolist and aestheticist movements, and the model of craftsman-like labor espoused by the arts and crafts movement and Rodin.²⁸ These models are legible in terms of the problems of finitude as I have characterized them in that each is concerned with the boundaries of the poetic self, that is, with the question of what part of poetry comes from or reaches to outside the poet. Does the poet, befallen by inspiration, project the significance that inspiration gives his feelings and sensations outward onto the objects of the external world? Or does he, instead, devote faithful and repeated attention to carefully chosen external objects that then organize and shape his impressions and sensations? Rilke appears to oscillate between these models throughout his career, sometimes combining both within a single volume or even poem.

Both models point to the increasing fluidity of the conception of selfhood as the nineteenth century turned to the twentieth. Whereas the problem of subjectivity appeared in Hölderlin as the subject's diremption (picked up from Kantian and post-Kantian philosophy), the self in Rilke's era appears to become porous and unstable. This stance toward selfhood, along with its epistemological implications, was developed by empiricist psychology; in the Austrian context, in particular, by Franz Brentano and Ernst Mach. Although both worked in the field of psychology, not philosophy, they differed from behaviorist psychologists in their interest in the

---

25. Rilke to Nanny Wunderly-Volkart, October 1925, in Rainer Maria Rilke, *Letters of Rainer Maria Rilke*, trans. Jane Bannard Green and M. D. Herter Norton, vol. 2, *1910–1926* (New York: W.W. Norton, 1969), 449–50.

26. Ibid.

27. For the centrality of the letters to Rilke's oeuvre and their connection to the main themes of his poetic and prose texts, see Ulrich Baer, "The Status of the Correspondence in Rilke's Work," in *The Cambridge Companion to Rilke*, ed. Karen Leeder and Robert Vilain (Cambridge: Cambridge University Press, 2010), 27–38.

28. There are, of course, other narratives of development that could be traced through Rilke's career: that of his relation to things, for example, or his relation to poetic tradition. Ryan describes Rilke's development first in terms of empiricist psychology (Ryan, *Vanishing Subject*) and then eight years later in terms of his move toward modernism (Ryan, *Rilke, Modernism*); I combine strains of both her narratives in my overview here.

philosophical and epistemological foundations of psychology.[29] In particular, this new psychology emphasized sensation and perception as essential to consciousness (rather than, say, thought or emotion). Thus Mach's *Analysis of Sensations* (1886) argues that

> the self includes—or, more precisely, is—what it sees. ... This position, followed to its logical extreme, had some astonishing consequences: it meant, in particular, that the familiar distinction between subject and object was no longer tenable, or at the very least it meant that it was tenable in a different way from that which had been supposed. The self was no longer firmly anchored in the body but in consciousness itself, and this was no longer a discrete unit but included everything that was within the individual field of perception.[30]

The porous nature of selfhood is registered in the visual arts (particularly in impressionism) and literature, especially in the lyric poetry of Hofmannsthal and the art history and fiction of Walter Pater.[31] Impressionism, Hofmannsthal, and Pater form the conduit between empiricism and Rilke's work, as he studied art history, worked for Rodin, took Hofmannsthal as a poetic model,[32] and reviewed Pater's novel *Marcus the Epicurean* and his volume on renaissance art.[33]

Thus Rilke's lifelong preoccupation with the boundaries and capabilities of poetic subjectivity does not come directly from empiricist psychology itself but instead from the combination of his engagement with literature and the visual arts with his own creative quandaries. In his earliest poetry, subjectivity often appears to be projected onto the world, organizing experience around the emotions and ideas it awakens in the mind, but this scheme coexists with poems suggesting that the self is indeed constituted by the senses.[34] Ryan reads such vacillation as a result of

---

29. Ryan, *Vanishing Subject*, 2. As in my reading of Hölderlin and idealism, I connect existing scholarship on Rilke and the discourses of his era to a general anthropological problematic and the attendant view of language that places greater weight on poetic than theoretical discourse. Ryan's depiction of empiricism is corroborated by scholarship on literary authors more directly influenced by empiricism, especially Robert Musil. See, e.g., Patrizia C. McBride, *The Void of Ethics: Robert Musil and the Experience of Modernity* (Evanston, IL: Northwestern University Press, 2006). Oddly, Ryan rewrites her account of Rilke almost completely in *Rilke, Modernism and Poetic Tradition*, where she links Rilke to Freudian psychology but never to empiricism. The later book offers a very useful account of Rilke's relation to his time, and I draw on it extensively in that capacity, but without accepting Ryan's teleological reading of Rilke's career in which everything in any text that approaches an (undefined) "modernism" is privileged over other poetic attributes.

30. Ryan, *Vanishing Subject*, 9.
31. Ibid., 19 and 58.
32. Prater, *Ringing Glass*, 42.
33. Ryan, *Vanishing Subject*, 25 and 57–58.
34. See Ryan for a reading of Rilke's early period as "making us aware of the machinery of self-projection—what we now call the pathetic fallacy—that Rilke had inherited from Romanticism" (Ryan, *Rilke, Modernism*, 26); Joachim Storck refers to an emotional subjectivity determining the early work (Storck, "Leben und Persönlichkeit," in *Rilke Handbuch: Leben—Werk—Wirkung*, ed. Manfred Engel with Dorothea Lauterbach [Stuttgart: Metzler Verlag, 2004], 8).

two competing poetic influences, "Hofmannsthal, the poet-empiricist, and George, the poet-prophet. Rilke makes little attempt to mediate between them."[35] In both empiricist and inspired models of poetic production, it becomes difficult to see where the subject ends and the object or the other begins; as my investigations of more narrowly epistemological questioning demonstrated, once the problems of finitude—here the problems of the boundaries of the self—are raised, there are no universal rules or limitations that can satisfy the desire for certainty in drawing such boundaries once and for all.

Rilke's poetry strikes perhaps his most virtuosic balance between subject and object in the years he spent working with Rodin. Even at the end of his life, Rilke credits the sculptor with helping him overcome "a lyrical superficiality and a cheap approximation (stemming from lively but undeveloped feelings)" by showing him his obligation to work "like a painter or sculptor, from nature, . . . relentlessly comprehending and imitating."[36] The comparisons to the work habits of painters and sculptors indicate the degree to which Rilke viewed his *Neue Gedichte* (New Poems)—published in two volumes in 1907 and 1908—through the lens of the visual arts. Programmatically, at least, the *New Poems* are concerned with concrete objects imitated from nature; they are "focused on objects in all their three-dimensional reality, removing them from time and situating them in space."[37] The unsentimental approach to objects in Rodin and Cezanne is part of Rilke's "argument with symbolism and aestheticism, movements from which he repeatedly tries to fight free—not always with complete success."[38] In their place the Rilke of the *New Poems* puts a poetics of craftsmanship, influenced not only by Rodin but also by his own activities as an art critic.[39] The poems thus "testif[y] to Rilke's desire to break out of the self-containment urged by proponents of poetic autonomy . . . turning away from a poetics of inspiration to a poetics of craftsmanship."[40] Rilke's first explicit commentary on the poetics of inspiration is thus a turning away—previously, he had picked up traditions of inspiration without explicit commentary—toward an ostensible objectivity that privileged not the writing poetic subject but the observed object or "thing."

---

35. Ryan, *Vanishing Subject*, 56.
36. Rilke to "a young friend," 17 March 1926, in Rainer Maria Rilke, *Briefe aus Muzot: 1921 bis 1926*, ed. Ruth Sieber-Rilke and Carl Sieber (Leipzig: Insel Verlag, 1937), 409–10; my translation. There exists no complete or authoritative collection of all of Rilke's letters, much less a complete translation. Where possible I have cited from published English versions; when none was available, the translations are my own.
37. Ryan, *Rilke, Modernism*, 50. At the same time, Rilke was fascinated by the way in which both Rodin and Cezanne worked with multiple surfaces of objects viewed from multiple perspectives, and neither artist, of course, produced solely mimetic depictions of preexisting objects, although both worked from models and from life (50–51).
38. Ryan, *Rilke, Modernism*, 51.
39. Ibid., 92.
40. Ibid., 81–82.

But the poems themselves repeatedly exceed this program and call it into question: Rilke is concerned with the "experience of objects," such that the poems "show consciousness captivated by its own perceptual field."[41] The thing-poem is predicated on the tension between the object of observation—what is sensorially perceived—and the evocation of a spiritual dimension.[42] Because the thing-poems depict not so much things (in) themselves as things *seen*, Rilke "examines, in poem after poem, the ways in which poetic subjectivity reproduces, deforms, metamorphoses, or creates the object it portrays. Claiming to be writing a poetry of 'things,' Rilke in fact demonstrates the impossibility of any attempt at objective representation. The poems perform a balancing act between the subjective and the objective."[43] One of his primary techniques for achieving this balance is the simile, in which things are described as *like* something evoked in the mind of the poet that nonetheless gives an increasingly precise depiction of the thing described.

This balancing act is a tenuous one: even as the poetic subject selects the object ostensibly to be depicted and actually whose observation is to be observed, organizing subjective experience around a concrete thing, the poems invert the traditional subject/object hierarchy between the viewer and the object viewed.[44] While in the *New Poems*, "with their unprecedented capacity to make inwardness and outwardness reciprocal,"[45] this inversion is celebrated, it testifies at the same time to the porousness and instability of the poetic self that will come to haunt Rilke in the writing of *Malte*.[46] Finally, the similes that Rilke deploys so skillfully throughout the *New Poems* frequently break down the distance between subject and object on which the program of careful observation is predicated. The poem "Spanische

---

41. William Waters, "The New Poems," in *The Cambridge Companion to Rilke*, ed. Karen Leeder and Robert Vilain (Cambridge: Cambridge University Press, 2010), 67–69.

42. Annette Gerok-Reiter, *Wink und Wandlung: Komposition und Poetik in Rilkes "Sonette an Orpheus"* (Tübingen: Niemeyer Verlag, 1996), 207–8.

43. Ryan, *Vanishing Subject*, 56. See also Winfried Eckel, "Bild und Figur in der Lyrik des Symbolismus: Beobachtungen zu Baudelaire, Mallarmé und Rilke," in *Das lyrische Bild*, ed. Ralf Simon, Nina Herres, and Csongor Lorincz (Munich: Wilhelm Fink, 2010), 112–53; and William Waters, "The Elusiveness of Things in Rilke's *Dinggedichte*," ibid., 320–36.

44. Ryan sees this inversion as adapted from Baudelaire's *Flowers of Evil*: "In the modern cityscape of *The Flowers of Evil*, objects disconcertingly return the gaze of their beholder, subverting the traditional supremacy of the viewer over the thing seen. For Baudelaire, this is part of an oppositional gesture that fundamentally puts into question the power relationships of modern society. Rilke is less concerned with power relationships in the socio-political sense than with the subject-object relationship . . . . [Baudelaire's ideas are thus] broadened to an essentially philosophical, rather than a social application" (Ryan, *Rilke, Modernism*, 86).

45. Michael Hamburger, ed. and trans., *An Unofficial Rilke: Poems 1912–1926* (London: Anvil Press, 1981), 11.

46. Both Hamburger and Ryan remark that the novel uncovers difficulties the poems were able—largely as a result of their virtuosic forms—to gloss over: Hamburger claims that Rilke is "helpless as soon as the prose work brought him up against rifts his verse had simply skated over" (*Unofficial Rilke*, 11), while Ryan comments that *Malte* "emerges, as does so much early modernist writing, from the ruins of a cultural world visible only in fragmentary and often incoherent form," about which the novel is more open than the *New Poems* (*Rilke, Modernism*, 97).

Tänzerin" (Spanish Dancer), for example, establishes an equivalence of dancer (or dance) and flame. As the poem's imagery blends dancer, dance, and flame, the annihilation of the flame at the end of the dance introduces the problem of the temporality of the subject and the thing-poem's negative side—the discovery that the folding together of subject and object in the completion of the artwork can, or even must, lead to the loss of the self.[47]

Crisis: *The Notebooks of Malte Laurids Brigge*

The thing-poems' problematization of the relation between finite poetic subjectivity and the poetic object, with the attendant quandary of the heteronomy or even loss of the self, prepares perhaps Rilke's most extended unfolding of the fears and difficulties of world orientation in his only novel, *The Notebooks of Malte Laurids Brigge*.[48] In the novel the worry about the relation between mind and world does not concern their discontinuity or isolation from one another (as for Hölderlin), but precisely the opposite: mind and world, self and other, seem to have become interpenetrating to an alarming and uncontrollable degree, leaving the subject vulnerable and exposed.[49] Rilke's repeated turns to traditions of inspiration or craftsmanship, seen in this light, represent attempts to control or channel this interpenetration; what in Rilke's letters appears as a question of proper poetic making appears in the novel as an investigation of *any* institutions or authorities (political, legal, religious, and familial, as well as writerly) that might shore up the subject against the vulnerability experienced in the absence of clear boundaries between self and other/outside. This vulnerability or exposure occurs, in the novel, in the form both of an impossibly deep recognition of other minds and of a sudden resonance with or even penetration by the external world of things.

Rilke's self-characterizations, moreover, suggest that the crises documented in the novel were felt by its author as well as its protagonist. Rilke's letters admit that

---

47. Gerok-Reiter, *Wink und Wandlung*, 203.
48. Rainer Maria Rilke, *The Notebooks of Malte Laurids Brigge*, trans. Stephen Mitchell (New York: Random House, 1990). This is not to say that either the *New Poems* or *Malte* alone is the single initiating point of a crisis distinct from Rilke's lifelong struggle to find how to write; Winfried Eckel analyzes the uncollected poems from 1906 and after as preparations of the late work and part of the expression of a first crisis of the thing-poem concept. See Winfried Eckel, "Einzelgedichte 1902–1910," in Engel, *Rilke Handbuch*, 347. Hamburger reads the novel as making Rilke aware of the limitations of the early and middle periods (*Unofficial Rilke*, 11).
49. This is, of course, the empiricist version of the self as constituted by its sense perceptions; Ryan reads *Malte* as Rilke's most empiricist work: "Like the Machian self, which consists in nothing more than a conglomeration of sense impressions, Malte subsists in what he hears and sees"; he is thus "totally permeable to the outside world"; "An overwhelming sense of the imminent dissolution of world and self pervades the novel, which thus becomes the record of one young poet's struggle to save the vanishing subject" (Ryan, *Vanishing Subject*, 57–59). The thought that the dissolution of the self might also entail the dissolution of the world is one of the literary insights into the implications of empiricist psychology not followed out by the psychologists themselves (Ryan, *Vanishing Subject*, 36).

Malte's difficulties are to some extent his own, even while insisting that Malte is an invented figure.[50] Even after the novel's completion Rilke leaves open whether he will escape or share the fate of its protagonist, wondering "whether [Malte], who is of course in part made out of my dangers, goes under in [them], in a sense to spare me the going under, or whether with these [notebooks] I have really got . . . into the current that is tearing me away and driving me across."[51] While the novel's intertextual references, aesthetic shapings, and invented protagonist of course preclude any direct identification of Rilke with Malte, Rilke's use of material from his own letters in the novel, together with his characterizations of his engagement with the problems its protagonist faces, renders it a central source text for Rilke's struggle with the problems of finitude as they appeared in his epoch.[52]

Early in the work, Malte—a young Dane of aristocratic descent living in Paris at the end of the nineteenth century and attempting to become a writer—states a kind of writerly program that at once celebrates the porousness of the self and anticipates the breakdown in identity he experiences: "I am learning to see. I don't know why it is, but everything enters me more deeply and doesn't stop where it once used to. I have an interior that I never knew of. Everything passes into it now. I don't know what happens there."[53] Not only does Malte not know the reason or cause for this deeper penetration; he also seems powerless to select its objects (although he can and does identify them), specifying that *everything* goes deeper within him. Moreover, the location this penetration reaches is one that he had not known of, and he does not know what happens there—whether to him or to "everything" is not clear.[54] Far from worrying about our access to the external world, then, *Malte's* protagonist exists in a condition of being himself penetrated by and potentially determined by the things of the external world.

Because the novel explicitly locates the protagonist in his sixth-story room in Paris, it may seem to offer a specifically urban, fin-de-siècle depiction of the

---

50. Rilke to Rudolf Zimmermann, 3 February 1921, in Rainer Maria Rilke, *Mitten im Lesen schreib ich Dir: Ausgewählte Briefe*, ed. Rätus Luck (Frankfurt a.M.: Insel Verlag, 1996), 263–64. In his commentary on the novel, August Stahl suggests that Rilke's very insistence that Malte is fictional is an attempt to protect himself from the dangers in which he had entangled his "young Dane" (KA 3:879–80).

51. Rilke to Lou Andreas-Salomé, 28 December 1911, in Rilke, *Letters of Rainer Maria Rilke*, 2:32.

52. Rilke's assertions of the protagonist's failure should not be taken as indicative of the *novel's* failure—it documents a richly textured struggle in a literary form commensurate with that struggle; it is widely read and widely translated; it remains a candidate for the title of "first modernist German novel." I am not, then, speaking of the kind of incompleteness or failure by their own lights that plagues Hölderlin's theoretical texts—in part because the kind of aesthetic shaping they call for is at least to some degree present in Rilke's novel, while it is forbidden to philosophical language—even as I use the novel as a documentation of the problems the lyric will need to address.

53. Rilke, *Notebooks*, 5.

54. It should thus be clear that "this inwardness is not a reliable core of autonomous selfhood but rather a means by which the self is opened up toward the intimate depths of the world" (Jennifer Anna Gosetti-Ferencei, *The Ecstatic Quotidian: Phenomenological Sightings in Modern Art and Literature* [University Park: Pennsylvania State University Press, 2007], 120).

struggles of a single subject caught between aristocratic and bourgeois worlds. (Indeed, this is indisputably *one* of the things the novel does.) But understanding Malte's early program of "learning to see" as an effort to embrace the porousness of the self in the interest of creating artworks offers a key to the unity of the novel: whereas its first part dwells on Malte's experiences of Paris, the second expands into examinations of mad kings, false emperors, dying aristocrats, and popes of divided authority that interrupt Malte's reliving of his childhood in Denmark.[55] If the novel as a whole is understood as investigating the possibilities of poetic production in the absence of institutions that formerly organized or oriented the self among its objects, these diffuse episodes in the novel's second part come into focus as examinations of previous systems of world-orienting institutions under threat or stress. What Rilke eventually describes as Malte's "failure," then, appears not as a deviation from, abandonment of, or contrast to the earlier writerly programs of the novel, but as their direct result: having learned to see that everything has the capability to penetrate inside the subject, Malte finds that the (historical) institutions supposed to control such interpenetration consistently break down.

Both Rilke's letters discussing *Malte* and passages from the novel itself depict an era in which previous forms of world orientation have lost their grip, leaving us helpless and fearful, in the face of what he calls the "elements of life." Rilke thus writes some four years after the completion of the novel that "[what is expressed, no, suffered in Malte Laurids Brigge] is really only *this* . . . : how is it possible to live when after all the elements of this life are utterly incomprehensible to us? If we are continually inadequate in love, uncertain in decision and impotent [*unfähig*] in the face of death, how is it possible to exist?"[56] Human impotence or incapability (*Unfähigkeit*) in the face of the elements of life appears as a symptom of the absence of meaning-granting institutions, whether religious or political, that would both make those elements graspable and help ensure our success and certainty in questions of love, death, and finitude—but both in the novel and in his later texts, Rilke emphasizes that these institutions end up being distracting mediators between us and the acknowledgment of our finitude.

The novel's primary mode of response to the absence of verifications and orientations is fear. And yet precisely that fear turns out to be the form taken by human

---

55. For the most through treatment of these episodes, see Eric L. Santner, *The Royal Remains: The People's Two Bodies and the Endgames of Sovereignty* (Chicago: University of Chicago Press, 2011), 188–245. Santner's is one of relatively few treatments of the novel to consider seriously the relation between its parts. Ryan characterizes the more remote episodes as mere "projections" of Malte's emotions (Ryan, *The Vanishing Subject*, 60), while other treatments of the novel ignore its second volume; e.g., Andreas Huyssen, "Modernist Miniatures: Literary Snapshots of Urban Spaces," *PMLA* 127, no. 1 (2007): 27–42; Ihor Junyk, "'A Fragment from Another Context': Modernist Classicism and the Urban Uncanny in Rainer Maria Rilke," *Comparative Literature* 62, no. 3 (2010): 262–82; and Michael Cowan, "Imagining Modernity through the Ear: Rilke's *Aufzeichnungen des Malte Laurids Brigge* and the Noise of Modern Life," *Arcadia* 41, no. 1 (2006): 124–46.

56. Rilke to Lotte Hepner, 8 November 1915, in Rilke, *Letters of Rainer Maria Rilke*, 2:146.

capacities that subjects have displaced from themselves. Indeed, in Malte's analysis, these capacities are so displaced that they are no longer recognizable as human. Toward the middle of the novel, Malte describes his nights of fear and their development away from his fearfulness as a child, explaining that as an adult he has learned to fear "with real fear, which only increases when the energy [*die Kraft*] that engenders it increases."[57] And this energy (or strength, or force), despite the fact that we feel it only in fear, turns out to be our own: "And yet for some time now I have believed that it is *our* energy, all our energy, which is still too strong for us. It is true that we don't know it, but aren't we most ignorant about what is most our own?"[58] Malte's discussion of fear continues with an anthropological analysis of how it is that we now fail to recognize our own powers:

> Sometimes I think about how the sky [heaven] came to be, and death: because we moved outside ourselves what is most precious to us, since there was still so much else to do first and it wasn't safe with us in all our busyness. Now much time has passed over this, and we have grown accustomed to smaller things. We no longer recognize what belongs to us and are terrified by its extreme vastness. May this not be so?[59]

We view heaven, a separation of the earthly world from our future, and death, the marker of that caesura, as fearsome because we have distanced them from ourselves in an effort to forget our finitude in the face of their magnitude.[60] I understand Rilke's use of repeated questioning—here and throughout the novel—to be part of his effort to redirect his readers' (and possibly his own) attention from what makes us *Beschäftigten* (busy ones), so that we have deprived ourselves of what is most precious to us.

He continues this technique in one of the most famous passages of the novel, in which Malte seems to state his calling to write by asking repeatedly if it is possible that human attention to life and its difficulties and possibilities have gone so thoroughly awry. Malte begins by reflecting in amazement that it is quite possible that all the millennia of human experience have failed to apprehend "anything real and important" as expressed in the question "Is it possible that despite our discoveries and advances, despite our culture, religion and science, we have remained on the surface of life?"[61] He then answers, as he does for all the passage's statements, "Yes, it is possible."[62] Rilke seems to share Malte's bafflement at these omissions

---

57. Rilke, *Notebooks*, 166.
58. Ibid.
59. Ibid., 166–67.
60. Hence, once again, the necessity of questioning and interrogating our own finitude, even or perhaps especially when doing so leads to disorientation, discomfort, and alienation. See the section "Skepticism and/in the Ordinary" in chapter 1.
61. Rilke, *Notebooks*, 22–23.
62. Ibid., 23.

and distractions, as it appears even more strongly in his letters; he explains that the novel's accusations are directed not (as it might seem) at the conditions of life but are instead "the [realizations] that, for lack of strength, through distraction and inherited errors we lose almost completely the countless earthly riches that were intended for us."[63] The "Is it possible?" passage in the novel ends with the call to writing of this specific subject in its specific place and time, but I argue that the themes of misdirected attention and bungling or incapability in the face of properly human tasks highlight the wider historical and anthropological weight of this program. My readings of the phenomenologies of skeptical argumentation have suggested that abdication from the greater part of subjective powers—the shift to knowledge from acknowledgment or from ethics to epistemology; the painting of metaphysical finitude as an intellectual insufficiency—is one paradigmatic line of response to the disappointments of human finitude.

But, as Rilke admits, the novel depicts our powers of living in the world only negatively; Malte is arrested, tormented, and disoriented by the absence of institutions or authorities to reinstate the hierarchy between subject and object. Rilke admits that the novel seems to end with "proof that life is impossible,"[64] and explains it as the negative imprint of human capacities:

> I tried once before, years ago, to write about Malte, to someone who had been frightened by the book, that I myself sometimes thought of it as a hollow form, a negative mold, all the grooves and indentations of which are agony, disconsolations and most painful insights, but the casting from which, were it possible to make one (as with a bronze the positive figure one would get out of it), would perhaps be happiness, assent,—most perfect and certain bliss.[65]

Even here, Rilke uses the subjunctive—there is no way to be sure that the figure yielded by the positive side of *Malte* would be "most perfect and certain bliss"—and in the novel itself the fear and uncertainty generated by unsponsored modernity and its lack of orientation are far more present than their inverses.

The novel documents the fear of heteronomy repeatedly; given the lack of meaning-granting and subject-orienting institutions, the interpenetration of individual subjectivity by the external world and other minds traps the subject in inevitable and terrifying intimacies. I turn to two further moments of the novel, in particular, that document the variety of potential appearances of that fear, first in relation to things, then in relation to other subjects. First, Rilke depicts the things of the external world as taking on agency of their own and projecting back into the subject. (This phenomenon goes beyond earlier scenes in the novel, vivid though

---

63. Rilke to "a young girl," undated, in Rilke, *Letters of Rainer Maria Rilke* 2:257–58.
64. Ibid., 257.
65. Rilke to Lotte Hepner, 8 November 1915, in Rilke, *Letters of Rainer Maria Rilke* 2:147.

they are, in which Malte finds himself in resonance with external objects.[66]) In this episode, Malte describes the noise that occurs when his neighbor drops what sounds like the top of a tin container so that it rolls and clatters on the floor.[67] The noise occurs unusually often, and when his neighbor leaves (apparently after a nervous breakdown), Malte imagines with relief that the lid has been left behind, placed neatly on top of its container. He reflects that only a damaged or poorly fitting lid would fall as often as this one has, and complains of how few lids still value (the German phrase is "noch zu schätzen wissen"[68]) sitting quietly on top their proper containers. What follows is apparently a unidirectional comparison of ill-fitting lids to humans ill suited to their vocations:

> For humans—if it is permissible to compare them, just in passing, with tin lids—humans sit upon their occupations ungracefully and with extreme unwillingness. Some because in their haste they haven't found the right one; some because they have been put on in anger, crooked; some because the corresponding rims have been dented, each in a different way.[69]

The comparison picks up the themes of misguided attention and distraction that occupied Malte both in the programmatic "Is it possible?" passage and in his diagnosis of fear as a misunderstanding of our own strength. Humans are busy and loud and distracted because they are not paying attention to where they fit, and they are placed hastily. Because they end up in occupations—*Beschäftigungen*, recalling the earlier description of humans as *wir Beschäftigten* (we, the busy or occupied)—to which they are ill suited, they, like lids, spring free at the first opportunity. But here Rilke (Malte?) adds elements of violence and anger ("because they have been put on in anger, crooked") and indicates that not only the lids/humans but also the containers/world are distorted or bent. The feeling of hostility—both from subject to world and vice versa—perhaps motivates the initial reluctance in the comparison,

---

66. One especially vivid example of intimacy with and exposure to the external world appears in a passage early in the novel in which Malte is captivated and horrified by the ruins of a row house (KA 3:484–87), one whose structure is taken a step further later in the novel. Although the row house description ends with Malte's realization that the house is somehow *inside* him, it could be argued that the operation at work here is still one of recognition of one's own interior in a quality of an external thing. Eric Santner has read this scene as an "attunement" or a resonance of "the narrator's own sense of exposure, of a certain *skinlessness* with respect to excitations from the outside" with "the flayed surface of the outside." That is to say, Malte recognizes his own condition of skinlessness in the exposure of the house lacking its outside walls. See Eric Santner, *On Creaturely Life: Rilke, Benjamin, Sebald* (Chicago: University of Chicago Press, 2006), 50–51.

67. In *Malte*, as Santner has argued, the neighbor is a central figure for the existence of an other whose calls and claims upon me cannot be fully absorbed, and who demands that I recognize both his "signifying stresses" (that which cannot be recouped into the symbolic order) and my own; this demand is, I would argue, what the skeptic turns to questions of "knowing" the other to avoid, as I shall read in detail below apropos the last section of the novel.

68. KA 3:582.

69. Rilke, *Notebooks*, 183.

which is qualified with "if it is permissible" and "just in passing," as if to protect the maker of the comparison from its conclusions.

But the tentative beginning is abandoned in the direct statement of the causes and consequences of this poor fit—Malte claims he is speaking candidly, and, in the use of the first-person plural, seems to claim fairly universal validity for his simile: "Let us admit in all sincerity that basically they [humans] have just one thought: as soon as they get a chance, to jump down and roll around and clatter. Otherwise, where do all these so-called amusements [*Zerstreuungen*, also meaning "distractions"] come from, and the noise they make?"[70] Human activities are directly designated as distractions; "noise" tightens the comparison between subjects and lids by referring back to the noisy clattering of the lid on the floor of the neighbor's apartment. (Particularly in its description of humans as jumping down and rolling around and clattering, the scene has a grotesque humor that turns threatening.)

And then the perspective switches to that of the things, attributing to them the capability to observe and even imitate human behavior across centuries; that behavior is precisely the neglect of essential capacities and questions that occupied Malte earlier in the novel:

> For centuries now, things have been looking on at this. It's no wonder that they are corrupted, that they lose their taste for their natural, silent functions and want to take advantage of existence, the way they see it being taken advantage of all around them. They make attempts to evade their duties, they grow listless and negligent.[71]

While the direction of the comparison is still from human to thing, the agency shifts to the things themselves, which take on human characteristics.[72] These characteristics are, moreover, those of negligence and listlessness that, in human subjects, led to the problem of lack of fit in the first place. In the "Is it possible?" passage, Malte registers astonishment that despite progress, religion, and culture, "we" have remained on the surfaces of life; here, it appears that even the surfaces (in the edges of the lid and container that are supposed to fit together) are distorted by the neglect of what the earlier passage calls "anything real and important."[73]

---

70. Ibid.
71. Ibid.
72. Gosetti-Ferencei reads the episode of the tin lid in a Heideggerian vein as an instance of an object becoming *vorhanden* (present to hand) rather than *zuhanden* (ready to hand), although she does not identify the shift of agency to things rather than people and misinterprets the line "For centuries now, things have been looking *at* this" as meaning "Malte attempts to comfort himself by insisting . . . that things have been looking *like* this for centuries" (Gosetti-Ferencei, *Ecstatic Quotidian*, 30; my emphasis). Heidegger himself uses *Malte* to explore the *zuhanden/vorhanden* distinction in *Grundprobleme der Phänomenologie*, drawing on the bifurcated picture of Being and beings that I critiqued in chapter 1; "Important for Heidegger is that in Rilke's description Being 'leaps toward us from the things'" (Gosetti-Ferencei, *Ecstatic Quotidian*, 32).
73. Rilke, *Notebooks*, 22.

Malte remarks that people are largely annoyed but not alarmed by the bad behavior of things, knowing it all too well from themselves. When, however, things are confronted by a person who is *not* distracted or fit poorly to his vocation, they take revenge, underscoring the hostility of the external world and the exposure of the subject to that hostility:

> But wherever there is someone who gathers himself together [*recht rund auf sich beruhen wollte*], some solitary person, for example, who wants to rest roundly upon his whole circumference, day and night, he immediately provokes the opposition, the contempt, the hatred of those degenerate objects which, in their own bad consciences, can no longer endure the knowledge that something can actually hold itself together and strive according to its own nature. Then they combine to harass and frighten and confuse him, and they know they can do that.[74]

The hostile lack of fit between mind and world enables a malevolent intimacy in which the external world mimics and torments the mind. The malice of the tin lid underscores the oddity of attributing agency to things—things have complex emotions, form plans and cohorts, and can have a bad conscience. The malevolence of the things combined with the nervous breakdown of the neighbor returns to the idea of fear in the earlier passage about learning to fear with real fear. Here this fear seems to come from the idea that the things of the external world can reach back into the subject. The possibility of shared vulnerability between the subject and the external world portrayed earlier in the novel shifts entirely onto the side of the subject; the responsiveness of mind to world becomes a dangerously exposed intimacy.

Moreover, this distressing intimacy is not limited to material objects; throughout the novel Malte feels himself inexplicably close to or implicated by others. He creates a category for one such group of others whom he calls "the outcasts" (*die Fortgeworfenen*), the urban poor of Paris who seem to recognize him as one of their own.[75] Several individual members of this class appear in the novel—a man with a nervous tic that infects Malte, a newspaper vendor, an old lady selling pencils—and Malte is torn between attempts to avoid them and an interest in investigating what it is in him that pulls him toward these others. His connections to the "outcasts" occur without warning or reason; simply sitting down across from someone in a café can trigger recognition. Malte relates an encounter with a man in a *crémerie*, introduced only as "he," who Malte feels has been waiting for him: "After all this

---

74. Rilke, *Notebooks*, 184; KA 3:583. The formulation *auf sich beruhen* seems to undercut the analogy I have drawn between subject/world and lid/container; this passage (along with much of the rest of the novel) suggests that the response proposed to such absolute vulnerability is one of avoiding intimacy by way of hermeticism or asceticism, becoming a closed entity referring only to oneself. As I have anticipated, Rilke will eventually deepen the idea of being at one to include the idea of being at one with the world in oneself.

75. Rilke, *Notebooks*, 55; KA 3:492. See Santner, *On Creaturely Life*, xvi-xvii for a biopolitical reading of the outcasts as a new class of uncanny human remnants.

[the episode with the exposed house; see note 66], I was rather tired—I would even say, exhausted—and so it was really too much that *he* had to be waiting for me."[76] He flees from the *crémerie* and then reflects on what had happened to unnerve him. He realizes he had apprehended the man's motionlessness and its sinister implications immediately on sitting down:

> The bond between us was established, and I knew that he was numb with terror. I knew that terror had paralyzed him, terror at something that was taking place inside him. Perhaps one of his blood-vessels had burst; perhaps, just at this moment, some poison he had long been afraid of was trickling into a ventricle of his heart.... Yes, he knew that he was now withdrawing from everything in the world, not merely from human beings.[77]

Words like "terror," "burst," "feared," and "poison" underscore that uncontrolled exposure to others is, indeed, something to be feared; far from worrying about the possibility of knowing other minds, Malte is immediately and uncontrollably able to sense an invisible physical or biological process and the shock or horror that takes hold within this other subject as a result. The emotional impact of this passage underscores just how narrow the epistemological response of asking about *knowing* others (from behavior, from criteria, etc.) is in the face of the overwhelming presence of someone or something other but accessible to the subject.

Further, this process of mutual implication does not stop at the present; Malte can perceive its eventual end point, legible in terms of the struggle for world orientation that the novel persistently investigates: "One more moment, and everything would lose its meaning, and this table and the cup and the chair he was clinging to would become unintelligible, alien and heavy. So he sat there, waiting for it to happen. And he no longer bothered to defend himself."[78] The crisis is specifically one of loss of meaning—the familiar, ordinary things will become strange and incomprehensible. This vision presents an extreme form of the loss of world orientation, as even the objects of the physical world lose their familiarity. It is the logical end point of the removal of systems or hierachies for organizing attention commenced in the thing-poems and carried out fully in the novel; it is, further, prepared by Malte's programs of learning to see (in which he allows himself to be penetrated by objects) and of redirecting attention—when no cultural systems decide what is "real and important" (*Wirkliches and Wichtiges*), nothing protects the subject from cathexis with dangerous or threatening objects.

Malte interprets his own sensitivity or vulnerability to the man's crisis of disorientation as the result of a similar process in himself, one that he himself is still resisting:

---

76. Rilke, *Notebooks*, 48.
77. Ibid., 50–51.
78. Ibid., 51.

"I am defending myself though I know that my heart has been torn out [*schon heraushängt*] and that even if my torturers left me alone I couldn't live."[79] The progression that began with Malte's attunement to or resonance with the exposed house and continued in the reaching of the malevolent things back into the mind of the subject here reaches its final stage: identification with the other leads to a radical externalization, as Malte admits his heart *heraushängt* (Mitchell translates "has been torn out," but the action is not so clear; *heraushängt* means simply "hangs outside"), an ultimate expression of vulnerability. This vulnerability is the logical end point of the heteronomy of the subject as Rilke picked it up and adapted it from empiricist psychology. In connecting the problem of heteronomy to more general problems of finitude, I open up the possibility of a reading of Rilke's novel as not merely the sufferings of a hypersensitive poet-subject (which it is) nor as only a response to its era (which it also is), but as bound up in the fundamental human tendency to yearn for certainty in our relations to the world and to other minds. *Malte* confirms the impossibility of certainty; Malte eventually falters on the desire for it; Rilke subsequently begins to work out the possibility of a different reaction to its impossibility, one that takes uncertainty as the starting point for the discovery of our implication and at-homeness in the world.

The end of the episode narrating the encounter in the *crémerie* hints at a more positive interpretation of the scene, one that doesn't prove that life is unlivable but only very difficult; it even suggests that if such difficulty could be incorporated into a fuller vision of subjective possibilities, it would become bliss. Malte reminds himself that if he were less afraid, it would be a comfort "that it's not impossible to see everything differently and still remain alive."[80] Although he cannot sustain the thought that a complete alteration of perspective or experience does not necessarily mean the loss of the world, he can recognize its (uncomforting) plausibility. And Malte identifies himself as "like someone standing in the presence of something great,"[81] lacking only a step from misery to bliss: "It would take so little for me to understand all this and assent to it. Just one step, and my misery would turn into bliss. But I can't take that step."[82] This step is furthermore associated with poetic production in an adaptation of Christ's prophecy of the destruction of Jerusalem in Mark 13. Here, however, instead of stones that will be ripped apart, words and sense will be dissolved: "The time of that other interpretation will dawn, when there shall not be left one word upon another, and every meaning will dissolve like a cloud and fall down like rain."[83] This dissolution will be one in which the subject

---

79. Rilke, *Notebooks*, 52; KA 3:490.
80. Ibid.
81. Ibid., 53.
82. Ibid.
83. Ibid., 52–53. The biblical passage is Mark 13:1–2: "And as he went out of the temple, one of his disciples saith unto him, Master, see what manner of stones and what buildings are here! And Jesus answering said unto him, Seest thou these great buildings? There shall not be left one stone upon another, that shall not be thrown down" (King James Version).

does not write but is written. This vision is akin to the view of language taken by poststructuralism that I critiqued in the introduction to this book; in the novel, it is a deeply ambivalent step that promises bliss as it destroys the self via a change in perspective that recalls the feared loss of meaning in the café. It also, however, suggests a fundamentally recast relationship between subject, language, and world in which vulnerability appears as ecstatic openness.[84]

The novel does not fulfill this promise. *Malte*'s final episode, a retelling and interpretation of the story of the prodigal son, depicts the prodigal son as succumbing to the skeptical syndrome of avoidance in relation to others. This avoidance denies responsibility to the other so long as I cannot *know* her completely; it is the inverse of "acknowledgment," understood as my responsibility and attunement to others and the world as beings or entities separate from but not inaccessible to me.[85] Cavell investigates Shakespearean tragedy as depicting the living out of skepticism (and thus the rejection of acknowledgment), using the idea of avoidance.[86] He discusses this response at length in a reading of *King Lear*, in which he understands Lear's behavior as an effort to avoid the claim that Cordelia's love places upon him.[87] In contrast to readings of Lear as deluded or senile, Cavell understands the opening bargain as a deliberate bribe on Lear's part: rather than actually demanding love, "he wants something he does not have to return *in kind*, something which a division of his property fully pays for."[88] Cavell explains that "[Lear] cannot bear love when he has no reason to be loved, perhaps because of the helplessness, the passiveness which that implies, which some take for impotence."[89] This unbearable demand exposes the fears of closeness, intimacy, and exposure to another being without *reasons* that would control my ties to the other. Reasons for love would once again anchor our lives with each other in the arena of knowledge, demanding that the other prove to be not-separate from me, and enabling me to withhold love, help, and acknowledgment if this proof does not emerge.[90]

Being loved without reasons, then, is a "terrible position,"[91] and, I want to say, the problem of being with and being separate from others who love illuminates

---

84. What the theological underpinnings of this passage imply is somewhat unclear; they participate in the novel's project of referring back to lost forms of world orientation, here, religious ones; they may also be part of the failed project of ecstatic openness I discuss in relation to the novel's final episode. I will argue that Rilke's later work discovers, contra *Malte* or Malte, that this ecstatic openness does not entail the annihilation of the subject.
85. See the section "From Knowledge to Acknowledgment" in chapter 1.
86. Stanley Cavell, "The Avoidance of Love: A Reading of *King Lear*," in *Disowning Knowledge in Seven Plays of Shakespeare*, updated ed. (Cambridge: Cambridge University Press, 2003), 39–123.
87. See chapter 1, note 30 for a discussion of acknowledgment as noncognitive relation to the other that brings Cavell's thought in proximity to that of Levinas; see chapter 1, "From Knowledge to Acknowledgment" for a discussion of epistemology itself as a form of avoidance.
88. Cavell, "Avoidance of Love," 61–62.
89. Ibid., 61.
90. In the terms of *King Lear*, love meted out according to reasons can be paid for with a third of a kingdom.
91. Rilke, *Notebooks*, 254.

Malte's discussion of the story of the prodigal son, the "legend of a man who didn't want to be loved,"[92] as a parable not of forgiveness but of avoidance. Rilke gives no direct explanation for the son's denial of love, but analyzes at least some elements of his avoidance: he refuses to take even his dogs to play with him, "because they too loved him; because in their eyes he could see observation and sympathy, expectation, concern; because in their presence too he couldn't do anything without giving pleasure or pain."[93] The fact that one can do nothing "without giving pleasure or pain" echoes the skeptic's fear of interpenetration of and by other subjects without the assurance of knowledge to render those subjects transparent. Moreover, the prodigal son's agonies over the welcoming and recognition that await him on his return from childhood expeditions prompt him to contemplate a final departure, which he characterizes specifically in terms of precision, truthfulness, and individual will (as opposed to what is approximate or deceitful and affinity or commonality with the members of his family): "Can he stay and conform to this lying life of approximations which they have assigned to him, and come to resemble them all in every feature of his face? Can he divide himself between the delicate truthfulness of his own will and the coarse deceit which corrupts it in his own eyes?"[94] The resounding "no" ("No, he will go away"[95]) that answers the question bears traces of an accusation of imperfect knowledge: he runs away from birthday gifts that are "badly guessed."[96] What the prodigal son flees, then, is love that is not based on knowledge or reasons. The avoidance of love is justified by claims of imperfect knowledge, trickery, or falsity: if those others do not *know* the prodigal son, he can deny their love.

The prodigal son's return is predicated upon his forgetting his family's existence; his homecoming occurs after only four sentences in the parable,[97] but in Rilke's retelling, the prodigal son's travels extend over several pages and several centuries.[98] The realization that love without reasons, love based on imperfect knowledge, can be avoided or denied enables him to remain at home once he has returned, and when his family's love reasserts itself, he avoids its pertinence to him:

> He, the one who was *recognized*, had no longer thought, preoccupied [*beschäftigt*] as he was, that love could still exist. It is easy to understand how, of everything that happened then, only this has been handed down to us: his gesture, the incredible gesture

---

92. Ibid., 251.
93. Ibid.
94. Ibid., 253–54.
95. Ibid., 254.
96. Ibid.
97. Luke 15:11–32.
98. The implications of the episode's narrative complexity, including several shifts in focalization, temporal jumps, and a discussion of the conventions of depictions and other retellings of the story, exceed the scope of my argument here, though I do not think they contradict it. Among other things, they raise the parable to an archetype of cultural experience.

which had never been seen before, the gesture of supplication with which he threw himself at their feet, imploring them *not to love*. . . . It must have been an indescribable relief for him that, in spite of the desperate clarity of his posture, *they all misunderstood him*. He was probably able to stay. For every day he *recognized* more clearly that their love, of which they were so vain and to which they secretly encouraged one another, *had nothing to do with him*. He almost had to smile at their exertions, and it was obvious how little they could have him in mind.

How could they know who he was?[99]

The passage is divided between love and recognition, on the one hand, and knowledge and (mis)understanding, on the other. And the identification of the prodigal son as preoccupied (*beschäftigt*) recalls the description of subjects as *wir Beschäftigten* (we, the preoccupied or distracted) and the condemnation of our inappropriate *Beschäftigungen* (occupations), already calling into question the success of his attempts to avoid love with either knowledge or, as I discuss below, absolute love. The prodigal son's initial begging not to be loved in the face of recognition is Rilke's particular inflection of the parable (in the biblical version, the pleading gesture is interpreted as begging for forgiveness); it enables the prodigal son's final avoidance, one that does not demand physical distance. Instead, he distinguishes between loving and understanding, and the passage appropriates the verb "to recognize" (*erkennen*) to describe his freeing realization rather than the miraculous and loving recognition offered by his family. His staying is enabled by a statement or accusation not only of misunderstanding but of ignorance: his family does not *know* who he is, and so he continues his avoidance in their presence because their love is invalidated by a lack of knowledge.

There is one source of love that the prodigal son does desire precisely because it is exempt from the accusation of incomplete knowledge, and its absence underscores the tone of negativity and failure that closes the novel: "He was now terribly difficult to love, and he felt that only One would be capable of it. But He was not yet willing."[100] This desire is for a divine and fully penetrating love ("penetrating, radiant love"[101]), one that renders the subject entirely transparent, thus knowable. (It also radicalizes the experiences of interpenetration and intimacy in the episodes of the tin lid and the *crémerie*). The prodigal son initially attempts to find such fully illuminating and penetrating love (that he believes mirrors his own) in human lovers:

For he had loved again and again in his solitude, each time squandering his whole nature and in unspeakable fear for the freedom of the other person. Slowly he learned to

---

99. Rilke, *Notebooks*, 259–60; my emphasis.
100. Rilke, *Notebooks*, 260.
101. Ibid., 257.

let the rays of his emotion shine through into the beloved object, instead of consuming the emotion in her. And he was pampered by the joy of recognizing, through the more and more transparent form of the beloved, the expanses that she opened to his infinite desire for possession.

    Sometimes he would spend whole nights in tears, longing to be filled with such rays himself.[102]

The desire not for absolute knowledge but for absolute being-known is what Cavell describes as the inverse of skepticism, which he calls fanaticism: "fanaticism of unconditioned or hyperbolic love as a contrary face of the skepticism of unconditioned or hyperbolic doubt—skepticism under a reverse sign."[103] The prodigal son is unusual, perhaps unique, in experiencing both skepticism and fanaticism, the drives toward both absolute knowledge and absolute being-known. His yearning seems to correspond to what Rilke elsewhere refers to as "intransitive love," which exceeds its object and ends in the absolute; in his letters, Rilke asserts clearly that the ability to love in this way belongs exclusively to women, perhaps another reason why the prodigal son fails, and perhaps Malte, taking him as a model, does too.[104] In either case, the prodigal son's dual stances toward human finitude and absolute love (skeptical and fanatical) enable the novel to portray every contour of what Rilke calls the negative mold of human subjectivity and possibilities, the shape whose cast I argue his later works begin to achieve.

After *Malte*: Being-Here

Rilke's letters and later prose sketches begin to trace a fuller view of the possibilities of living in the world under the sign of finitude, where no certainty in or protection from orientations to the world can be unequivocally achieved. In his early and middle periods, then, Rilke sought to use first subjective projection and then mimetic depiction to provide hierarchical orientations of attention that direct and ensure proper attunement to the world. *Malte*, in the crises it depicts and the crisis it expresses for its author, responds to the terrifying realization that there can *be* no

---

    102. Ibid., 254.
    103. Cavell, *Disowning Knowledge*, 18.
    104. "No one will change my conviction concerning what becomes evident through this extremest lover and her ignominious partner: that this relationship definitely brings to light how much all that was achieved, borne, accomplished on the one side, the woman's, contrasts with the man's absolute inadequacy in love" (Rilke to Annette Kolb, 23 January 1912, in Rilke, *Letters of Rainer Maria Rilke*, 2:47). Cavell, too, genders fanaticism as opposed to skepticism in the context of Shakespeare: "skepticism on the feminine side" functions differently; it is also a drive for unconditionedness, expressed as a claim of absolute love; "And what masculine philosophy knows as skepticism feminine philosophy will know as fanaticism" (Cavell, *Disowning Knowledge*, 17). For an extended meditation on this gendering of philosophy (in Cavell's work as a whole and in academic philosophy more generally), see Naomi Scheman, "A Storied World: On Meeting and Being Met," in *Stanley Cavell and Literary Studies: Consequences of Skepticism*, ed. Richard Eldridge and Bernard Rhie (New York: Continuum, 2011), 92–105.

certainty in our affective investments, commitments, and relations to others, and that we are nonetheless condemned to risk them. Crucially, the development I see in this realization in Rilke's late period is neither a quietist resignation to blindly conditioned cathexis nor a celebration of death and pain (the themes so present in the novel) as strengthening the human race.

Rather, what Cavell helps me to uncover is that Rilke is interested in our investigation and our testing of our investments and attachments, our honest attention to what interests us in the phenomenal world, as *themselves* the best and only possible modes of inhabiting our inevitable finitude. Any orientations within this finitude must be worked out anew each time in poetry; in what follows, I look at documents from Rilke's decade-long struggle to risk the writing of that poetry. In these documents, Rilke dwells on ways of acknowledging the body, including praise of sexuality and a pronounced anti-asceticism; he also insists on a recast relationship to death, one that does not see it as antithetical to life but rather at life's center. Finally, both of these ideas inform his rejection of *Jenseits-Denken* (thinking the beyond) and his insistence on *das Hiesige* (what is here, the earthly) as the proper object of attention and love. In all of these arenas, Rilke deliberately includes the pain, fear, and difficulty that characterized *Malte*; acknowledging human finitude as something to be inhabited rather than overcome hardly makes these struggles go away. Using both prose texts and letters, I outline a series of ideas and problems that are, as I see it, indicative of Rilke's interest in and awareness of those themes in the periods immediately before and during the writing of the *Sonnets to Orpheus*.

Rilke's insistence on the importance of the body and his refusal of asceticism appear in both letters and texts, beginning in a fictionalized introduction to "Das Testament," a short text written to some extent as a justification of his failure to finish the *Elegies* in the winter of 1920/21. In it, the speaker expresses frustration that the material concerns of life have inhibited his poetic production and blames himself, but remarks: "Askese freilich ist kein Ausweg; sie ist Sinnlichkeit mit negativem Vorzeichen" (Asceticism is admittedly no escape: it is sensuality preceded by a negative sign).[105] The idea of "sensuality with a negative sign" suggests that asceticism is itself a kind of indulgence or distraction, a misdirection of the attention to self-denial rather than to poetic making. Although Rilke concedes that to saints denial may be a useful heuristic, he bans *Absage* (renunciation) from anyone involved in artistic making: "Whoever is obligated by his senses to take appearance for pure and form for true on earth, how could he begin with renunciation!"[106] I understand taking "appearance for pure and form for true on earth" to be artistic, possibly specifically poetic tasks, anticipating the training of attention on the earthly that I elaborate below.

---

105. KA 4:721; my translation.
106. KA 4:721; my translation.

142   Lyric Orientations

Inevitably bound up with the joy of life *on earth* and the embodiedness of human subjects is the theme of human sexuality. In perhaps his most antireligious text, "The Letter from a Young Worker" ("Brief eines jungen Arbeiters"), Rilke's critique of modern bourgeois Christianity is predicated partially on its censure of sex: "It is, if I may say so, harder and harder for me to comprehend how a doctrine which puts us in the wrong in the point where the whole of creation enjoys its most blessed right can with such steadfastness, if not actually prove its validity, nevertheless affirm it in all quarters."[107] The speaker deploys the moral language of "right" and "wrong" against the arbiter of that morality, the teaching that physical enjoyment is precisely "wrong." The acknowledgment of the body is not, however, limited to pleasure—in keeping with his refusal to elide the difficult or negative aspects of earthly life, Rilke also demands attentiveness to and acceptance of physical pain.[108] In a letter written in 1924 while he was suffering from (undiagnosed) leukemia, he endeavors to take the signs of his body seriously in the midst of considerable pain: "I have never been one of those who could establish an elevation of the spirit at the price of a weakening of the body; all of my work has been nothing but an increasingly dense unity of all my physical and spiritual faculties, and this body has collaborated with great intensity in the richness of my soul."[109] The first sentence reexpresses the anti-ascetic idea that the body cannot be sloughed off in the interest of soulful purification. Rilke goes on to express that his work is not enabled by but *is* itself nothing other than an ever denser (in German, *dichter*) unification of body and soul; the body itself has collaborated in the soul's richness. Rilke continues to use this vocabulary of collaboration, referring to his body as "my companion and my collaborator" (*mein Gefährte und mein Mitarbeiter*).[110] This relation to the body is, for Rilke, part of according expressivity to human subjects here on earth. And acknowledging the importance and expressivity of the body is a crucial element of inhabiting our own finitude: if the body is a companion to and a collaborator with our expressions, we are as finite, vulnerable, and exposed as it is.[111]

---

107. Rainer Maria Rilke, *"Letters to a Young Poet" and "The Letter from the Young Worker,"* trans. Charlie Louth (New York: Penguin, 2011), 84.

108. Rilke's full acknowledgment, expression, and interrogation of his pain offers a corrective (before the fact) to the professional-philosophical reduction of suffering to something known (or not known) about based on behavior or criteria. On acknowledging the pain of others, see the section "From Knowledge to Acknowledgment" in chapter 1.

109. Rilke to Nanny Wunderly-Volkart, 2 January 1924, in Rainer Maria Rilke, *Briefe an Nanny Wunderly-Volkart*, ed. Rätus Luck (Frankfurt a.M.: Suhrkamp, 1977), 2:962; my translation.

110. "Admittedly, I am trying also to *understand*: my body has been too much my companion and my collaborator for me to decide now to take up a frame of mind that hoped to extract something over its head or even against it" (Rilke to Nanny Wunderly-Volkart, 8 February 1924, in Rilke, *Briefe an Nanny Wunderly-Volkart*, 2:966; my translation).

111. This acknowledgment of the body is, further, part of nonskeptical, nonepistemologizing relations to other minds in that it recognizes the possibility of legibility without certainty. Cavell calls acknowledging the body in this way "letting oneself matter": "To let yourself matter is to acknowledge not merely how it is with you, and hence to acknowledge that you want the other to care, at least care to

The second relation Rilke seeks to reshape is the expression of human finitude tout court: our relation to our own mortality. As the passage about the origins of heaven and death from *Malte* suggests, even within the novel Rilke begins to elaborate a stance toward death whereby it is not the interruption or opposite of human existence, but rather native to us.[112] And indeed, Rilke asserts that he holds the view "that death is *anything but* the opposite and the refutation of life."[113] Instead of thinking it an opposite or refutation, Rilke writes: "I have tended ever more strongly to make death the middle of life, as if we were really properly secured and preserved in it as in the greatest and deepest familiarity."[114] He uses the subjunctive, and does not say that death *is* the middle of life, but rather that he has been inclined to *make* it so—the task is not to investigate the nature of death as a matter of knowledge, but rather to achieve a stance that makes it "familiar."

This thought is underscored by Rilke's critique of religious attitudes toward death as preventing such a stance: "I reproach all modern religions for having handed to their believers consolations and glossings over of death, instead of administering to them the means of reconciling themselves to it and coming to an understanding with it [*sich mit ihm zu verständigen*]."[115] Importantly, the sentence demands not understanding *of* death but an understanding *with* death: "sich *mit* ihm verständigen," not "ihn verstehen." Comprehension and comfort are precisely *not* the means of achieving familiarity or understanding with death; indeed, they make matters worse. Instead, Rilke uses an astronomical simile to explain the potential of a nonnegative, nonoppositional relation to death: "Like the moon, life surely has a side permanently turned away from us which is not its [opposite] but its complement toward perfection, toward consummation, toward the really sound and full sphere and orb of *being*."[116] The shift in perspective from opposite to completion is the shift Rilke hopes to bring about. Crucially, it is not one that he sees as demanding any cognitive understanding of death; nor does taking death and life

---

know. It is equally to acknowledge that your expressions in fact express you, that they are yours, that you are in them. This means allowing yourself to be comprehended, something you can always deny. Not to deny it is, I would like to say, to acknowledge your body, and the body of your expressions, to be yours, you on earth, all there will ever *be* of you" (Stanley Cavell, *The Claim of Reason: Wittgenstein, Skepticism, Morality, and Tragedy*, new ed. [Oxford: Oxford University Press, 1999], 383).

112. This elaboration might be understood as a continuation of the famous theme of "dying one's own death" in *Malte*, with its juxtaposition of the death of Malte's grandfather and the anonymity of dying in a hospital. Although the description of the brigadier's death privileges it over the hospital deaths, the episode dwells on the horror (*Entsetzen*) and struggle of that death; I suggest that the later texts attempt to maintain the individuality and acknowledge the pain present in the episode, but work to reinterpret the antagonism to mortality and to the surrounding world during death that appears in the novel.

113. Rilke to Anita Forrer, 22–24 March 1920, in Rilke, *Mitten im Lesen*, 260; my translation and emphasis.

114. Ibid.; my translation.

115. Rilke to Countess Margot Sizzo, 6 January 1923, in Rilke, *Letters of Rainer Maria Rilke*, 2:316; *Die Briefe an die Gräfin Sizzo: Aus Rainer Maria Rilkes Nachlass* (Wiesbaden: Insel Verlag, 1950), 36–37.

116. Rilke to Countess Margot Sizzo, 2:316.

together to be the completion of the "sound and full sphere and orb of *being*" have to do with making death more accessible or less mysterious—the moon's obscured side is always turned away from us.[117]

Instead, Rilke takes up another task: attention to what he calls *das Hiesige* (what is here, the earthly), and, accordingly, a rejection of any kind of religious or metaphysical beyond (*Jenseits*) as a distraction from this task. Our improper relation to death (one that seeks comfort, understanding, or denial) has also corrupted our relation to the things of the phenomenal, present world. The leaders of modern religions, in the view of Rilke's young worker, "are so zealous they cannot stop making the Here and Now, which we should take pleasure and have trust in, base and worthless,"[118] in favor of a comforting or beautiful hereafter, and in consequence leave the earth to those who subject it to the depredations of profit and progress.[119] The speaker decries the madness and trickery of religious distractions and conceptions of heaven—"What madness, to divert us towards a beyond when we are surrounded by tasks and expectations and futures here. What deceit, to divest us of images of earthly delight in order to sell them to heaven behind our backs!"[120]—and ends the passage with a call for the return of the earth's borrowed bliss.[121] While the vehemence of this particular text's critique perhaps belongs more to its fictional author than to Rilke himself, both the fictionalized letter's rejection of *Jenseits-Denken* and its call for a turn to *das Hiesige* are repeated in Rilke's personal letters.[122] Rilke's unusual contrast reveals the valences of his differentiation: normally *Jenseits*, the beyond, is opposed to *Diesseits*, this life, what is "this side," while *hiesig* means "local"; *ein Hiesiger* is a local inhabitant. The contrast he draws is not between the binary *Jenseits/Diesseits*, but rather between the vaguely metaphysical and an earthly, place-bound everyday.

And in Rilke's descriptions of the "tasks of our earthly life" some of the difficulty and struggle that characterized *Malte* reappears—it is *not* automatic or easy to attend to the tasks of earthly life: "The tasks of our earthly life are so numerous, the millennia of humanity, far from mastering them, seem, as it were, still to be stuck in the first discoveries."[123] Here, as in *Malte*, the millennia of human experience have

---

117. This letter and its discussion of being toward death were, unsurprisingly, what attracted Heidegger's attention to Rilke.
118. Rilke, *Letter from a Young Worker*, 74.
119. "So more and more they deliver the earth into the hands of those who are prepared to turn it, the failed, suspect earth which is good for nothing better, to temporal, quick profit" (Rilke, *Letter from a Young Worker*, 74).
120. Rilke, *Letter from a Young Worker*, 73.
121. "All the loans that have been made on her [the Earth's] felicity" (Rilke, *Letter from a Young Worker*, 74).
122. So he writes to the Countess Sizzo in more moderate tones: "I do not [love] the Christian conceptions of a Beyond, I am getting farther and farther away from them, naturally without thought of attacking them" (Rilke to Countess Margot Sizzo, 2:314–15).
123. Rilke to Anita Forrer, 260; my translation.

not yet led us to an understanding of our earthly existence, of our human existence. The reason Rilke gives for this failure of experience is precisely that our attention has been misdirected and our judgments of worth or value misassigned. In our eagerness to rush into the hereafter, into "hypotheses about the periphery of the divine," we have become "less definite, less earthly."[124] Becoming *bestimmt* and *irdisch* is the task Rilke takes up in his late poetry; in the letter cited here, he continues with the assertion that becoming earthly is part of our task "solange wir *hier* sind, und verwandt mit Baum, Blume und Erdreich" (so long as we are *here* and akin to tree, flower, and soil)[125]—a list that recalls the command in Rilke's *Ninth Elegy* to "say . . . the things" and its suggestion that we are placed on earth only to *say*:

House.
Bridge. Fountain. Gate. Jug. Fruit-tree
Window.[126]

In a letter to his translator, Witold von Hulewicz, Rilke links the projects of the *Sonnets* and the *Elegies* more closely than I would wish to do.[127] In the letter, Rilke joins the two in recognizing the subjection of humans and nature to the passing of time, our fundamental finitude, but nonetheless asserts the rights of the earthly against the beyond: "It is our task to imprint this provisional, perishable earth so deeply, so patiently and passionately in ourselves that its reality shall arise in us again 'invisibly.' "[128] Rilke describes this relation of internalization and inhabitation as *Verwandlung*, or transformation—which will be the formal and thematic center of the *Sonnets*. In the next chapter, I demonstrate that the *Sonnets to Orpheus* are quite literally involved in the "saying" and transformation of the earth, as they list trees, flowers, fountains, birds, fruits, fish, and countless other objects of *Hiersein* (being here).

The argument of the current chapter has been that the significance of such *saying* derives from its discovery that the relation of human subjects to each other and to their world is not a matter shaped, vouchsafed, or ensured in advance by any projection of the subject or description of the material world; my reading of *Malte* has claimed throughout that Rilke never discards the terror of such uncertainty and the potential for disorientation and self-loss inherent in it. The late poetry,

---

124. Rilke to Countess Margot Sizzo, 2:315.
125. Ibid.; Rilke, *Die Briefe an die Gräfin Sizzo*, 35.
126. Rilke, *The Ninth Elegy*, in *Sonnets to Orpheus; Duino Elegies*, trans. Jessie Lemont (New York: Fine Editions Press, 1945), 106.
127. This linking is perhaps due to his describing the poetological projects of each in discursive language. I will differentiate between the two works at the outset of the next chapter, forming a starting point for my reading of the contributions of the *Sonnets to Orpheus*, in particular, to the lyric shaping of world orientation.
128. Rilke to Witold von Hulewicz, 13 November 1925, in Rilke, *Letters of Rainer Maria Rilke*, 2:374.

I want to suggest, completes the transformation Malte anticipates, in which horror (*Schrecken*) overturns to bliss (*Seligkeit*), with two central differences. First, this change does *not*, as suggested by the novel, involve the annihilation of the subject in an ecstatic and self-destructive openness; second, it cannot be a *single* step that, once taken, leaves fear and pain behind. Rather, Rilke wrests his—our—attention away from the destroyed forms of meaning granting, away from the vague consolations of religion, and redirects them in repeated poetic work to human subjectivity: embodied, sexual, in pain, in love, mortal, and earthly.

In chapter 5, I follow these themes and the problems of finitude they take up into Rilke's final poetic cycle, the *Sonnets to Orpheus*. Embodiment (including pain and sexuality), the shifting relation toward mortality, attention to the earthly, and responsiveness appear in a number of interrelated poetic versions; I will demonstrate that Rilke gathers them using an organizing and shaping poetics of figurality. This poetics of the figure takes a plastic and formal as well as thematic and acoustic approach to the workings of language on the boundary between mind and world; as I have been arguing throughout, understanding this poetics in the Cavellian horizon of skepticism lets us understand the ways in which Rilke's figurality makes lyric poetry world orienting.

Rainer Maria Rilke, *Sonette an Orpheus* (Excerpts)

Sonnets appear here in the order cited in chapter 5, not the order in which they appear in the cycle. Modifications to translations are in square brackets.

I.11[1]

Sieh den Himmel. Heißt kein Sternbild "Reiter"?
Denn dies ist uns seltsam eingeprägt:
dieser Stolz aus Erde. Und ein Zweiter,
der ihn treibt und hält und den er trägt. [4]

Ist nicht so, gejagt und dann gebändigt,
diese sehnige Natur des Seins?
Weg und Wendung. Doch ein Druck verständigt.
Neue Weite. Und die zwei sind eins. [8]

Aber *sind* sie's? Oder meinen beide
nicht den Weg, den sie zusammen tun?
Namenlos schon trennt sie Tisch und Weide. [11]

---

1. Rainer Maria Rilke, *Kommentierte Ausgabe in vier Bänden*, ed. Manfred Engel, Ulrich Fülleborn, Horst Nalewski, and August Stahl, vol. 2, *Gedichte 1910–1926*, ed. Ulrich Fülleborn and Manfred Engel (Frankfurt: Insel Verlag, 1996), 246; hereafter KA, followed by volume number and page number.

Auch die sternische Verbindung trügt.
Doch uns freue eine Weile nun
der Figur zu glauben. Das genügt. [14]

I.11[2]

Look at the sky. Is there no constellation
called '[Rider]'? For this pride from earth we bear
strangely engraven. And a second's there,
who rides and spurs and guides its destination. [4]

Is not this being whipped and then restrained
like our existence, the sinew and the bone?
Highway and turning. But a touch explains.
New open vistas. And the two are one. [8]

But *are* they that? Or do not they both mean
the road they go together? Then between,
the utter separation of table and trough. [11]

Even stellar conjunctions can deceive.
But let us rejoice a short time to believe
the figure as a symbol. That's enough. [14]

I.12[3]

Heil dem Geist, der uns verbinden mag;
denn wir leben wahrhaft in Figuren.
Und mit kleinen Schritten gehn die Uhren
neben unserm eigentlichen Tag. [4]

Ohne unsern wahren Platz zu kennen,
handeln wir aus wirklichem Bezug.
Die Antennen fühlen die Antennen,
und die leere Ferne trug... [8]

Reine Spannung. O Musik der Kräfte!
Ist nicht durch die läßlichen Geschäfte
jede Störung von dir abgelenkt? [11]

---

2. Rainer Maria Rilke, *Sonnets to Orpheus*, with English translations and notes by C. F. MacIntyre (Berkeley: University of California Press, 1960), 23; hereafter MacIntyre, followed by page number.
3. KA 2:246.

Selbst wenn sich der Bauer sorgt und handelt,
wo die Saat in Sommer sich verwandelt,
reicht er niemals hin. Die Erde *schenkt*. [14]

I.12[4]

Hail to the spirit that can unite us;
for we live really in figures. Always
go the clocks with little strides
along with our intrinsic days. [4]

Without knowing our proper place
we act as if from true relations.
The antennae feel their sister-stations,
and the emptiness of space [8]

bore ... pure tension. O music of forces!
Aren't the interruptions turned away
by the indulgent affairs of the day? [11]

However the peasant works and sows,
he never reaches those deep sources
where seeds turn into summer. Earth *bestows*. [14]

I.6[5]

Ist er ein Hiesiger? Nein, aus beiden
Reichen erwuchs seine weite Natur.
Kundiger böge die Zweige der Weiden,
wer die Wurzeln der Weiden erfuhr. [4]

Geht ihr zu Bette, so laßt auf dem Tische
Brot nicht und Milch nicht; die Toten ziehts—.
Aber er, der Beschwörende, mische
unter der Milde des Augenlids [8]

ihre Erscheinung in alles Geschaute;
und der Zauber von Erdrauch und Raute
sei ihm so wahr wie der klarste Bezug. [11]

---

4. MacIntyre 25.
5. KA 2:243.

Nichts kann das gültige Bild ihm verschlimmern;
sei es aus Gräbern, sei es aus Zimmern,
rühme er Fingerring, Spange und Krug. [14]

I.6[6]

Does he belong here? No, from both
realms his ample nature has grown.
One to whom the roots were known
could bend more deftly the willow's growth. [4]

Never leave milk on the table or bread
when you go to sleep; that lures the dead.
But let him who conjures them to rise,
under the gentle lids of his eyes [8]

mix their ghosts with all he perceives;
may the spell of fumitory and rue
be real for him as the clearest things. [11]

Nothing impairs the [image] that's true;
be it from houses, be it from graves,
let him praise bracelet, pitcher, and ring. [14]

I.8[7]

Nur im Raum der Rühmung darf die Klage
gehn, die Nymphe des geweinten Quells,
wachend über unserm Niederschlage,
daß er klar sei an demselben Fels, [4]

der die Tore trägt und die Altäre. —
Sieh, um ihre stillen Schultern früht
das Gefühl, daß sie die jüngste wäre
unter den Geschwistern im Gemüt. [8]

Jubel *weiß*, und Sehnsucht ist geständig, —
nur die Klage lernt noch; mädchenhändig
zählt sie nächtelang das alte Schlimme. [11]

---

6. MacIntyre 13.
7. KA 2:244.

Aber plötzlich, schräg und ungeübt,
hält sie doch ein Sternbild unsrer Stimme
in den Himmel, den ihr Hauch nicht trübt. [14]

I.8[8]

Only in the land of Praise can Lamentation
work: the guardian nymph of the weeping source,
she watches over our precipitation,
that it run clearly on the rocky base, [4]

the same on which the gates and altars stand.
See, around her tranquil shoulders broods
the dawning feeling: she, of all the band,
is the youngest of the Passions' sisterhood. [8]

Rejoicing *knows* and Longing is contrite:
only Lament still learns; and night by night
tallies with girlish hands the ancient evil. [11]

But suddenly, unpracticed and awry,
she holds a star-sign of our voices high
against a sky her breathing does not trouble. [14]

I.9[9]

Nur wer die Leier schon hob
auch unter Schatten,
darf das unendliche Lob
ahnend erstatten. [4]

Nur wer mit Toten vom Mohn
aß, von dem ihren,
wird nicht den leisesten Ton
wieder verlieren. [8]

Mag auch die Spieglung im Teich
oft uns verschwimmen:
Wisse das Bild. [11]

---

8. MacIntyre 17.
9. KA 2:245.

Erst in dem Doppelbereich
werden die Stimmen
ewig und mild. [14]

I.9[10]

Only whoso has raised
among the Shades his lyre
dares, with foreboding, aspire
to offer infinite praise. [4]

No one but that one
who has eaten with the dead
their poppies will never forget
the softest tone. [8]

Though the picture in the pool
before us grow dim:
Make the image yours. [11]

Only in the dual
realm will voices become
eternal and pure. [14]

II.12[11]

Wolle die Wandlung. O sei für die Flamme begeistert,
drin sich ein Ding dir entzieht, das mit Verwandlungen prunkt;
jener entwerfende Geist, welcher das Irdische meistert,
liebt in dem Schwung der Figur nichts wie den wendenden Punkt. [4]

Was sich ins Bleiben verschließt, schon *ists* das Erstarrte;
wähnt es sich sicher im Schutz des unscheinbaren Grau's?
Warte, ein Härtestes warnt aus der Ferne das Harte.
Wehe —: abwesender Hammer holt aus! [8]

Wer sich als Quelle ergießt, den erkennt die Erkennung;
und sie führt ihn entzückt durch das heiter Geschaffne,
das mit Anfang oft schließt und mit Ende beginnt. [11]

Jeder glückliche Raum ist Kind oder Enkel von Trennung,
den sie staunend durchgehn. Und die verwandelte Daphne
will, seit sie lorbeern fühlt, daß du dich wandelst in Wind. [14]

---

10. MacIntyre 19.
11. KA 2:263.

II.12[12]

Will the transformation. Oh, be inspired by the burning
flame in which something that boasts of transformation withdraws;
that scheme-devising spirit, which masters earthly laws,
loves nothing so much in the soaring of [figures] as the point of turning. [4]

What shuts itself in abiding *is* already numb. It believes
itself safe in the shelter of unostentatious gray?
Wait, a hardest forewarns the hard from far away.
Alas, an absent hammer upheaves! [8]

He who pours out himself as a spring is perceived by Perceiving,
that conducts him enraptured through all the cheerful creation,
which often ends at the start and begins at the end. [11]

Every happy space is a child or grandchild of Leaving
in which they wander astounded. And Daphne, since transformation,
feeling herself laurel, wills that you change to a wind. [14]

II.18[13]

Tänzerin: o du Verlegung
alles Vergehens in Gang: wie brachtest du's dar.
Und der Wirbel am Schluß, dieser Baum aus Bewegung,
nahm er nicht ganz in Besitz das erschwungene Jahr? [4]

Blühte nicht, daß ihn dein Schwingen von vorhin umschwärme,
plötzlich sein Wipfel von Stille? Und über ihr,
war sie nicht Sonne, war sie nicht Sommer, die Wärme,
diese unzählige Wärme aus dir? [8]

Aber er trug auch, er trug, dein Baum der Ekstase.
Sind sie nicht seine ruhigen Früchte: der Krug,
reifend gestreift, und die gereiftere Vase? [11]

Und in den Bildern: ist nicht die Zeichnung geblieben,
die deiner Braue dunkler Zug
rasch an die Wandung der eigenen Wendung geschrieben? [14]

---

12. MacIntyre 79.
13. KA 2:266.

II.18[14]

Dancer: O you translation
of all transiency into action, how you made it clear!
And the whirl of the finish, that tree of motion,
didn't it wholly take in the hard-won year? [4]

And didn't its summit, so that your flourish just now could swarm
about it, blossom with stillness? And up in the blue
wasn't it summer and sunlight, with the warm
immeasureable warmth from you? [8]

But it also bore, it bore, your tree of rapture.
Aren't these its peaceful fruits: the pitcher
striped with ripening, and the more ripened vase? [11]

And in the [images]: has not the drawing
endured, the dark line your eyebrows traced
swiftly in the texture of their own turning? [14]

II.28[15]

O komm und geh. Du, fast noch Kind, ergänze
für einen Augenblick die Tanzfigur
zum reinen Sternbild einer jener Tänze,
darin wir die dumpf ordnende Natur [4]

vergänglich übertreffen. Denn sie regte
sich völlig hörend nur, da Orpheus sang.
Du warst noch die von damals her Bewegte
und leicht befremdet, wenn ein Baum sich lang [8]

besann, mit dir nach dem Gehör zu gehn.
Du wußtest noch die Stelle, wo die Leier
sich tönend hob —; die unerhörte Mitte. [11]

Für sie versuchtest du die schönen Schritte
und hofftest, einmal zu der heilen Feier
des Freundes Gang und Antlitz hinzudrehn. [14]

---

14. MacIntyre 91.
15. KA 2:271–72.

II.28[16]

Oh, come and go. You, almost a child, complete
for an instant the dance-figure, that it be
a pure constellation by which we beat
the order of [dull] nature transiently. [4]

Yes, for it was nature that first stirred
fully just to listen to Orpheus' song.
You were excited from the time you heard
and felt it strange when any tree thought long [8]

whether it would go with you by ear.
You still knew where the lyre was raised to call,
resounding—the unheard-of center. Therefore, [11]

you tried the lovely steps and hoped to turn
the eyes and footsteps of your friend to learn
for once the whole and healing festival. [14]

---

16. MacIntyre 111.

5

FIGURING FINITUDE

Rilke's Sonnets to Orpheus

The asymmetry between Hölderlin's and Rilke's engagement with finitude (addressed in the opening of chapter 4) also characterizes the relation between chapters 2 and 3 and chapters 4 and 5. Whereas Hölderlin's poetologies allowed me to identify his goals for successful poetry, in reading Rilke I used prose texts supported by personal letters to read *themes* that took up the problems of finitude as they developed across Rilke's career. In characterizing the *Sonnets to Orpheus* as centrally engaged with the human inhabitation of finitude, I will be guided by those overlapping themes as they are taken up and altered in poetic form. First, and most obviously, Rilke's struggles to acknowledge and inhabit finitude appear in his repeated attempts to recast and recharacterize human relationships to death. Second, this recasting directs attention away from a metaphysical or religious "beyond" and toward earthly existence. Third, Rilke insists that subjectivity is defined by being embodied: sexuality, pain, and sensory particularity form vital components of human existence. And finally, these themes all require responsiveness—to and of the body, the world, other minds, and our own finitude. This responsiveness acknowledges the impossibility of certainty and the costs of defenses of avoidance; it accepts the uncertainty in subject and world orientations that makes these strategies so seductive. The importance of embodiment, the earthly, and human relations to death is not news for Rilke scholarship; what I add to these themes is the idea of a responsiveness that is not merely described but modeled and undertaken in the *Sonnets* themselves using strategies available specifically to poetic form, thus creating world orientations in lyric poetry that inhabit human finitude.

While Rilke himself does not make the claim, like Hölderlin, that poetry addresses finitude in ways that prose, poetology (general or individual), or theory cannot, I contend that his treatment of the sonnet form deploys material qualities of language to *perform* orientations in poetic form that his prose can only identify as absent or desirable (as, for example, in his description of *Malte* as the "hollow form" or "negative" of bliss).[1] I describe this plastic treatment of language using Rilke's poetics of the figure, a term that describes its own work of shaping and orienting. Understanding Rilke's poetics of figurality as a response to finitude illuminates several of the *Sonnets*' most striking and sometimes baffling features: their mixing of concretion and abstraction, the relation between individual sonnets and the cycle as a whole, and the exceptionally plastic and self-actualizing qualities of the sonnets as they expand and interrogate the sonnet form. All of these qualities open to and seek the responsiveness of the reader as she is invited to form organizing orientations within and between sonnets and across the entire cycle. As with my readings of Hölderlin, without the view of language in which language and world are mutually shaping, it becomes difficult if not impossible to understand how Rilke can celebrate the temporary, constructed, and equivocal orientations his sonnet figures achieve; the *Sonnets* repeatedly perform and present the view that any orientation reaching from language to the world, rather than vice versa, is not an illusion but an achievement.

Orphic Implications: The Place of the *Sonnets to Orpheus* in Rilke's Late Work

Rilke's career, like Hölderlin's, is typically broken into several overlapping phases: an initial period from his earliest publications until (roughly) 1902 and characterized by the emphasis on projected subjectivity that Rilke later criticized; a middle phase from 1902 to 1910, including both the extensive engagement with the visual arts in the *New Poems* and the crisis thematized in *Malte*; a "late" period outlined by the beginning and completion of the *Duino Elegies* (1911–22); and finally the inelegantly named "latest" work, beginning with the *Sonnets to Orpheus* (1922) and including the German and French poems that Rilke wrote up until his death in 1926.[2]

---

1. Rilke to L[otte] H[epner], 8 November 1915, in Rainer Maria Rilke, *Letters of Rainer Maria Rilke*, trans. Jane Bannard Green and M. D. Herter Norton, vol. 2, *1910–1926* (New York: W.W. Norton, 1969), 147.

2. See Manfred Engel, "Vier Werkphasen," in *Rilke Handbuch: Leben—Werk—Wirkung*, ed. Manfred Engel with Dorothea Lauterbach (Stuttgart: Metzler Verlag, 2004), 175–81. Engel's outline acknowledges the overlaps between periods that make unequivocal distinctions difficult, while Judith Ryan argues against this periodization even as her chapter titles more or less conform to it. See Judith Ryan, *Rilke, Modernism and Poetic Tradition* (Cambridge: Cambridge University Press, 1999). Many of

The precise situation of the *Sonnets to Orpheus* is complicated first by their composition during the completion of the *Duino Elegies*,[3] and second by Rilke's own varying assessments of them: initially unconvinced of their quality compared to his finally completed "great work,"[4] he later linked the projects in a letter to his Polish translator, Witold von Hulewicz:

> *We are*, let it be emphasized once more, *in the sense of the Elegies, we are these transformers of the earth; our entire existence, the flights and plunges of our love, everything qualifies us for this task* (beside which there exists, essentially, no other). (The Sonnets show details from this activity which here appears placed under the name and protection of a dead girl whose incompletion and innocence holds open the gate of the grave so that, gone from us, she belongs to those powers that keep the one half of life fresh and open toward the other wound-open half). Elegies and Sonnets support each other constantly—, and I see an infinite grace in the fact that, with the same breath, I was permitted to fill both these sails: the little rust-colored sail of the Sonnets and the Elegies' gigantic white canvas.[5]

Many of the themes I have drawn out as indicative of Rilke's engagement with problems of finitude are attributed in the letter to both the *Sonnets* and the *Elegies*: the theme of transformation, the emphasis on the earthly, and the complementary relation between life and death as two halves of existence.

But despite Rilke's description of them in (and as) the same breath, the two cycles differ significantly in their treatment of finitude and thus in their treatment of language, and it is because of this differing relation to language and finitude that I focus on the *Sonnets* and not the *Elegies* here.[6] The most apparent differences

---

the uncollected poems from the middle and late periods anticipate both stylistically and thematically some of the attributes I draw out of the *Sonnets to Orpheus*, especially Rilke's discussions of abstraction in modern art: "An die Musik" (1915), for example, already deploys similar metaphors, and spatial figures "prepare for a move toward abstraction in his late elegies and the *Sonnets to Orpheus*" (Ryan, *Rilke, Modernism*, 158).

3. Rilke gave the following account of their writing to Katharina Kippenberg: "The two parts came about from the beginning of February and (part II) now, in the past days. Between them the great storm of the *Elegies* roared in.—So the order (with two exceptions, where poems were replaced with others) within the two parts remains chronological; I lacked the detachment for any reorganization. And this order, in which they were written, may bring its own justification, as it often happened that many sonnets appeared on the same day, indeed almost simultaneously, so that my pencil had difficulty in keeping up with their appearance" (Rilke to Katharina Kippenberg, 23 February 1922, in Rainer Maria Rilke, *Rainer Maria Rilke-Katharina Kippenberg: Briefwechsel*, ed. Bettina von Bernhard [Wiesbaden: Insel Verlag, 1954], 455; my translation).

4. Donald Prater, *A Ringing Glass: The Life of Rainer Maria Rilke* (Oxford: Clarendon Press, 1986), 350.

5. Rilke to Witold von Hulewicz, 13 November 1925, in Rilke, *Letters of Rainer Maria Rilke*, 2:376.

6. In doing so I am not implying any kind of aesthetic judgment or argument that the *Sonnets* are to be preferred to other poems from other parts of Rilke's career. I am, however, claiming that Rilke's earlier "official" poetic projects do draw on programs or institutions that purport to overcome finitude or obviate its problems, even as many of the poems themselves exceed Rilke's own characterizations of them both in their aesthetic interest and in their approach to problems of finitude; still others of his uncollected poems gain a more responsive and open stance toward finitude by virtue of their independence from Rilke's own programs. On the contrast between Rilke's collected and uncollected poems, see Michael Hamburger, ed. and trans., *An Unofficial Rilke: Poems 1912–1926* (London: Anvil Press, 1981).

between the two cycles are their forms and their guarantors or interlocutors. While the *Elegies* are ten long poems mostly in free rhythms (with occasional fragments of elegaic distichs), the *Sonnets* form a cycle (loosely construed) of fifty-five sonnets in a variety of regular meters. The apparent dedication of the cycle *an Orpheus* (to Orpheus) in the title is complicated by a further dedication, appearing on the title page: "Written as a grave monument for Wera Ouckama von Knoop" ("Geschrieben als ein Grabmal für Wera Ouckama von Knoop"). Knoop, a young woman Rilke met briefly and with whose mother he corresponded, had died two years earlier; her presence in the dedication adds a female and human subject to the mythical presence of Orpheus, under whose auspices the cycle's title places it.[7]

Orpheus's and Wera's mortality thus distinguishes the Orphic program of the *Sonnets* from the appeal to the angel in the *Elegies*, emphasizing the *Sonnets'* particular engagement with finitude: while the angel is native to the realm of the beyond or invisible, Orpheus traverses the boundary between life and death, at home in both,[8] while Wera is an unequivocally human figure whom Rilke identifies as helping him keep the door to death—the "other half of life"—open.[9] Orpheus also, unlike the angels of the *Elegies*, has a physical, destructible, and suffering body, as indicated by its violent rending at the hands of the Maenads in the myth and as described in I.26.[10] This traversal, moreover, is not foreign to the capability of human subjects: while Orpheus performs these crossings more adeptly than we could do, the subject's tentative crossing into death nonetheless aspires to be the same step into (and within) continuous existence.[11] The two guarantors of the *Sonnets to Orpheus*, then, underscore that the cycle's project is an earthly or human one that takes up the themes of transformation and death as central components of life.

---

7. The beginning of the twentieth century saw a surge of interest in Orpheus as a figure of cultural critique, but Rilke's handling of the mythological material, in particular on a formal/linguistic level, distinguishes him from popular- or occult-scientific investigators. See Sandra Pott, *Poetiken: Poetologische Lyrik, Poetik und Ästhetik von Novalis bis Rilke* (New York: de Gruyter, 2004), 333–80. Pott's claim is that much of Rilke's Orpheus thematic reacts to texts on popular and occult science (343). The *Sonnets*, particularly in their discussions of technology, do seem to participate in some kind of critique of modernity, but their aesthetic shaping supersedes the vulgar-sociological themes and normative judgments of these ostensible "source" texts.

8. See, e.g., Thomas Martinec, "The Sonnets to Orpheus," in *The Cambridge Companion to Rilke*, ed. Karen Leeder and Robert Vilain (Cambridge: Cambridge University Press, 2010), 99.

9. See Manfred Engel, "Die Sonette an Orpheus," in Engel, *Rilke Handbuch*, 411. For a phenomenological reading of this task, see Jennifer Anna Gosetti-Ferencei, *The Ecstatic Quotidian: Phenomenological Sightings in Modern Art and Literature* (University Park: Pennsylvania State University Press, 2007), 126. Wera's presence also underscores the difficulty of changing human relations to death: in treating the deaths not only of distant and/or fictional mythical figures but also of real and familiar others, Rilke acknowledges that pain and loss cannot be elided in poetic work; appropriately he describes the half of life Wera helps keep open as *wundoffen*, "wound open," using a bodily metaphor of pain and vulnerability to depict what the cultural and religious narratives he criticizes portray as a metaphysical beyond or comforting heaven.

10. Orpheus's continued existence in death—according to the myth, his severed head continued to sing as it was washed out to sea—also establishes him as the founding figure in a cultic religion of unity that stands in opposition to Christian distinctions between this world and the next. See Uwe Spörl, "Kulturräume und Literaturen—Antike," in Engel, *Rilke Handbuch*, 36.

11. Spörl, "Kulturräume und Literaturen," 36.

And this emphatic turn toward the earthly—announced programmatically in the *Ninth Elegy* but called into question by the otherworldly *Tenth*—shifts the *Sonnets*' relation to language. While the language conception of the *Elegies* derives from a painfully perceived difference or distance between language and being, the *Sonnets* no longer operate with such a distinction.[12] The *Elegies* thus end with an allegorical journey through the country or landscape of the dead, while from the outset the *Sonnets* "sugges[t] . . . that Orpheus' song is not merely a lament for something lost, but also the creation of something new."[13] Even as the *Elegies* turn away from a transcendent "beyond" toward the transformation of the earthly, the *Sonnets* assert repeatedly that the world's mysteries are not transcendent or separate from the everyday.[14] The blending of the transcendent and the everyday has a striking effect on the cycle's language: unifying for the first time the poetologies of inspiration and craftsmanship that he struggled with throughout his career,[15] Rilke creates sonnets that themselves are shaped, plastic figures, working with language as a constructed and constructive medium that he stylizes as *Diktat* (dictation)—but without specifying any divine or transcendent source. (The sonnets are *to* or *for* Orpheus, but not *from* him.)

This dictation from nowhere that demands responsive openness from the poet without a reassuring source creates a poetics of hearing that combines with the visual metaphors of the figure to create a synesthesia between hearing and seeing. Both the poetics of the figure and Rilke's more general Orphic program blur distinctions between different perceptive faculties (here, vision and sound) in a synesthetic celebration of sensory, embodied existence. The *Sonnets*' self-actualizing language brings together concrete oppositions while leaving the full resonances of

---

12. KA 2:722. Engel and Fülleborn identify a departure from the high pathos of the *Elegies*; the *Sonnets* attend instead to the earthly (ibid., 726). Judith Ryan likewise distinguishes the *Elegies* and the *Sonnets* because in the former, "sign and signified fall radically apart" (Ryan, *Rilke, Modernism*, 183).

13. Ryan, *Rilke, Modernism*, 171.

14. Gosetti-Ferencei, *Ecstatic Quotidian*, 124. Gosetti-Ferencei elsewhere draws the distinction between the *Elegies* and the *Sonnets* in terms of a (phenomenologically based) distinction between "vertical" transcendence ("a crossing . . . from the realm of earthly, human limitation and finitude, to a realm metaphorically above and beyond") and "horizontal" transcendence ("a virtual line in the distance against which what is experienced or known can be projectively interpreted"). See Gosetti-Ferencei, "Immanent Transcendence in Rilke and Stevens," *German Quarterly* 83, no. 3 (2010): 275–76. She rightly points out that the *Sonnets* do engage with and refer to the first kind of transcendence as something unattainable even as they privilege the second kind, but she occasionally slides into the language of "beyond" that Rilke so categorically rejects. For example, she claims that the "pure transcendence" (*reine Übersteigung*) of the first line of the first sonnet refers to Orpheus (ibid., 279), whereas in fact it refers to a tree that becomes a figure of Orpheus's song: "Da stieg ein Baum! O reine Übersteigung! / O Orpheus singt! O hoher Baum im Ohr." (KA 2:241; "There arose a tree! Oh, pure transcension! Oh, / Orpheus sings. Oh, tall tree in the ear!" Translation: Rainer Maria Rilke, *Sonnets to Orpheus*, with English translations and notes by C. F. MacIntyre [Berkeley: University of California Press, 1960], 3.) The transformation of invisible song into a visible object in an impossible place, and the transformation of a fairly mundane verb of motion into an abstract and seemingly metaphysical noun is, as I discuss below, a paradigmatic linguistic strategy of the *Sonnets*, as they are suspended between the abstract and the concrete.

15. See the section "Rilke's Epoch and Influences: Problems of Finitude around 1900" in chapter 4.

their coexistence open. In doing so, their language extends the poetology of hearing from the poet to the reader/hearer. Furthermore, in keeping with the tension between inspiration and craftsmanship, visible and invisible, the *Sonnets* exist in a tension between the sensory precision of Rilke's images and a curious abstraction or ambiguity of meaning.[16] The interplay of ambiguity and concretion supplies a further element of openness to the reader, as the individual poems display their own disjunctions and contradictions without certainty in their resolution, even as they are held together by the sonnet form.

The ways in which Rilke's treatment of language takes up his engagement with finitude are, of course, best seen in detail in individual sonnets, but identifying a few particularly striking features of that treatment underscores that the treatments of language I analyze are central to the cycle as a whole. Rilke's use of syntactic and formal strategies dynamizes the normally static and syllogistic sonnet form without destroying its shape; the sonnets are all clearly recognizable as sonnets even as they use different meters, line lengths, and rhyme schemes. Precisely this formal dynamization enables the sonnets themselves to become figures of relation without ossifying those relations into closed or rigid structures.[17] Rilke further uses both thematic and formal or linguistic/lexical strategies of metamorphosis to create continuities between individual sonnets or among groups within and between each half of the cycle.[18]

These techniques, fully in keeping with the self-actualizing poetological and concrete progression of the *Sonnets* as a whole, foreground the expressive force of the acoustic and optical levels of language, as word metamorphoses occur using prefixes, suffixes, or single sounds. Appropriately, Rilke also uses unusual rhyme words—often insignificant or normally unemphasized parts of speech—further undoing distinctions between types of words and thus underscoring their phonetic rather than semantic components.[19] His privileging of acoustic material contributes

---

16. For example, he mentions bananas, oranges, and apples explicitly and then reminds the reader that the sweetness of the latter derives in part from their incorporation of the buried dead (I.13 and I.14), thus relating a particular, concrete object to an ontological concept (death) but in such a rapid and cryptic way that he renders those concrete everyday objects mysterious and meaningful. Fülleborn and Engel point to the tension between what they call Rilke's poetic exactness and a multiplicity of suspended meanings (KA 2:714–15). This rapidity is one of Rilke's strategies for "recasting . . . mundane things" and "awakening" consciousness "from its tendency toward a prosaic grasp and reception of the world, its tendency to objectify and dominate things" (Gosetti-Ferencei, *Ecstatic Quotidian*, 132) by putting them in relation to finitude and death: "The life of poetic consciousness, death's semi-transcendence holds and protects for Rilke the mystery of presence and invests the quotidian with a mysterious depth, glimpsed in natural phenomena. Finitude is the horizon which gives shape and possibility to all things" (129).

17. He describes the *Sonnets* as "the freest, as it were most transformed that can be understood as belonging to this otherwise so static and stable form" (Rilke to Katharina Kippenberg, 23 February 1922, in Rilke, *Rilke-Kippenberg*, 455; my translation).

18. This technique creates a complex interplay of self-similarity and self-relationality throughout the cycle. See Wolfram Groddeck, "Kosmische Didaktik: Rilkes 'Reiter'-Sonett," in *Gedichte von Rainer Maria Rilke*, ed. Wolfram Groddeck (Stuttgart: Reclam, 1999), 206.

19. Annette Gerok-Reiter, *Wink und Wandlung: Komposition und Poetik in Rilkes "Sonette an Orpheus"* (Tübingen: Niemeyer Verlag, 1996), 83.

greatly to the musicality of the work and reiterates the blurring of boundaries between abstraction and concretion on a linguistic level. The radical revaluing of linguistic elements becomes a powerful tool for the creation of figures, as Rilke deploys a simultaneously celebratory and baffling combination of neologisms, foreign words, colloquial phrasing, and archaic flourishes.[20] The precise effects of Rilke's language use—in particular, the ways in which he uses language to make the poems themselves figures—must of course emerge over the course of individual readings. Understanding figurality in relation to the interlocking problems of language and finitude that Rilke takes up in historically specific forms shows that the creation of poetic figures is not a flight into a play of forms but *itself* a mode of world orientation. The organizations of material, the linking of oppositions, the sensory blending, and the temporality his sonnet figures investigate are modes of organizing and attending to not only language but the world—hence, again, Rilke's insistence on attention to the earthly and embodied in the face of dissolution and death.

The concepts of finitude and organization, with their shared blending of concretion and abstraction, introduce the theme of *Bezug*, (relation), which likewise forms Rilke's late and last connection to the visual arts and his strongest tie to classical modernism.[21] Shortly before writing the *Sonnets* and completing the *Elegies*, Rilke devoted his attention to the work of Paul Klee, particularly as treated in Wilhelm Hausenstein's 1921 volume, *Kairuan oder eine Geschichte vom Maler Klee und von der Kunst dieses Zeitalters* (Kairouan or a History of the Painter Klee and of the Art of This Era). Several of the terms Hausenstein used to analyze Klee's work became central for Rilke's own:

> Hausenstein saw Klee's work as a response to the disappearance of the object in the modern world. Instead of the concrete reality of objects, Klee, in Hausenstein's view,

---

20. Ibid., 116. As I reflect below, this shift of emphasis is analogous to modernist painting's attention to brushstrokes, surfaces, and framing.

21. The term "abstraction" and the figurality I discuss below do not, however, refer to the disappearance of sensory particularity or concretion onto a calculated grid of quasi-mathematical relations, any more than "abstraction" in modern art describes schematization and the disappearance of medial particularity. Quite the contrary: in Rilke's late poetry, as in modernist drawings or paintings such as Klee's or those of Wassily Kandinsky or Jackson Pollack, the absence of representation in favor of depictions of the relationality of elements such as brushstrokes, lines, and surfaces heightens the particularity and concretion of the medium of painting or language (in Rilke's case, the kind of word and sound components I described above). For a narrative of sensory particularity and modernist painting as working precisely *against* schematization, see J. M. Bernstein's claim that "having the familiar world of the senses first liquefy and then disappear into mathematical knowing is a fable for the fate of things in the modern world, and by extension a fable of modernity itself with which we have yet to get on level terms" (J. M. Bernstein, *Against Voluptuous Bodies: Late Modernism and the Meaning of Painting* [Stanford, CA: Stanford University Press, 2006], 22). It is within this context that one should read Winfried Eckel's assertion that Rilke's poetics of the figure is his most important contribution to the abstraction processes of classical modernism. See Winfried Eckel, "Bild und Figur in der Lyrik des Symbolismus: Beobachtungen zu Baudelaire, Mallarmé und Rilke," in *Das lyrische Bild*, ed. Ralf Simon, Nina Herres, and Csongor Lorincz (Munich: Wilhelm Fink, 2010), 139.

represented the extraordinary complexity of their relationships to one another; Klee's art manifests the 'Bezogenheit' (relatedness) of things, transforming it into 'intersphärische Trigonometrie' (interspherical trigonometry) that makes his paintings 'inwendig lauter Figur' (inwardly nothing but figure). In Rilke's late poetry, 'Bezug' (relation) and 'Figur' (figure) are used in a similar sense.[22]

The idea of relationality, in particular the complexity of the relations between things, is taken up in Rilke's paradoxical and productive poetics of the figure: figurality will often appear as the balancing or relating of relations among objects that creates a preserving or shaping tension between them. The *Sonnets to Orpheus* differ from Rilke's earlier work in their awareness and celebration of their own role in not merely observing or picking up but *constructing* such relations.[23] Such self-awareness and constructedness do not mean, however, that the poems represent (only) the play of language within itself: Rilke's calls for the preservation of the ordinary even as it disappears by way of the delineation of its relations within finitude shows that the figures the *Sonnets* create not only consider but enact world orientation, where the mutual influences of subject, language, and world are taken up, tested, dissolved, and reformed again and again.

Figuring Figurality: Rilke's Constellations

These interlocking themes and characteristics indicative of Rilke's engagement with the problems of finitude are gathered nondiscursively in the poetics of the figure that define the *Sonnets to Orpheus*.[24] Rilke, as I show in readings of individual sonnets, uses the sonnet form in particular to make the poems *themselves* figures that reshape and redirect human attention. Figures undertake this reshaping by relating and holding together opposed elements of life in a poetic-material presentation of what Rilke calls *Bezug* (relationality). To illustrate how the Rilkean figure takes up the themes and features I have traced as continuing Rilke's engagement with human finitude in poetic form, I use his most self-interpreting figure,

---

22. Ryan, *Rilke, Modernism*, 157.
23. Whereas in the *New Poems*, for example, reciprocity between subject and object threatened to collapse the distance between them required for the ostensible program of observation and mimesis, which the poems themselves constantly challenge and undermine. See the section "Rilke's Epoch and Influences: Problems of Finitude around 1900" in chapter 4.
24. The standard approach to elucidating Rilke's poetics of the figure has been to define *Figur* using a combination of general characteristics extracted from Rilke's oeuvre as a whole. In part because one function of figurality is the holding together of opposed attributes or principles, such efforts tend to culminate in extreme abstraction or paradox (or both). Manfred Engel and Ulrich Fülleborn also identify the poems as linguistic *figures*, which bring opposites together and into each other. Because they are only introducing the cycle, Engel and Fülleborn give no detailed sense of how these thematic and formal figures bring together categorically or ontologically opposed components of human existence (KA 2:727); nor, I contend, could one do so in abstraction from the specific imagistic and formal working-through of individual poems.

that of the constellation, to derive the central characteristics of the figural poetics of the *Sonnets*.[25] Constellations are human organizations of nature: the stars are, of course, there, but the traces between them appear only on astronomical or astrological maps, and Rilke himself describes constellations in August 1921 as "spatial distances between fixed points."[26] They are thus necessarily relational structures, ways of putting together separated components that need a human consciousness to collect them.[27] In doing so, that consciousness creates a further relation between earthly and heavenly: the act of looking up organizes natural material into an image, a Stern*bild* (literally, "star *image* or picture").

Furthermore, constellations are always already relativized in several senses, and are thus themselves finite and nonabsolute: they are temporal and temporary, in that they move (or turn) across the sky and change with the seasons (thus also taking part in a wider cycle of the earth's revolution around the sun). Likewise, they are both geographically and culturally contingent: the Northern and Southern hemispheres perceive different constellations in each season. Perhaps even more importantly, constellations are culturally received: two cultures that see the same sets of stars at the same time need not group them in the same way, and, even if the groupings are the same, need not see the same image or give it the same name.

The cultural specificity of constellation names emphasizes their curious combination of myth and geometry (which in turn makes them ideal candidates for Rilke's sensory concretion and portrayals of relationality or *Bezug*): while the spatial relations between stars are fully explicable by lines, planes, and shapes, the myths that describe the creation of each constellation (such as the myth of Orpheus's lyre being placed in the sky after his death) are culturally and aesthetically specific. But nor are constellations, once imagined or described, merely a matter of individual projection; they also serve to orient subjects in (for example) maritime navigation, enabling progress through otherwise undifferentiated and unorganized spaces. In that constellations are both imagined and received, both organized and orienting, both culturally specific and world describing, they add an aesthetic dimension to the idea of convention as the lines along which a culture and a subject intersect in a form of life.[28]

---

25. Although the *Sonnets to Orpheus* in particular and Rilke's poetics of the figure in general form perhaps his most decisive step into modernism, the idea that there is a special expressive potential to the "movement" of language created by unusual word order, syntax, punctuation, etc. (Eckel, "Bild und Figur," 142) has a poetic long tradition.

26. "Räumliche Distanzen zwischen Fixpunkten"; cited by Jana Schuster, "'Tempel im Gehör': Zur Eigenbewegtheit des Klinggedichts am Beispiel des ersten der Sonette an Orpheus von Rainer Maria Rilke," in *Textbewegungen 1800/1900*, ed. Matthias Buschmeier and Till Dembeck (Würzburg: Königshausen und Neumann, 2007), 356.

27. This makes them, of course, a paradigmatic example of Rilke's concept of *Bezug* or relationality.

28. See chapter 1, "Language, Grammar, and Forms of Life"; and Cavell, *The Claim of Reason: Wittgenstein, Skepticism, Morality, and Tragedy*, new ed. (Oxford: Oxford University Press, 1999), 11ff.

Implicit in this commonsense description of the attributes of constellations as Rilke's leading figure of figurality are several characteristics that take up problems of finitude in poetic form and as they will emerge in the *Sonnets*: first, the poems persistently treat and perform the relation between temporal persistence and decay (a trope of finitude in general and an instance of *Bezug* as Rilke picked it up from Hausenstein's discussion of Klee); second, they instantiate a related contrastive connection between fluidity and form that complicates the theme of relationality (placing problems of finitude in relation to the *Sonnets*' key theme of transformation or *Verwandlung*); both of these contrasts unfold within what I have called the figure's self-actualization or performativity.[29] Rilke's conception of the temporality and time-containing qualities of the figure dynamizes what might normally be considered a solely spatial and static phenomenon,[30] and raises the second tension inherent to the Rilkean figure: that between temporal or spatial dynamism and the search for a shape or measure to organize that fluidity.[31] And temporality and *Bezug* (relationality) play a central role in the *Sonnets*' performativity or self-actualizing quality. This quality refers to the tendency of the *Sonnets* to announce or unfold their own poetological principles, as well as to the interplay between lexical, acoustic, optical, and formal structures that occurs within and between poems. The *Sonnets*' enactment of their own themes, like their synesthetic concreteness, also corresponds to the theme of earthly attention: they themselves give or posit the principles to which they adhere, rather than drawing such principles from a (metaphysical or transcendent) "beyond." And finally, both the idea of relationality as world orientation and the performative qualities of the sonnets bespeak their partaking in the projects of acknowledgment and responsiveness as they seek to open orientations to the reader without recourse to any authority outside themselves.

---

29. Eckel remarks that the concept of the figure is constitutive for its own construction and that the Rilkean figure is not observed but undertaken or performed ("will vollzogen werden"; Eckel, "Bild und Figur," 140 and 143). Perhaps motivated by the desire to avoid the speech act theory ramifications of the term "performativity," others have referred to this quality as *Eigengesetzlichkeit*, "self-lawgiving-ness" (KA 2:717), and *Eigenbewegtheit*, "self-movingness" (Schuster, "'Tempel im Gehör,'" 354). Since English efforts to avoid the word "performativity" in describing the quality of a work's own enacting the programs or principles presented in it become unwieldy quite rapidly, I will continue to use "performativity" nonetheless.

30. And indeed, Rilke sometimes uses the word *Figur* to describe sculpture or painting, sometimes dance, the flight of birds, or the parabola traced by a ball. In all these cases, however, he uses the word to describe abstract relations and structures of elements. Ironically, given de Man's famous insistence on Rilke's rhetorical figurality, Rilke never uses the term to describe rhetorical figures. Compare Eckel, "Bild und Figur," 140; and Paul de Man, *Allegories of Reading: Figural Language in Rousseau, Nietzsche, Rilke, and Proust* (New Haven, CT: Yale University Press, 1979), esp. chap. 2. See also Beda Allemann, *Zeit und Figur beim späten Rilke: Ein Beitrag zur Poetik des modernen Gedichts* (Pfullingen: Neske, 1961); and Anke Bosse, "'Auch die sternische Verbindung trügt': Aspekte der Rilke-Lektüre Paul de Mans," *Germanistische Mitteilungen: Zeitschrift für deutsche Sprache, Literatur und Kultur* 54 (2001): 10.

31. Gerok-Reiter, in a reading heavily influenced by Allemann's, describes the *Sonnets* as taking up the problem of how transient matter or material can be given shape or form without destroying it (Gerok-Reiter, *Wink und Wandlung*, 211).

The figure of the constellation as a structure or organization that holds together separated or distant points (creating a relation or *Bezug* between them) furthermore describes the relationship between sonnets across the entire cycle (recall again Rilke's designation of constellations as "distances between fixed points"). One of the difficulties raised by the *Sonnets* is that of their unity or difference: they all belong to the same cycle, of course, and as such are members of the category or genre of *a* "Sonnet to Orpheus."[32] But Orpheus does not appear directly in every sonnet, nor does Wera, the cycle's second guarantor.[33] Rather, the family or genre of the "Sonnet to Orpheus" encompasses a fairly large number of characteristics and themes; all the *Sonnets* have some of these themes, and some of the *Sonnets* have all of them.[34] Within this family or genre, then, it is possible to trace numerous networks or constellations of sonnets linked by theme or content, formal attributes, or even sonic structures. This activity is a large-scale version of the finding and testing of relations or *Bezüge* that form a central component of Rilke's figures; it also extends the performative attributes of the *Sonnets*—themselves thematizing the creation of relationality—to the macrostructural level of the cycle. And the relations between change and identity, persistence and transience, that emerge between sonnets in these constellations take up the Orphic principle of transformation or metamorphosis (*Verwandlung*), which appears on the level of words, motifs, poem groups, and further in the relation of the two parts of the cycle to each other. The constellation, itself a figure of figurality as such, forms the central motif of a network (or constellation) of sonnets with related themes and structures, specifically those containing the words *Sternbild* (constellation), *Bild* (image), or *Figur*

---

32. I am indebted for this way of characterizing the *Sonnets* to Christoph König and the participants in the workshop of the Peter-Szondi Kolleg with the Deutsches Literaturarchiv and the Fritz Thyssen Stiftung, Marbach (November 2012).

33. Appropriately, the figures of Orpheus and Wera appear as frames of both parts of the cycle: the first and last sonnets of both the first and second parts refer to Orpheus (either directly or in dedications), while the second and penultimate sonnets of each refer to Wera (either in dedications or in second-person addresses to a dancer, Wera's primary attribute in the cycle). See Gerok-Reiter, *Wink und Wandlung*, 41.

34. Although the idea of a genre already addresses the relationship of similarity and difference between each sonnet, the Wittgensteinian notion of a *family* is also helpful here: in discussing similarities and difference between types of game, Wittgenstein remarks: "I can think of no better expression to characterize these similarities than 'family resemblances'; for the various resemblances between members of a family: build, features, colour of eyes, gait, temperament, etc., etc. overlap and criss-cross in the same way.—And I shall say: 'games' form a family.

"And for instance the kinds of number form a family in the same way. Why do we call something a 'number'? Well, perhaps because it has a—direct—relationship with several things that have hitherto been called number; and this may be said to give it an indirect relationship to other things that we call the same name. And we extend our concept of number as in spinning a thread we twist fibre on fibre. And the strength of the thread does not reside in the fact that some one fibre runs through its whole length, but in the overlapping of many fibres" (Ludwig Wittgenstein, *Philosophical Investigations/ Philosophische Untersuchungen*, trans. G. E. M Anscombe, 3rd ed. [Malden, MA: Blackwell Publishing, 2001], 28e).

(figure).³⁵ Using readings of the sonnets that make up this network, I demonstrate that and how the *Sonnets to Orpheus* programmatically invite the reader to engage in the finding and testing of such networks in a larger-scale version of the subject and world orientations that occur in the plastic and thematic shaping of the figure.

Sternbild, Bild, Figur

Having established more general themes and characteristics of the *Sonnets*, I can now turn to the sonnets in the network created by the themes of *Sternbild, Bild,* and *Figur* across the work. These three terms establish a network of eight poems: I.6, 8, 9, 11, 12 and II.12, 18, and 28.³⁶ I begin with two sonnets that explicitly discuss the creation of figural constellations and the significance of those figures for poetic production: I.11 and I.12. Reading the poems in this network fills in and deepens the attributes of the constellation and of figurality, as the poems deploy a variety of formal and thematic strategies for the presentation of the fullness of life and the shaping, finding, and testing of its limitations. My claim is that these activities (presenting, shaping, finding, testing) identify the desire for certainty, eternity, or transcendence but in response to that desire persistently turn or re-turn to an ordinary of immanent transcendence that discovers aptnesses of expression that orient language and world, text and reader, to each other.

I.11 "Sieh den Himmel."

The eleventh sonnet of the first part combines direct discussion of figures and figurality with several characteristics of the *Sonnets to Orpheus* that I identified as exemplary for the cycle as a whole. In presenting a series of questions and self-interpretations instead of a "plot," the poem thematizes processes of argumentation and questioning; it further represents those processes via physical tropes of paths and turns (*Weg* and *Wendung*). Both this concretization and the sonnet's deployment of volta-like structures not only in the traditional location in the sonnet

---

35. The *Sternbild/Bild/Figur* constellation is, of course, not the only network into which the sonnets I will read could be placed; the genre or family designation of the *Sonnets* necessarily means that different connections will exist between different groups. Moreover, one could go on building relations that would eventually encompass the entire cycle: I have excluded sonnets that mention stars (*Sterne*) rather than constellations (*Sternbilder*), but if the stars were included, they would link the topos I have identified here to flowers (flower blossoms are described as stars in II.5) and then to fruit, which in turn connects to the topos of the seasons that appears in the cycle, etc., etc. It should be clear from these linkages that I make no claim that the network I identify here is the only or even the most important one in the *Sonnets*; rather, it is the one in which the self-interpreting attributes of the cycle are most apparent because of the self-interpreting nature of I.11, which explicitly presents figurality.

36. These sonnets are reproduced in full in both German and English directly preceding this chapter. Line numbers cited in the discussion of the sonnets in this chapter correspond to the German text and translations there provided.

but in nearly every line support the claim that the sonnet is itself the kind of figure it describes, in which abstraction and plasticity merge in poetic form. But this performance also foregrounds its own temporary nature, openness, and even contingency: the constellation the poem imagines does not exist. The figure created is solely a joining of matter in perception, but it is nonetheless celebrated and, in the presentation of the poem, shared. Rilke's poetic inhabitation of human finitude that does not give up on orientations outside the subject appears, I want to say, in precisely this kind of world organization that does not deny its lack of absolute or universal certainty but seeks to create attunement both with the world and, in its performative openness to the reader, to other minds.

The sonnet opens with a command: "Sieh den Himmel." (1; "Look at the sky.") It then questions the existence of what turns out to be a fictional constellation, *Reiter*, the rider: "Heißt kein Sternbild 'Reiter'?" (1; "Is there no constellation / called '[Rider]'?").[37] Rather than answering the question directly, the poem proceeds with an *interpretation* of the figure of the rider and an insistence on its familiarity:

> Denn dies ist uns seltsam eingeprägt:
> dieser Stolz aus Erde. Und ein Zweiter,
> der ihn treibt und hält und den er trägt.
>
> (2–4)

The lines appear to create a dichotomy between earthly/animal and human, and the subsequent quartet extends the contrasts in the constellation to the *Natur des Seins* (nature of being) while continuing the idea of natural movement joined to rational control:

> Ist nicht so, gejagt und dann gebändigt,
> diese sehnige Natur des Seins?
>
> (5–6)

Beda Allemann points to the coexistence of animals and stars as a coherency of extremes essential to Rilke's poetry,[38] but emphasizes that the turn to *Natur des Seins* focuses on the central relationality or relatedness of being rather than a hierarchical distinction between stars, animals, and humans or body and mind.[39] (In typical

---

37. Groddeck observes that *Reiter* is the cycle's only instance of a word inside quotation marks, and as such is a *Fremdkörper* (foreign body) in the textual body of the *Sonnets* (Groddeck, "Kosmische Didaktik," 208). He also points out that Rilke names a constellation "rider" in the Tenth *Elegy*'s depiction of the constellations of its *Leidland* (land of sorrow). As my discussions of I.8 and I.9 below will make clearer, the relation between the *Elegies* and the *Sonnets* is in part predicated on a thoroughly different relationship to both *Leid* (suffering) and *Klage* (lament), which Groddeck does not take into account.
38. Allemann, *Zeit und Figur*, 88.
39. The realization of the relation between horse and rider is a recognition of the relational character of being as such (Allemann, *Zeit und Figur*, 88).

Rilkean fashion, the nature of being is described as a "sinewy nature," linking physical and ontological with an image of the connective tissue of the body.)

And indeed, the seventh line turns its attention from the dualistic constitution of the rider (of man and horse) to the path and turns they trace as a single constellation and to the means of communication that unites them:

> Weg und Wendung. Doch ein Druck verständigt.
> Neue Weite. Und die zwei sind eins.
>
> (7–9)

While it seems that the animal movement is contained or turned by the human intelligence in *Weg und Wendung* (path and turning), Wolfram Groddeck points out that in fact either movement or redirection might be initiated by either being. Extending this point, I suggest that the figure of unity is predicated on a relationship of physical touch: pressure, *ein Druck*, makes the two *understand* each other (*verständigt*), collapsing the distinction between mental and physical. That touch, moreover, links horse and rider together as they move through the space opened up by the poem, *Neue Weite* (8; New open vistas). Their unification seems predicated on the contrast between living, concrete beings whose bodies trace the same arc and the undefined spatiality through which they move.

Unlike many of the *Sonnets*, I.11 appears to have a traditional volta at the beginning of the tercet that questions the unity asserted at the end of the quartet: "Aber *sind* sie's?" (9; "But *are* they that?") What has gone before seems to be called into question as mere appearance; the last two verses seem to interpret the first two. But on further investigation, the structures of questioning, contradicting, or reinterpreting appear in virtually every line of the sonnet. Its alternation of apparently rhetorical questions and their logical support or answers (introduced by *denn*, *auch*, *und*, and *doch*; "for," "also," "and," and "however") plays on the traditional syllogistic structure of the sonnet, but it is not in fact easy to tell whether the answers to these questions should be understood as positive or negative. The structure "Heißt kein . . ." of the first question typically expects an affirmative answer, but since there is (except in the *Tenth Elegy*) *not* any such constellation, the reader is caught between the two possibilities. In the second question, the negative structure that anticipates affirmation ("Is it not so that . . .") is repeated, only to have its assertion questioned by the opening of the tercet: "Aber *sind* sie's?" (9) seems to expect the answer "No."

This impression is enhanced by the sonnet's seeming to present an alternative interpretation, one that complicates the relation between horse and rider, on the one hand, and constellation and path, on the other:

> Oder meinen beide
> nicht den Weg, den sie zusammen tun?
>
> (9–10)

The word *meinen* (to mean, to indicate) suggests signification, in keeping with the poem's general tendency toward self-interpretation, and supports the idea that horse and rider are united only insofar as they trace a common path through an expansive space. Indeed, the final line of the first tercet seems to confirm the thought that when this "path" is ended, the constellation dissolves: "Namenlos schon trennt sie Tisch und Weide" (11; "the utter separation of table and trough"). With the end of the path, and the end of the poem, Rilke returns to the constellation and admits its dissolution as well: "Auch die sternische Verbindung trügt" (12; "Even stellar conjunctions can deceive"). But the subsequent lines make clear that the deceptive nature of our projection (what we thought *must* be a constellation because it so perfectly represented our notion of being) is not a matter of disappointment or a reason for discarding the figure it creates. Instead the poem ends by reclaiming the pleasure and aptness of the figure:

Doch uns freue eine Weile nun
der Figur zu glauben. Das genügt.

(13–14)

In its insistence on simultaneous aptness and temporariness, the poem offers an important reminder of the temporal limitations of figurality.[40]

The falling together of the end of the figure and the end of the poem already suggests a poetological interpretation of the sonnet as a whole: it itself is a poetic figure that enacts the belonging together of antinomies.[41] Perhaps the key description of how the poem's figurality works appears in the alliterative phrase *Weg und Wendung* at the poem's midpoint in the seventh line. The horse and rider's common path can be interpreted as movement in whose course the figuration is constructed and then, in the "turning," deconstructed, making the *Weg und Wendung* the progress and pivot of the poem itself, the figure it itself describes.[42] I suggest further that *Weg* and *Wendung*, the turning of meaning (which is not separate from form or figure) as it interprets itself, fully characterize the formal qualities of the poem.

As I indicated earlier, the rhetorical questioning followed by interpretation applies the technique of the volta throughout the entire sonnet, appearing in nearly every line, occasionally within single lines. Several of the subsequent sonnets highlight the importance of turning for the formed quality of the figure; appropriately for a poem that thematizes the formative or *shaping* capacity of this turning, I.11

---

40. See Allemann's remark that "herein lies... the insight into the essence of the figure, that always asserts its connectedness only for awhile" (Allemann, *Zeit und Figur*, 73; my translation).

41. This conclusion is generally agreed on in the scholarship; see, e.g., Groddeck, "Kosmische Didaktik," 209. The difficulty, however, is to say *how* the poem does this.

42. Where Bosse understands this deconstruction as the dismantling of the figure, I suggest that it is interpretable as self-interpretation, self-questioning, and a demonstration of fictionality or self-reflection that does not preclude the satisfaction of the figure at the poem's close. See Bosse, "Auch die sternische Verbindung," 10.

is remarkably contained by sonnet form, without the pronounced enjambment that Rilke uses in many of the other sonnets to render the sonnet form fluid. But in keeping with the linguistic proximity between *Wendung, Wandlung*, and *Verwandlung* (turning, transition, and transformation), the transformative or metamorphic principles that guide the cycle as a whole, sonnet I.11 is not static. The migration of the volta within strophes and even lines—indicated by the sentences beginning with *denn, und, doch, und, aber, oder*, and *auch* ("for," "and," "however," "and," "but," "or," and "also")—is the formal instantiation of the poem's perpetual self-interpretation and self-questioning. Following these turns, the reader repeatedly recasts the potential relations between horse and rider, sense and sound, matter and mind, shifting the constellation's image across the space of an interpretive sky until its aptness emerges out of its very temporariness and self-questioning. This shifting or alteration invites the reader to test her world attunements and recognize the fit between mind and world even as it recognizes the temporary and conditioned (because human and subjective) nature of such a fit.

I.12 "Heil dem Geist..."

Sonnet I.12 continues I.11's discussion of figures and figurality along several lines. Most centrally, it introduces the idea of *Bezug* (relationality), one of Rilke's central terms for characterizing the work of balancing shaping tensions and contradictions accomplished by and within poetic figures. Not only do figures shape relations between differing and potentially opposing elements of life; they themselves are also shaped by tensions between images, ideas, and personae. The shaping created by such tension enables a further relation between form and formlessness, one that Rilke maps onto the opposing temporal qualities of persistence and transience. Both the attention to transience and the introduction of distinctions between true and untrue, actual and inactual, or literal and nonliteral reiterate the inadequacy and finitude of singular human orientations. The figurality that seeks orientation within human finitude thus simultaneously places that finitude in relation to forces outside itself, forces that are unknowable and yet familiar.

The sonnet begins by using the terms *wahr* (true), *eigentlich* (actual), and *wirklich* (real), implicitly contrasting them with *falsch/unwahr* (wrong or untrue), *uneigentlich* (inactual or nonliteral), and *unwirklich* (unreal). But this contrast itself opposes the commonsense distinction between figural and nonfigural speech:

Heil dem Geist, der uns verbinden mag;
denn wir leben wahrhaft in Figuren.

(1–2)

Truthfulness is found in figures; even more strongly, according to the second line, we *live* in them. Using the word *Verbindung* (connection) as itself a connection between the sonnets,⁴³ Rilke underscores the relational capabilities of the figure: *Verbindung/verbinden* not only links the two sonnets but has the potential to link human (?) subjects through the *Geist* (spirit) of (presumably) Orpheus. The next four lines (3–6) reiterate the distinctions of the first two along the lines of actual/ inactual and real/unreal applied first to a temporal (in *Tag*, "day") and then to a (loosely speaking) spatial concept (*Bezug*, "relation"). In the third and fourth lines, the parallel between chronometer or measured time (here emphasized by the device of measurement, namely, the clock) is shifted from the temporal to the spatial realm by the claim that the two types of time move *neben* or "next to" each other, apparently without interference. Likewise, the relation between two kinds of space: our unknowing location (we have a *wahren Platz*, a "true place," but do not know what it is) works simultaneously within our *wirklichem Bezug* (real relation), a relation temporalized by the verb *handeln* (to act).

The normative vocabulary of *wahr* and *wirklich* (in our "true place" and "actual relation") and their distinction from the *Geschäfte* (businesses) in line 10 restate in poetic form the distinction between full attention to the subject's placement in the world and the businesses of modern life that Rilke first delineated in *Malte* and that I followed into his calls for a fuller existence in his late prose texts and letters.⁴⁴ This "true place" and "actual day" (*eigentlicher Tag*, 4; MacIntyre translates this as "intrinsic day") take up the call for an existence that places subjects in relation to death—our *wirklichem Bezug*. Thus it is appropriate that we should not know or recognize our full existence completely from within one part of it ("Ohne unsern wahren Platz zu kennen" [5; "Without knowing our proper place"]), but our creation of figures that illustrate fullness and the holding together of relations enables us to feel our *relation* to that wholeness (despite our lack of *knowledge*, we nonetheless act within our true relationality). This suggestion is substantiated by the sonnet's next image, which combines modern technology and the insect world in a figure of relationality: "Die Antennen fühlen die Antennen" (7; "The antennae feel the antennae"⁴⁵). Strange as the image is, it is not the first time Rilke uses it to describe not only existential but intersubjective communion or communication: a month before the composition of the sonnets he describes Wera in a letter to her mother: "Oh how, how she loved, how she reached out with the antennae of her heart beyond all that is graspable and encompassable here."⁴⁶ But whereas Wera's love is described as reaching beyond or over (*über*) everything earthly, the antennae of the sonnet reach toward

---

43. The *Sonnets* progress from *Verbindung* (connection) in I.11.12 to *verbinden* (to connect) in I.12.1.
44. See the section "After *Malte*: Being-Here" in chapter 4.
45. MacIntyre translates this as "the antenna feel their sister-stations," emphasizing the technological element and enabling the rhyme with "relations" in line 6.
46. Rilke to Gertrud Ouckama Knoop, [?] January 1922, in Rilke, *Letters of Rainer Maria Rilke*, 2:284.

each other, relating relations across what is described as *die leere Ferne* (empty distance, 8).

In a particularly clear instance of the *Sonnets'* self-actualizing or performative qualities, the distance and void (perhaps commensurate with the *Neue Weite*, "New open vistas," in I.11.8) are represented by an ellipsis and missing syllables: while the sixth line, with which line 8 rhymes, has nine syllables, line 8 has only seven. Moreover, the ellipsis and the continuation of the sentence it indicates create the tension the first line of the first tercet describes. The virtuosity of the sonnet becomes clear as this tension appears on three levels: first, it draws out the space between the second quartet and the first tercet, taking advantage of the structure of the sonnet form, which expects some sort of event in the transition from quartets to tercets, to increase tension and anticipation. Second, the sentence and its syntax delay their resolution by delaying the object of the verb *tragen*, "to carry or bear." (*Tragen* in the sense of "to bear weight"—"to hold up"—thus reverses the significance of *trügt*, "deceives," in I.11.12 even as the sonic affinity between *trug/trügt* rejects the binary distinction.) And third, both form and syntax correspond to the image being created, which is one of a relation tensed across space like a string across an instrument, anticipating and illuminating the apostrophe that closes the ninth line: "O Musik der Kräfte!" (O music of forces!). The shape of the poem itself on the page continues the Rilkean topos of the world as an instrument across which the relations of existence are stretched and against which they resonate.[47]

Whereas sonnet I.11, then, was a figure of the turning and shaping of constellations as figures that unite the contrasting forces of existence, I.12 attends to the tension created by these relations, likewise a shaping force. The two sonnets thus present two related but differing versions of figures as figurations of relationality. In the remaining five lines, I.12 returns to the vocabulary of technology and antennae in the word *Störung* (disturbance): the *läßlichen Geschäfte* (indulgent affairs, 11) of human actions divert disturbance from the true tensile relations that enable the *Musik der Kräfte*. This is an extraordinarily benign presentation of the human distraction condemned in *Malte*, and the use of a semitechnical word (in conjunction with antennae, *Störung* sounds like an interruption of a connection) anticipates that human behavior will not always be so harmless—sonnets I.17, 18, 19, 22, 23, and 24 contrast the hastiness of and damage done by an instrumentalizing worldview to the slower and deeper transformations of the earth. These earthly transformations appear in an abbreviated form at the end of I.12, as human actions seem perpetually

---

47. See, e.g., "Am Rande der Nacht" and de Man's reading of it (de Man, *Allegories of Reading*, 33ff.). MacIntyre is obliged to sacrifice this effect in the interest of the rhyme scheme; he places the ellipsis in the ninth line.

to fall short of an earth that comes forward to meet them. Without any explicit connection to the previous lines, the last tercet insists:

> Selbst wenn sich der Bauer sorgt und handelt,
> wo die Saat im Sommer sich verwandelt,
> reicht er niemals hin. Die Erde *schenkt*.
>
> (12–14)

The generosity of the earth and the vocabulary of sowing and seeds prepare the next group of sonnets centered around fruit and trees (I.13–15). The subject's concern and care foreshadows not only the husbandry of natural products but their intertwining with death and loss; the sweetness of fruit comes from the dead: "die Toten . . . die die Erde stärken" (I.14.5; "The dead . . . who strengthen the earth"). In this progression of themes, the *Sonnets* demonstrate that figurality is not merely a poetological principle or a linguistic trick; figurality, in the logic of the cycle, opens onto the themes of the earthly, sensuality, and death that I read as central to Rilke's engagement with problems of human finitude.

I.6 "Ist er ein Hiesiger?"

The sixth sonnet of the first part, the first sonnet in the cycle to use the word *Bild* (image), likewise presents the concept of *Bezug* (relation) for the first time, linking it, moreover, explicitly to visuality. Whereas the first five sonnets focus on the ear, hearing, and singing, the sixth turns to the eye and *das Geschaute*, "that which is seen." (That *Bezug* is likewise a sonic relation should already be clear from I.12; the interplay between visuality and orality is a fundamental part of the cycle's synesthesia.) And this visuality is introduced by way of a series of contrasts between Orpheus's nature or being and a second group, referred to only as *ihr* ("you," plural)—possibly other poets, or human subjects more generally. Rilke contrasts the two specifically along the lines of their relation to death. While Orpheus comes from *beiden / Reichen* (both / realms, 2–3), the addressees have an antagonistic or oppositional relation toward death, as explicated in the second quartet. The sonnet ultimately extends the idea (present more implicitly in I.12) that a recast relation to death or mortality instantiates a shift in perception: the vagueness, mysticism, and hermeticism of occult practices become, for Orpheus, as clear as *der klarste Bezug* (the clearest relation, 11; MacIntyre translates "the clearest things" to rhyme with "ring" in line 14). And the sonnet figures this shift as an activity of mediating between clarity of relation and obscurity (or absence of differentiation), presenting a series of framing structures organized around images of blending, mixing, or dissolution. It thus enacts the organization of the relation between relation and non-relation it calls for as part of the human orientation toward mortality and finitude.

An Orphic relation to death changes human world-orientations, shifting fear and hostility to praise—an activity that, centrally, calls not for religious or mystical experience (Rilke has already rejected them in his late works) but for poetic production.

Like I.11, I.6 begins with a question, this time not about the external world (Does such and such a constellation exist?) but about Orpheus himself: "Ist er ein Hiesiger?" (1; "Does he belong here?"). The answer, "No," seems to separate Orpheus from the human and earthly, but it is immediately qualified to explain that his nature comes from "*both* / realms" (1–2; my emphasis). It seems that these realms might refer to either mortal/immortal or living/dead; although the previous sonnet's insistence on Orpheus's death and transience strongly suggests the latter, both would entail a recast relation to death. (His nature is also described as *weit*, "broad, ample, or far," linking it to the "Neue Weite" in I.11 in which figures turn, emerge, and decay.) Moreover, the subsequent lines root (literally) the dual nature of Orpheus in the earthly by way of an analogy to the relation between roots and branches of a tree:

> Kundiger böge die Zweige der Weiden,
> wer die Wurzeln der Weiden erfuhr.
>
> (3–4)

Experience of the subterranean and the ethereal elements of a natural object, the tree, would enable more skillful shaping (bending: *bogen*) of its visible parts. And the bending of branches recalls both the twisting of funeral or mourning wreaths and, in reference to the end of I.5, the bending of the lyre, itself a figure of Orpheus's transgression of the boundaries between death and life.[48] The analogy implies that Orpheus has a deeper and clearer relation both to the living and to the dead (those who are above and who are below ground) by virtue of his experiences in the underworld.

The second quartet differentiates Orpheus from an addressed group, *ihr*, who seem to have an antagonistic or hostile relation to the dead: they are commanded to avoid leaving milk and bread out overnight lest the dead be attracted by the nourishment they can no longer enjoy. Line 5 mentions going to bed, explicitly, returning to the topos of sleep central to the second sonnet of the first part, which connects sleep to death and to Wera.[49] The line likewise initiates a further contrast

---

48. See sonnets I.3 and I.5 in particular (KA 2:242–43; MacIntyre 7 and 11).
49. "Und alles war ihr Schlaf. / . . . Sie schlief die Welt. . . . / Sieh, sie erstand und schlief. / Wo ist ihr Tod?" (I.2, 5, 9, 11–12) "Her sleep was everything. / . . . She slept the world. . . . / She rose and fell asleep. / Where is her death?" KA 2:241; MacIntyre 5.

between mortals and Orpheus that emphasizes visuality even as it takes place in unseeing eyes under sleeping eyelids:

> Aber er, der Beschwörende, mische
> unter der Milde des Augenlids
>
> ihre Erscheinung in alles Geschaute;
>
> (7–9)

Orpheus seems to be able to call up the dead in dreams; the first tercet's portrayal of the magic of the plants rue and fumitory seem appropriate to the vagueness and otherworldly qualities of dreaming and the process of *mischen*, "mixing" (7).[50] But the final line of the first tercet denies such hazy mixing or occultism; for Orpheus, the appearances of the dead are as true as the *der klarste Bezug* (the clearest relation, 11) Particularly in conjunction with the meaning of *Raute* as "rhombus," *Bezug* reads as geometrical; its clarity forms the locus of comparison between human and Orphic practices of relation to the dead.

Clarity, truth, and definition, then, seem to prompt the emergence of the word *Bild* (image) in the first line of the last tercet. Without explanation, the line insists: "Nichts kann das gültige Bild ihm verschlimmern" (12; "Nothing impairs the [image] that's true"); what exactly that picture *is* remains unclear. It seems, however, to emerge from the relation outlined in *Bezug*, a figure of our relation to the dead traced more clearly by Orpheus than we could ever perceive it to be. The poem's final lines likewise link the realms of the living (contained in "rooms") and the dead (in graves) via their focus on concrete objects: ring, clasp, and jug. All of these objects, in addition to being commonly found at grave sites, represent figures of joining or turning: the circle of the ring mirrors the turning of the jug in its formation, while the clasp holds beginning and ending together, allowing all three to figure the unity rather than polarization of existence between the realms of the living and the dead. The call to praise these objects underscores the positive and open rather than hostile and protective relation toward death enabled by a recast stance toward mortality from an Orphic perspective.

The poem's contrast between image/clarity/visuality/relation and dreams/magic/mixing is taken up formally as well as semantically. Perhaps most strikingly, the enjambment that runs from line 8 to line 9 enacts the "mixing" it calls for in the optative (*mische*), as the sentence overruns the boundaries of sonnet

---

50. These plant names are themselves highly suggestive: fumitory is called "earth smoke" in English as well as in German, and the occult practices of burning herbs, the burial practice of funeral pyres, and the Hades-like connotations of smoke from the earth merge in its common name. *Raute* (rue) refers, first, to the plant buried with the dead, especially deceased children, to protect them from evil. See Thomas Krämer, *Rilkes "Sonette an Orpheus" Erster Teil: Ein Interpretationsgang* (Würzburg: Königshausen und Neumann, 1999), 80. But it also means "rhombus," the geometrical figure, thus mimicking the blending of myth and geometry found in the constellation.

form and mixes quartet and tercet. The poem thus performs repeated processes of framing and blending, putting interior and exterior in relation to each other in a figure of second-order relation *between* relation or shape and mixing or indeterminacy. So the extended description of blending or nondifferentiation is differentiated by the frame of the first quartet and last tercet, placing relation and the absence of relation into relation with each other. Several smaller instances of framed indeterminacy appear within each framing structure: the initiating question frames an enjambment as *beiden / Reichen* (both / realms) is divided between the first two lines, further framed by the *n* sounds of *Nein* and *Natur* (1, 4; No and nature); lines 7–9, calling for this mixing or blending, are surrounded by a further interior frame created by the contrast between the *ihr* ("you," plural), whose carelessness could create a blending between the realms of the living and the dead, and Orpheus, whose experience of this blending is one of clear relations. The sonnet's enactment of its own calls for forming and framing thus emphasize that mystery, difficulty, mortality, and lack of clarity are not alien to the Orphic standpoint or poetic act, but are rather to be incorporated within it. Because the form of the sonnet itself allows the tension between form and formlessness to persist, it demonstrates once again that Rilke's inhabitation of finitude does not entail shifting from one side of an opposition to another but rather the holding open of those polarities in a fuller relation to existence and finitude.

I.8 "Nur im Raum der Rühmung..."

In I.8, the theme of praise (*Rühmung*), initiated in I.6 and expanded in I.7, continues; whereas in I.6 and I.7 calls for praise contrast with presentations of death and mortality, I.8 creates an oppositional link between praise and lament (*Klage*), thus shifting from extrasubjective considerations of the relation between the realms of the mortal and the dead to a perspective within the mortal or human world, in which lament represents an emotional and subjective response to death. As it thematizes the relation between lament and praise, the sonnet likewise connects types of poetic production and modes of emotional experience; in doing so, it both personifies and spatializes these affects into the nymph Klage (Lament) and the *Raum der Rühmung* (land or space of Praise, 1). The movement of a (here, personified) living being through space recalls the movement of horse and rider in I.11, while the constellation (Stern*bild*) into which lamenting voices coalesce in the final lines makes the mutually constitutive relation between image and voice explicit for the first time. In doing so, the constellation evokes both the tension between organization and fluidity (present in the theme of *Bezug* paradigmatic for poetic orientation within finitude) and the synesthesia central to the cycle's presentation of embodied subjectivity. Finally, the themes of embodied subjectivity, affective responsiveness, and transience or temporal fluidity are combined in the literal fluidity of human tears contained within a spring. The image of the spring introduces the motifs of liquidity and containment that appear in multiple sonnets as figures of the shaping tension between transience and persistence. Here, as in I.11, Rilke combines orientations to human finitude with an emphasis on the shared but temporary nature of these orientations. He uses the sonnet form not merely to depict but to enact the shaping and fluidity, persistance and transience, that are central to such orientations within finitude.

The first appearance of constellations in the *Sonnets* does not occur until the penultimate line of I.8. At its outset, the sonnet continues the theme of praise that emerged in the final line of I.6 and was elaborated upon in I.7; in an apparent inversion of the relation of lament and praise presented in the *Elegies*, I.8 locates the spring formed by the tears of a personified Lament within the space of praise (*Raum der Rühmung*).[51] The sonnet introduces the need of a space of praise for the movement or presence of *Klage*, "lament"; this lament is personified using mythological details from the story of Byblis, whose unhappy incestuous love culminates in her tears being transformed into a spring by Lelegeian nymphs (Ovid, *Metamorphoses* 9.454–665). The fluidity of her tears links I.8 to the previous sonnet's images of the heart's blood as overflowing wine, as does the task Rilke gives the *Nymphe des geweinten Quells* (line 2) in the sonnet of watching over *unserm Niederschlage*, a metaphor of precipitation for human tears. This overflowing finds its representation in the poem's formal features: the first sentence overruns the first quartet (subtly through the use of commas, appropriate to a gently flowing spring). The spring takes on Orphic and thus poetological import by virtue of being the cliff that also holds (*trägt*, "carries": the same verb that Rilke used to describe the relation between horse and rider and the tension held by empty distances) the altars and gates of the *Tempel im Gehör* (Temple in hearing) erected to Orpheus in the first sonnet.

Lines 6–11 complicate the personification of *Klage* by describing her in relation to *Geschwiste[r] im Gemüt* (MacIntyre translates this as "the Passions' sisterhood," but *Geschwister* is the gender-neutral "siblings"), specifically Jubel (rejoicing) and Sehnsucht (longing). In doing so, these lines continue to elaborate the relation of joy and lament to one another and, as will appear in the figure of the constellation in line 13, to poetry. Klage is described as (potentially) the youngest of the *Geschwiste[r] im Gemüt*; she *lernt noch* (still learns, 10), and her activity is *mädchenhändig* (with girlish hands, 10). *Jüngste* also suggests that lament is the first emotion in reaction to loss, one that cannot achieve the perspective necessary to understanding the belonging together of death and life. Instead, Lament remains preoccupied with loss and absence:

---

51. In the *Tenth Elegy*, conversely, the *Quelle der Freude* is located in the *Landschaft der Klage* (landscape of lament) and flows from *Gebirgen des Ur-Leids* (mountains of primal sorrow), as Engel and Fülleborn point out (KA 2:734).

> mädchenhändig
> zählt sie nächtelang das alte Schlimme.
>
> (10–11)

The "knowledge" that belongs to joy or praise ("Jubel *weiß*" [Rejoicing *knows*]) and the openness or confession of longing ("Sehnsucht ist geständig" [Longing is contrite]) contrast with the unmediated grief of Klage. But (and here Rilke shifts the volta of the sonnet, this time placing it at the outset of the last tercet rather than at the transition from quartet to tercet) precisely Lament's newness or purity of feeling seems to relate it to specifically human feeling:

> Aber plötzlich, schräg und ungeübt,
> hält sie doch ein Sternbild unsrer Stimme
> in den Himmel, den ihr Hauch nicht trübt.
>
> (12–14)

The rhyme between *Schlimme* (evil, 11) and *Stimme* (voice, 13) suggests that it is the nymph Klage's lack of mediation or distance toward suffering that makes her capable of producing a constellation of *human* voices; the plural *uns* (us) implies that the voice is human, not that of the nymph Klage, while the singular *Stimme* creates a single image or *Bild*, underscoring the synesthesia of the constellation and poetic production as it hovers between orality and visuality.

Furthermore, the group ("we") designated by the repeated use of the first-person plural (*wir*) in I.11 and I.12 appears in I.8 only in the possessive *unser* (our) with reference to (human) tears and the (human) voice, insisting on the relation between tears and the voice, linked in the aesthetic production of the sonnet. The visualization of the voice in the constellation offers a potential figure of the relation between the written form of the sonnet and its traditional identity as a *Klinggedicht*, or "sound poem";[52] I show further the necessary relation between that poetic production and the tension between fluidity and formation in my reading of I.9. For the moment, I want to reiterate that, as itself a figure in the form of a sonnet, I.8 as a whole acts out the flowing, overlapping, and rippling back into itself of a spring, first through the subtle contrast between syntax and line endings, and then in the tercets in a conflict between meter and rhyme scheme. Lines 9, 10, 11, and 13 all have ten syllables and end with an unaccented syllable, while lines 12 and 14 have nine and end with an accented syllable. The rhyme scheme is *eef gfg*, which further disrupts the unity of each tercet: the first tercet appears to start with a couplet and

---

52. See, e.g., Groddeck's claim that the constellation is a visual metaphor of the voice, i.e., the transformation of the audible into the visual, like the written (legible) signs of the sound-poem/sonnet (Groddeck, "Kosmische Didaktik," 219).

then has an unrhymed line that does not receive its rhyme word until the second line of the next tercet. The sonnet genre as experimenting with fluid (literally liquid in depictions of bodies of water) thought encased in rigid form is of course a canonical topos, but Rilke's sonnet makes that form itself a representation of bounded fluidity, corresponding precisely to the overflowing tears that form a spring whose images will, in the next sonnet, take up the holding together of life and death, lament and joy.

I.9 "Nur wer die Leier schon hob..."

Sonnet I.9 takes up several of the central themes of I.8 in particular and the cycle as a whole, including the simultaneously aural and visual nature of poetic production (voice as creating a *Bild*, or "image"), the relation toward death and the dead, and the topos of liquidity in bodies of water. Most importantly, however, the theme of the tension between persistence and transience is extended into a new semantic field with new connotations. The final lines call for voices (whether those of poets, humans, or the dead is not clear) to become *ewig und mild* (eternal and mild), a set of terms that seems at least slightly contradictory (the strong or harsh might be expected to be more persistent than what is mild; Rilke addresses this expectation directly in II.12). Such voices, however, are eternal within a *Doppelbereich* (dual realm) that emerges, I contend, as neither the transient nor the persistent but the relation between them; the slight paradox of the persistence of mildness begins to elaborate the idea that transience will turn out to be not opposed to but necessary for persistence. As the poem figures the *Doppelbereich* it describes by way of metrical doubleness throughout its structure, Rilke tentatively elucidates poetic presentations of the call in his letters for individual and finite subjects to orient themselves toward death (that is, toward their own transience) not as other or alien but as a component of existence. What emerges in poetic figures (as opposed to more discursive prose texts or letters) is the more paradoxical idea that only in undertaking this reorientation can subjects begin to reach outside their own isolation toward something persistent or even "eternal" in its very passing away.

Several more specific elements also link I.8 and I.9: both sonnets refer to voices (although they are clearly human in I.8, and in I.9 it is not clear whose or what voices are described); the fluidity of the tears and the spring (*Quelle*) in I.8 return in the form of a *Teich* (pool or pond) and the *Bild* (image) that "blurs" (*verschwimmt*); finally, the description of (implicitly) the reflection in the water as a *Bild* hints at a connection between the myth of Narcissus (as a personification of the nexus of death, beauty, and poetry) and the topos of the figure that appeared as a constellation in I.8. The sonnet's first project, however, is to tighten the relation between Orpheus and a mode of poetic production emerging from death and absence, apparent in the reference to the lyre and its being played among the dead (the shades or shadows):

> Nur wer die Leier schon hob
> auch unter Schatten,
> darf das unendliche Lob
> ahnend erstatten.
>
> (1–4)

Here, too, the topos of the constellation occurs in the reference to Orpheus's lyre, itself placed among the stars after the singer's dismemberment by the Maenads.[53] Death thus appears as a necessary component of praise. This relation is complicated by a connection specifically to memory in the second quartet, which likewise emphasizes the *sonic* quality of Orphic poetry or singing:

> Nur wer mit Toten vom Mohn
> aß, von dem ihren,
> wird nicht den leisesten Ton
> wieder verlieren.
>
> (5–8)

Poppies, associated with forgetting, establish the complex relation between forgetting (transience to and in an individual subject) and poetic production: precisely the person who eats the food of the dead and has been among them will not lose (forget? miss?) the softest of tones.

Two important shifts take place in the shift from quartet to tercet: first, the sonnet moves from portrayal of Orpheus and the dead to the activities of an *uns* (us), and, second, the sonic register becomes visual without losing any of its fluid qualities. Given the mythic frame of reference, the figure of Narcissus resonates fairly immediately within the description of the *Spieglung im Teich* (reflection in the pool, 9), also anticipating the mirror sonnets of part II in a mythically and intrasubjectively inflected version of the self-commentary and self-interpretation of the figure that occurred in I.11. The seemingly contradictory relation between the fluidity or dissolution of the image in lines 9 and 10 and the command "*Wisse das Bild*" (*Know the image*; MacIntrye translates this as "*Make the image yours*") in line 11 continues the paradox of continuity and change that emerged around the tension between poppies and memory in the second quartet and places it explicitly in relation to one of the central tensions of the figure.

---

53. For an account of the myth, see Gertrud Höhler, "Rainer Maria Rilkes Orpheus," in *Mythos und Mythologie in der Literatur des 19. Jahrhunderts*, ed. Helmut Koopmann (Frankfurt a.M.: Klosterman, 1979), 380.

The final tercet seems to elaborate on the reasons for or achievements of following the command to know the image:

> Erst in dem Doppelbereich
> werden die Stimmen
> ewig und mild.
>
> (12–14)

It is not immediately clear what *the* double realm (the line uses the dative form of the definite article) refers to; the most immediate referent seems to be the doubling of the world in the reflection. But while reflection is precisely what dissolves (*verschwimmen*), *das Bild* (the image) is what the hearer/reader is commanded to *know*; I want to suggest that the double realm in which voices are both mild and eternal is that of the relation *between* reflection and world, and as such the *Bild* is not the reflection itself (after all, Rilke uses different words for reflection and image, *Spieglung* and *Bild*, respectively) but the doubleness of self-reflection.

The term *Doppelbereich*, moreover, provides insight into the techniques Rilke uses to make the sonnet a figure of doubleness that expresses the complex relation it presents between persistence and decay. The structure of the Italian sonnet, in general, exists in a double realm between multiples of two and multiples of three (quartet/quartet//tercet/tercet or octave/sestet); Rilke heightens this impression by alternating lines of three and lines of two strong syllables throughout the first eight lines. In the tercets the first two lines of each continue this pattern, while lines 11 and 14 preserve the pattern of two strong syllables but reduce the total syllables in each line (seven/five/four). This tapering does not interrupt the doubleness of the sonnet's meter, but it executes the mildness and fluidity that in the sonnet is the proper form of memory. The gentle fading away of the end of each tercet figures the necessity of decay, ending, and susceptibility to the passage of time for the human situation in the fullness of existence; knowing the figure of the sonnet requires the reader to recognize that what II.12 will call *Erstarren* (becoming rigid) and *Bleiben* (staying or remaining), antagonistic attempts to exceed temporality, are distorting forces that preclude the transformation of the earthly and ordinary that is the *Sonnets*' project.

II.12 "Wolle die Wandlung."

The first sonnet of the second part to mention the figure directly is II.12, the pendant sonnet to I.12 in which the program of figurality becomes a vehicle for confident praise. Sonnet II.12 is also the last sonnet in the cycle to mention *Figur* explicitly, in keeping with the second part's more diffuse presentation of themes and images from the first part following the death and dismemberment of Orpheus described in I.26. And here the theme of transience and persistence is linked most strongly to the tension between identity and change created by the cycle's central theme of metamorphosis or *Verwandlung*. This theme further describes the formal principle of the cycle, with its shifting and self-commentating network of images, formal features, and sounds that develop between individual sonnets, between groups, and between the two parts. *Verwandlung* is thus legible as the specifically human attitude of openness and responsiveness toward our own finitude in the infinity of existence, and, more concretely, the formal and semantic impulse of II.12. Under the auspices of the theme and structure of transformation, II.12 reiterates the paradox between persistence and decay even more strongly than the earlier sonnets, as attempts to achieve *Bleiben* (remaining) lead to violent destruction, while self-dissolution ("Wer sich als Quelle ergießt" [9; "He who pours himself out as a spring"]) offers continuity between beginning and end (11). And the poem enacts this relation between persistence and transience in the contrast between its unified sonic structure and the perpetual presentation of "turning points" as the sonnet becomes a figure for the relation between finitude and persistence that describes figurality's capacity for creating orientations within finitude.

II.12 also collects and reiterates numbers of the motifs I have traced in previous sonnets: not only the reference to *Figur* but the presence of *Geist* (spirit) connects it to I.12; like I.8, II.12 refers (here indirectly) to Byblis in line 9, and in line 12 to praise or happiness intimately made material in a physical space that is also related to separation and loss; both Byblis and, in the thirteenth line, Daphne, link the sonnet to Ovid's *Metamorphoses* and thus to the theme of metamorphosis (also translated as *Verwandlung*) more generally. Like I.11, II.12 begins with a command; here, the theme of transformation could hardly be more explicit: "Wolle die Wandlung" (1; "Will the transformation"). A further command spills over into the second line and transforms *Wandlung* into *Verwandlung*:

> O sei für die Flamme begeistert,
> drin sich ein Ding dir entzieht, das mit Verwandlungen prunkt;
>
> (1–2)

The flame in which *ein Ding* (a thing; MacIntyre translates this as "something") recedes seems to stand for the consuming and disappearing of all experience; *entziehen* (to withdraw) is the *Sonnets*' descriptor for the transition of objects from present to absent, from *Besitz* (possession) to *Bezug* (relation),[54] the latter being the spatialized version of connection or relation that traces figurality. Already this withdrawing implies that present and possessed objects are themselves no more than a component of figurality, and it is their transformation that enables them to exist in the tension between absence and presence, fictionality and aptness, that is

---

54. KA 2:753.

constitutive of the figure. The central moment of this transformation appears in the next line in what appears to be a justification for such enthusiasm for transformation and change:

> jener entwerfende Geist, welcher das Irdische meistert,
> liebt in dem Schwung der Figur nichts wie den wendenden Punkt.
>
> (3–4)

Schwung der Figur (soaring of figures) suggests the turning of constellations through the sky.[55] *Wendenden Punkt* (point of turning) can also be taken literally, as either the precise moment in which the thing recedes into relationality or simply the turning point of the poem.

And the next quartet does turn from praise of transformation or metamorphosis to a warning about the misguidedness of attempts at stasis or unchanging persistence:

> Was sich ins Bleiben verschließt, schon *ists* das Erstarrte;
> wähnt es sich sicher im Schutz des unscheinbaren Grau's?
>
> (5–6)

The rejection of *Bleiben* (remaining, abiding) and, even more strongly, *das Erstarrte* (the numbed or ossified) serves as an important reminder that the figure, properly conceived, is measured and shaped but not rigid or fixed. Although the question is not directly answered, the apparent safety (of, it appears in the subsequent lines, an unformed stone) is revealed as transient; something still more irrevocable and perhaps immaterial (*abwesender Hammer*) will transform it, too. Strong *w* sounds alternate breathlessly with *h* and long *e* sounds to spell or sound out the word *Wehe* (woe) four times: "W**a**rte, ein H**ä**rtestes w**a**rnt aus d**e**r F**e**rne das H**a**rte. / **Wehe**—: ab**we**sender H**a**mm**e**r holt aus!" (7–8; "Wait, a hardest forewarns the hard from far away! / Alas, an absent hammer upheaves!") Moreover, the eighth line, concerned with woe, violence, and absence, is itself noticeably shorter (nine syllables, with a clear break marked by an em dash and a colon after *Wehe*, "Alas" or "Woe"), reiterating the failure of *das Erstarrte* to persist and dynamizing the meter of the sonnet.

In a second *wendender Punkt*, "turning point" (this one at the standard volta locations between quartets and tercets), the tercets present the examples of "Wer sich als Quelle ergießt" (He who pours out himself as a spring; a reference to the story of Byblis abstracted to a potential activity for poet and/or reader) and Daphne as figures of transformation. The spatialization of creativity to *das Geschaffne* (creation, the created) through which the self-transforming and fluid subject is led is likewise temporalized in the relation of beginning and end in the eleventh line, as

---

55. Groddeck points out that *Wendepunkt* is an astronomical/astrological term as well (Groddeck, "Kosmische Didaktik," 220).

it "mit Anfang oft schließt und mit Ende beginnt" (11; "often ends at the start and begins at the end"). As beginning and end meet in a circular or cyclical conception of time, their meeting underscores the Orphic program of the wholeness or fullness of existence, which, as Rilke remarked in a letter to the Countess of Sizzo,[56] encompasses both life and death.

The poem reiterates this circularity sonically as well: the *w* sounds of *Wolle* and *Wind* open and close the poem. The *w* sounds that appear throughout the poem are in large part an effect of one of Rilke's grammatical permutations of *Wandlung* or *Wandeln* (transformation)—an effect itself sometimes grammatically referred to as *Wandlung*.[57] Transformation is grammatically transformed and linked with prefixes to *Ver-wandlung* and thematically to *Wendung*. But despite the poem's insistence on transformation, the sonic level of the poem is astonishingly consistent: *Wolle, Wandlung, was, wähnt, warnt, warte, wehe, wer, will, wandelst,* and *Wind,* in addition to the internal *w* sounds in *verwandelte* and *abwesend*, create an acoustic network across the poem.[58] This acoustic element remains constant in the grammatical and thematic *Verwandlungen* of the sonnet; as such, it demonstrates on a lexical or material level the complex relationship between persistence and decay, constancy and change, that I have followed in I.8 and 9 (perhaps also in the fictionality and temporariness of I.11) as a central tension of Rilke's figures. The tension between identity and change, even death, reminds the reader that the inhabitation of finitude entails neither an insistent and unidirectional projection of subjectivity onto the world nor self-relinquishing immersion in the flux of time or nature. II.12 acknowledges the desire for assured persistence or even eternity; its images show that attempts to achieve such persistence lead directly to an ossification that denies finitude and thus destroys the relation to the wholeness of existence opened up by Orphic transformation of the ordinary and transient.

II.18 "Tänzerin: o du Verlegung..."

Wera appears indirectly in her attribute as a dancer in II.18, making it a prelude to the penultimate sonnet (II.28), in which her biography is addressed more specifically. As with the Wera motif as a whole, II.18 is centrally concerned with human relations toward death and finitude: here, a dancer's final twist or turn mimics

---

56. "Like the moon, life surely has a side permanently turned away from us which is not its [opposite] but its complement toward perfection, toward consummation, toward the really sound and full sphere and orb of *being*" (Rilke to Countess Margot Sizzo, 6 January 1923, in Rilke, *Letters of Rainer Maria Rilke*, 2:316).

57. *Grimms Wörterbuch*, in its article on *Wandlung*, specifies that in linguistic tracts, *beugung* is "declinatio" (declension), *wandlung*, "conjugatio" (conjugation), *fügung*, "syntaxis" (syntax) (*Deutsches Wörterbuch von Jacob und Wilhelm Grimm*, online ed., s.v. "Wandlung").

58. This sonic consistency is much less striking in English: "will," "transformation," "what," "believes," "wait," "forewarns," "woe," "who," "will," "transforms," and "wind."

other figures of turning and completion, placing artistic accomplishment irrevocably in relation to death. Appropriately, the sonnet is caught in an ambiguity between praise and mourning—it celebrates Wera's accomplishments (or rather, those of the unnamed dancer) even as the ending of her movement falls together with the ending of her life. The poem's uncertainty manifests itself in the overwhelming presence of the negative *nicht* in its repeated questioning and in an overarching tendency toward repetition or redescription, as if the speaker sought to reinscribe lament as celebration, but remained unsure of success. Formally, the sonnet's pronounced variation between long and short line lengths reiterates both the dynamic of forward motion and controlled turning together with the tentativeness of its repeated questioning—it never moves into a full flow of equal line lengths uninterrupted by enjambment or punctuation. The sonnet thus enacts the movement of lament (here represented by negation and questioning) through a land of celebration (in the descriptions of the dancer's completeness and virtuosity) in a figuration of finitude's complex relation (*Bezug*) to grief and joy.

Like II.12, II.18 begins with an address; unlike II.12, that address is not a command and is directed to a specific person, a *Tänzerin* (dancer, 1). This apparent addressee complicates the most striking feature of the sonnet, namely, its deployment of questions. Because they seem to be addressed to the dancer (presumably but perhaps not only Wera), it is not clear whether they are rhetorical questions. Like the questions in I.11, they are posed in the negative form that initially seems to expect a positive answer. Whereas in I.11 this expectation was undercut from the outset by its reference to a fictional constellation, in II.18 the questions seem to work within the expectation of a positive answer. But by the end of the poem, the word *nicht* has been repeated six times in five questions ("nahm er nicht...?" 3; "Blühte nicht...?" 5; "war sie nicht... nicht...?" 7; "Sind sie nicht...?" 10; "ist nicht...?" 12), leading to the uncertainty that it really might *not* be the case that the questions are to be answered affirmatively. The speaker also consistently repeats and qualifies his questioning assertions, as in lines 7–8 ("die Wärme, / diese unzählige Wärme aus dir?") and line 9 ("Aber er trug auch, er trug..."; But it also bore, it bore...). Several lines seem to redefine or qualify their original object, so that the *Wirbel am Schluss* (whirl of the finish, 3) becomes a *Baum aus Bewegung* (tree of motion, 3), and the *Zeichnung* (drawing, 12) becomes a *Zug* (line or stroke, 13). The sonnet's tentative self-qualifications reiterate that there can be no unequivocal assurances in relations toward mortality or finitude.

This uncertainty is inherent to the *Sonnets'* engagement with human finitude and mortality, taken up so often in the tension between persistence and transience. In the second line the translation (*Verlegung*) of transience into movement (*Vergehen* to *Gang*, "gait") uses a grammatical-etymological transformation to describe the transformation of mortality or transience into aesthetic making. The end of the sentence (one of only two nonquestions in the sonnet) praises the addressee's bringing of her dance as an offering: "wie brachtest du's dar" (2; "how you made it clear!"). The figure of the tree encompasses both the deepening of the roots among the dead and the expansion of limbs and leaves into the air, and is as such itself a figure of the unity of death and life recalling the connections between roots and branches in I.6. But this "tree of motion" is itself the figure of completion of the dancer's spinning or turning (*Wirbel am Schluß* [whirl of the finish, 3]), which encompasses as tree and as turn *das erschwungene Jahr* ("the hard-won year," but *erschwungen* includes the participle of *schwingen*, "to swing"), recalling the turning point of transformation into figures in II.12. The warmth that radiates from the figure of the dancer, meanwhile, and the summer whose fruits appear in the first tercet, recall the earth's gift of the ripening of the seed at the end of I.12.

The tree's fruition is described specifically as *bearing* fruit ("er trug" [9; "it bore"]). The conjugated form of the verb *tragen* (past tense imperfect) links the figure to the bearing of the rider by the horse in I.11 but also to the *Be*trug (deception or fictionality) of the figure represented in the constellation. The natural act of ripening, which the farmer in II.12 cannot reach, extends in II.18 to artifacts as well: the vase and jug are described as *gereift* (ripened) in the eleventh line. Both the connection of the sweetness of fruit to the *Lehm* (clay) of the dead (I.14) and the vase or jug's connotations of rounding off or finishing of movement make them, too, figures of completion and death that depict the fullness of existence in their rounded forms.[59] This connection has, of course, already been made explicitly in the praise of *Fingerring, Spange und Krug* (ring, clasp, and jug) in I.6, with its direct consideration of Orpheus's shifting relations between the dead and the living. These figures indicate an aesthetic or craftsmanly synesthesia (a more physical complement to the interplay between visuality and aurality in the earlier sonnets): the tactile spinning and shaping of the pot and the visual and dynamic forming of the dancer combine with drawing (*Zug*, "stroke") and writing (*geschrieben*). Moreover, the image integrates relationality with embodied subjectivity as *Bezug* becomes *Zug*, and the wide spans of the cosmos are written not on but *by* a human face.

In addition, the tree recalls the *Baum im Ohr* (tree in the ear, I.1.1) evoked or created by Orpheus's singing and its poetics of hearing. Thus both Orpheus and Wera are present in the tercets, placed into relation by the movement of the dancer forming the Orphic tree and the Orphic poet writing the stroke of the dancer's face. That face, appearing *rasch an die Wandung der eigenen Wendung* (swiftly in the texture of their own turning, 14), recalls the face reflected in the pond of tears in I.9. There, the double realm of persistence and transience was portrayed in the double meter of the poem; here, the tension between absence and presence, life and death, constitutive of Rilke's figures appears in the placing of the network of several of those paradigmatic figures into the ambiguity between negative and positive answers to the questioning that shapes the sonnet. The poem creates the field for reflection (per I.9, a *Doppelbereich*, or double realm) in which the relation between

---

59. Gerok-Reiter, *Wink und Wandlung*, 216.

persistence and transience unfolds, turning *Zug* (stroke, line) into *Bezug* (relation) in its poetic shaping.

II.28 "O komm und geh."

Wera reappears in II.28, the penultimate sonnet, as it forms the interior frame of the double framing of the sonnets by Wera and Orpheus.[60] It is primarily concerned with human aesthetic production, particularly Wera's, as it unites her dance steps with other art forms in the kind of synesthetic blending characteristic of the cycle and its treatment of finitude. The sonnet itself both depicts and is a figure of the tension across an empty middle, familiar from I.12. Here this figure is affiliated directly with Orpheus's lyre; the shape of the lyre itself, as a frame around emptiness crossed by tensed strings, both corresponds to the sonnet's participation in the cycle's frame and refers to the conditions of possibility of song itself (emptiness in which to resonate). The dancer's activity and her glance (or perhaps Orpheus's) undertake the boundary crossing performed by the rider in I.11, thus linking the two sonnets; whereas in II.18 the dancer's movement was the shape around an empty middle, here, the dancer mimics the crossing of space by the strings of the lyre in her own enactment of the tensile boundary crossing of relationality or *Bezug*.

The first line addresses or commands Wera to perform the activity attributed to Orpheus in the fifth sonnet of the first part ("Er [Orpheus] kommt und geht" [I.5.6; "He comes and goes"): "O komm und geh" (1; "Oh, come and go").[61] She is directly implicated in the Orphic poetology by the strange image of a tree that responds to her movement, recalling both the tree *of* movement and silence in II.18 and the "tree in the ear" in the first sonnet of the cycle. The figure created by both dance and poetry is connected explicitly to a constellation that, like the constellation Reiter (rider), is temporary (*für einen Augenblick* [for an instant, 2]) but complete (*ergänze*, 1). That dance and its figures are the ordering in which humans, although transient, supersede the ordering of nature in its sheer physical there-ness. Constellations are both more fleeting and less concrete, but they gather and shape perceptions of the external world, allowing subjects to place themselves in that world and the world in themselves, thus exceeding (*übertreffen*) natural physicality as the line exceeds the quartet:

> darin wir die dumpf ordnende Natur
>
> vergänglich übertreffen.
>
> (4–5)

---

60. Gerok-Reiter, *Wink und Wandlung*, 41.

61. In fact this could also be a command to the reader, as the attributes that make clear that the *Du* (You) here addressed is Wera appear only gradually in the rest of the poem.

The joining of Stern*bild*, Tanz*figur*, dance, and singing/hearing recalls the Orphic synesthesia that has appeared throughout the cycle; here, however, aesthetic production appears to be motivated by an *unerhörte Mitte* (unheard-of center).[62] Curiously, the middle point of the poem is anything but empty—through a striking enjambment, it seems rather to stretch syntax over the space between strophes:

> wenn ein Baum sich lang
>
> besann
>
> (8–9)

This middle is initially not named as such but instead described as the originary space of Orphic poetry:

> die Stelle, wo die Leier
> sich tönend hob
>
> (10–11)

And then a representation of the unheard or unheard-of does appear, as the line is interrupted by an em dash and a semicolon: "sich tönend hob—; die unerhörte Mitte" (12; "resounding—the unheard-of center"). Although *unerhört* in fact carries the same idiomatic connotation in German as *unheard-of* in English, meaning "unprecedented or tremendous" (perhaps an echo of the excess of *übertreffen*, "to exceed," in line 5), it also, of course, comes from the verb *hören*, "to hear." I suggest that this empty middle is both unheard-of, in the sense of strange or fantastic—perhaps something human subjects have missed in their distractions—and in the sense of unheard. As such, it plays a role analogous to that of the *Weite* (distance) of I.11 and the *Spanne* (span) of I.12, as the space that the figure moves through or organizes; what the *Zug* or *Bezug* of relations drawn through space divide to create form, here described as the space of the resounding lyre. It is thus directly associated with Orphic poetic production, and the ringing (*tönen*) of the lyre seems to find expression in the *erhörte Mitte* created by the palindromic rhyme scheme of the tercets (*gehn*, "to go"; *Leier*, "lyre"; *Mitte*, "middle"; *Schritte*, "steps"; *Feier*, "festival"; *drehn*, "to turn"),[63] concentrating sonic repetition in the middle of the tercets.

---

62. There is an extensive scholarship on *Mitte* in Rilke, as it is an idea that appears in various guises throughout Rilke's work (e.g., in "Der Panther"); I am not treating it alone or discussing that scholarship here because it is, as I shall discuss, fully incorporated in the conception of figurality I have been advancing throughout.

63. MacIntyre changes the rhyme scheme from *efg gfe to efe ggf*.

The *unerhörte Mitte* is not only associated with poetic production by way of the lyre's link to Orpheus; it also *motivates* Wera's artistic activity, namely, dance: "Für sie versuchtest du die schönen Schritte" (12; "Therefore, / you tried the lovely steps"). But the desire for and power of the unheard/-of center undertake not only to emulate or create a relation to Orpheus. The genitive in the final lines of the poem creates an ambiguity that causes the poem's motions of boundary crossing (from death to life) to move in two directions. In the first reading (rendered easier to hear by the line break between 13 and 14), the lines refer to the hope of the dancer that she might, crossing death, draw the poet's attention to the solemn celebration of her dance: "du . . . / hofftest, einmal zu der heilen Feier / des Freundes Gang und Antlitz hinzudrehn" (12–14). *Freund* refers in the last sonnet (II.29) directly to Rilke/the poet (a note designates it as addressed to *einem Freund Weras*, "a friend of Wera's"); consequently the posthumous appeal of Wera's dance asks him to turn his own steps (*Gang*, "gait," like *Schritte*, "steps," in line 11) and perception toward the unacknowledged and as yet unformed continuity between life and death.

But in the second reading, the dancer would hope to turn her gaze toward the wholeness of Orphic celebration (*Freund* would then refer to Orpheus), across the boundary of death. In this reading, the unity or wholeness of life requires a redirection of human attention toward the unities of Orphic song. The sonnet ends by reaching outward—not only toward the poet (and the final sonnet) but past him toward the reader in an invitation to renewed attentiveness to the kind of holding together of the antinomies of existence that occurs in Rilke's figures. The *unerhörte Mitte* is thus also the space between reader and poet, hearer and speaker, mind and world; the poetology of the sonnets calls on human subjects to shape the relations between them in acknowledgment of the difficult, temporary, and dangerous yet fitting figures of the wholeness of existence.

In this chapter I have returned to the themes of openness to death and embodied subjectivity that form the locus of Rilke's poetic inhabitation of finitude. Human subjects are finite, mortal, and earthly; we can have no final assurances that our attunements either to the external world (in Rilke, to things) or to other minds are "accurate" or of how they will end; nor is there any "beyond" (religious or more generally metaphysical) that can or will intercede or vouchsafe the directions of subjective investment in the world. The crisis documented in *Malte* serves as a reminder of the ease with which human subjects take this uncertainty as precisely *not* obvious; what Rilke repeatedly calls our *Ablenkungen* or *Verdrängungen* represent subjective efforts to find certainty or despair at its absence. I have argued that the Orphic poetology of the *Sonnets to Orpheus* takes up precisely the themes of subjective relations to bodies, to others, to the world, and to death that engage with the problems of human finitude; the sonnets themselves seek provisional, open, and temporary inhabitations of that finitude that do not abdicate the possibilities of aptness, sufficiency, or communal experience.

But precisely because of the virtuosity with which Rilke handles the sonnet form, the poetics of figuration may seem like a flight from finitude into a play of infinitely changing forms. Rilke, further, seems less ambitious than Hölderlin: he never presents programs that strive to reform national or political life in the way that even Hölderlin's late poetry seems to do, and when Rilke takes up a strategy of undercutting traditional hierarchies of thought simliar to that of Baudelaire, he adapts it away from socioeconomic critique toward the self-questioning of the poetic subject.[64] But several attributes of Rilke's oeuvre as a whole—which not only appear but are instantiated in poetic form in the *Sonnets*—belie this apparent solipsism. First, Rilke's lifelong attention to human relations to objects, in particular in the late form of the project of rescuing them from the distraction that reduces them to commodification, indicates a more critical stance toward economic realities than his persuading Hertha Koenig to buy Picasso's *Acrobats* so that he could look at it suggests.[65] Second, his persistent preoccupation with the problems of and for writing *in his era*, marked by belatedness and the inaccessiblity of tradition (in some ways analogous to Hölderlin's treatments of childood and ancient Greece as lost eras of unreflective presence), and his hope that a shifted relation to objects and to death will change that era, show a poet unwilling to retreat to unquestioned tradition in the face of his culture. That his hopes for cultural renewal never take the form of political or national engagement is likely, as I suggested in chapter 4, due in part to the linguistic and cultural heterogeneity of his environments throughout his life (from multilingual Austro-Hungarian Prague to French- and German-speaking Valois). But surely the fact that he had seen and even briefly

---

64. See the section "Rilke's Epoch and Influences: Problems of Finitude around 1900" in chapter 4; and Ryan, *Rilke, Modernism*, 86.

65. Rilke is further not alone in treating human relations to the most insignificant and unassuming objects as central to a modernity critique that has far-reaching political implications: Theodor Adorno, in an aphorism from *Minima Moralia* even more pessimistic about technology's influence on modernity than Rilke is, makes a provocative link between door slamming and fascism: "Do not knock.— Technology is making gestures precise and brutal, and with them men. It expels from movements all hesitation, deliberation, civility. It subjects them to the implacable, as it were ahistorical demands of objects. Thus the ability is lost, for example, to close a door quietly and discreetly, yet firmly. Those of cars and refrigerators have to be slammed, others have the tendency to snap shut by themselves, imposing on those entering the bad manners of not looking behind them, not shielding the interior of the house which receives them. The new human type cannot be properly understood without awareness of what he is continuously exposed to from the world of things about him, even in his most secret innervations. What does it mean for the subject that there are no more casement windows to open, but only sliding frames to shove, no gentle latches but turnable handles, no forecourt, no doorstep before the street, no wall around the garden? And which driver is not tempted, merely by the power of his engine, to wipe out the vermin of the street, pedestrians, children and cyclists? The movement machines demand of their users already has the violent, hard-hitting, unresting jerkiness of fascist maltreatment. Not least to blame for the withering of experience is the fact that things, under the law of pure functionality, assume a form that limits contact with them to mere operation, and tolerates no surplus, either in freedom of conduct or in autonomy of things, which would survive as the core of experience, because it is not consumed by the moment of action" (Theodor Adorno, *Minima Moralia: Reflections on Damaged Life*, trans. E. F. N. Jephcott [London: Verso, 2005], 40).

participated in the nationalistic fervor of the First World War and lived through its consequences warned him of the dangers of being swept away on the current of nationalist feeling.

Rilke turns instead, I would argue, to the possibility of speaking out of the particularity of an individual, finite, subjective voice, but this voice is not one that isolates itself from the world and speaks to itself regardless of who hears. The weaving together of letter productivity and poem productivity throughout his life lends credence to the thought that the equivocal transformations he strove to undertake in poetic form were intended for his readers as well; I have undertaken to show how the *Sonnets to Orpheus* work to reach and change their readers. In letter after letter Rilke seeks and attempts to offer help and advice, even as he denies the easy consolations of religion, for example, in condolence letters or self-reckonings written to both friends and strangers. While the idea of the poet as a guide to life is surely too simplistic (indeed, Rilke's own reception of Hölderlin is an example of the dangers of interpreting poetry directly for one's current situation), the intersubjectivity toward which his poems and letters persistently strive raises the possibility of a poetic rather than national community of speaking subjects.

Central to the creation of this community is the absence of any prescriptive or universal procedures or rules for its creation and its delineation. This is precisely the kind of community that undertakes what I used Charles Bernstein and Stanley Cavell to characterize as a "convening on its conventions," a calling into question of relations to and in language that uncovers our injustices and seeks "ecstasies of exactness" that change subjective relations both to language and to the world.[66] And because of this absence of rules or prescriptions, the "we" of this community will necessary be one that strives for rather than assumes agreement, aware of its own finitude and fragility. Thus Rilke's figures that display their own uncertainty and transience undertake findings and testings of orientation in the service of a community that "consists of any or all of those persons who have the capacity to acknowledge what others among them are doing."[67] This acknowledgment takes place between finite subjects whose relations to the world and to each other are fundamentally uncertain. The fragility of subjectivity appeared already in the crisis of *Malte* and is openly displayed in the *Sonnets*; as I turn in my conclusion to Paul Celan, that subjectivity becomes ever more threatened even as Celan offers its particularity as the only remaining route to the acknowledgment of finitude in poetic communication.

---

66. See the section "Language, Grammar, and Forms of Life" in chapter 1.
67. Lyn Hejinian, "Who Is Speaking?," in *The Language of Inquiry* (Berkeley: University of California Press, 2000), 34.

Epilogue

"Desperate Conversation"—
Poetic Finitude in Paul Celan and After

In opening and ending this project with the works of Paul Celan, I hope to suggest some of the ways in which the struggles of acknowledgment in the inhabitation of finitude continue after Hölderlin and Rilke into the second half of the twentieth century and perhaps through the beginning of the twenty-first. Here, I read Celan's speech *Der Meridian* (The Meridian) as suggesting the ways in which his poetry takes up the problems of finite subjectivity as it lives in and with language.[1] In particular, Celan's engagement with finitude appears in the *Meridian*'s treatment of poetry's individual and historical particularity, its communicative or intersubjective dimension, and its role in the conflict between art and artificiality, which Celan treats in the speech under the rubrics of *Dichtung* (poetry) and *Kunst* (art).

As in the case of Hölderlin and Rilke, these themes, which I identify as bespeaking Celan's engagement with finitude, are familiar to Celan's readers. But the account of finitude I have developed throughout helps show, first, how Celan's language, even or especially at its most difficult and distant from everyday speech,

---

1. Paul Celan, *Der Meridian: Endfassung—Entwürfe—Materialien*, ed. Bernhard Böschenstein and Heino Schmull, with Michael Schwarzkopf and Christiane Wittkop, vol. 4 of Paul Celan, *Werke, Tübinger Ausgabe*, ed. Jürgen Wertheimer (Frankfurt a.M.: Suhrkamp, 1999); Paul Celan, *The Meridian*, trans. Rosemarie Waldrop, in *Selections*, ed. and intro. Pierre Joris (Berkeley: University of California Press, 2005), 154–69.

can take part in the project of what I called "convening on conventions," in which language and world index and alter each other in what Celan, like Hölderlin, calls "conversation" (*Gespräch*). Second, the idea that finitude is inhabited most authentically via the unfulfillable desire to transcend it provides one possible frame for understanding the baffling and circular interplay between poetry and art in Celan's work. For my sketch of Celan, as in my longer treatments of Hölderlin and Rilke, the account of finitude and its reciprocal relation to language is at once a mode of approach to the poet and is itself changed and challenged by the poetic, temporally specific responses individual poets offer to the problems of inhabiting finitude.

The *Meridian*, delivered on the occasion of Celan's acceptance of the Büchner Prize in Darmstadt in 1960 and published in 1961, is a complex interweaving of references and citations, most prominently to and of Georg Büchner, the German dramatist and pamphleteer for whom the prize was named.[2] A conclusion is not the place to tease out these references (to Kafka, Benjamin, Buber, Scholem, Levinas, Schestow, and others); nor can I give an overview of Celan's biography or poetic career, situate him fully in aesthetic debates of his era, or even provide a complete accounting of the ways in which his speeches and letters elaborate the difficulties of inhabiting finitude. Both for reasons of space and because of my noncomparative approach, I also do not analyze the ways in which Celan refers to and writes poetry that takes up the tradition of Hölderlin and Rilke (especially the former).[3] Like them, Celan attracted the attention of Martin Heidegger, but because (unlike Hölderlin or Rilke) he lived during the philosopher's lifetime, Celan also read and responded to Heidegger as the twentieth century's most prominent thinker on poetic language and finitude, first enthusiastically and then critically as Heidegger failed to address either his involvement in the Nazi Party or his silence on the Shoah after the war.[4]

---

2. On quotation in the speech, particularly as part of Celan's response to critical reviews in conjunction with the spurious accusations of plagiarism tinged with anti-Semitism initiated by Claire Goll, see Helmut Müller-Sievers, "On the Way to Quotation: Paul Celan's Meridian Speech," special issue, *New German Critique* 91 (Winter 2004): 131–49. Kristina Mendicino describes Celan's treatment of quotation as *er-innern*, literally, "internalization," from Celan's repeated rhetorical formula "Sie erinnern sich" (You will remember) in the speech. See Kristina Mendicino, "An Other Rhetoric: Paul Celan's *Meridian*," *MLN* 126, no. 3 (2011): 640. Alexandra Richter notes Celan's citation of every interlocutor except Büchner by way of a Jewish mediator (e.g., Pascal via Schestow, Malebranche via Benjamin, etc.) and thus sees the speech as a dialogue between German and Jewish traditions whose pleas for attentiveness she reads convincingly as a call to political alertness in light of reviving anti-Semitism in Germany. Alexandra Richter, "Die politische Dimension der Aufmerksamkeit im *Meridian*," *DVjS* 77, no. 4 (2003): 659–76.

3. See, e.g., Aris Fioretos, "Nothing: History and Materiality in Celan," in *Word Traces*, ed. Aris Fioretos (Baltimore: Johns Hopkins University Press, 1994), 295–341; and Anja Lemke, "Andenkendes Dichten—Paul Celans Poetik der Erinnerung in 'Tübingen, Jänner' und 'Todtnauberg' in Auseinandersetzung mit Hölderlin und Heidegger," in *Die Zeitlichkeit des Ethos: Poetologische Aspekte im Schreiben Paul Celans*, ed. Ulrich Wergin und Martin Jörg Schäfer (Würzburg: Königshausen und Neumann, 2003), 89–11.

4. Pierre Joris, "Introduction: 'Polysemy without Mask,'" in Celan, *Selections*, 21. Indeed, the *Meridian* speech has been read as a criticism of Heidegger in terms similar to those in which I take issue with

Rather than elaborating all of these developments and connections (which would furnish the material for several monographs), I touch on Celan's themes of historical and individual particularity, the intersubjective nature of poetry, and the conflict between art and artificiality. In placing these themes in relation to my account of finitude (far more briefly than I have done with Hölderlin and Rilke), I hope to give some idea of one way the problems of finitude change in the latter half of the twentieth century and, conversely, show how the account of poetic quests for the inhabitation of finitude I have developed might help us understand the persistent questions of Celan's poetry and speeches: how can poets seek any orientation between subject, language, and community; indeed, how can poets speak at all in light of the traumas of individual and historical experience? Although the *Meridian* should not be read as directly applicable to or explanatory of any of Celan's poetry (any more than Hölderlin's poetological texts or Rilke's letters were of their poems), its repeated thematizations of what poetry attempts to do illuminate what Celan seeks to "add here, today, to the old hopes" of poetry.[5]

The accusation of a flight into poetic virtuosity I saw as raised by and refuted in Rilke's *Sonnets to Orpheus* was leveled repeatedly at Paul Celan, whose early reviewers suggested that his work "escape[d] the bloody horror chamber of history," "ris[ing] to the ethereal domain of pure poetry."[6] But in his consideration of what differentiates poetry "here today" from poetic tradition, Celan foregrounds not the pure timelessness of poetry but rather the historical particularity of poetic speech, and thus also poetry's connection to, and power to intervene in, its particular time.[7] Contrary to notions of poetry as a timeless, universalizing mode and to the idea that poetry must purify itself of worldly contamination,[8] Celan

---

him in chapter 1: Heidegger elides subjectivity, individual particularity, and historical specificity in his subsuming of the poem to his historico-philosophical schema of the gradual saying of Being in poetry. See, e.g., Dennis J. Schmidt, "Black Milk and Blue: Celan and Heidegger on Pain and Language," in Fioretos, *Word Traces*, 110–29; and Lemke, "Andenkendes Dichten." Christopher Fynsk goes so far as to read both of Celan's major public addresses as saying: "Here is what must be said about poetry after Heidegger" (Christopher Fynsk, "The Realities at Stake in a Poem: Celan's Bremen and Darmstadt Addresses," in Fioretos, *Word Traces*, 159).

5. Celan, *Selections*, 163.

6. Celan, *Selections*, 163. Hans Egon Holthusen, "Five Young German Poets," in *Der Merkur*; cited by Joris, "Introduction," 21. Holthusen, "an enthusiastic member of the SS before the fall of the Reich," made the criticism specifically with reference to Celan's now-canonical "Todesfuge"; "This negation of the context of the poem was not a singular aberration but happened with regularity throughout the fifties and sixties" (ibid.). The *Meridian* may thus be read as offering a critique of a historiography of poetry as becoming increasingly self-absorbed, culminating in the hermeticism of "sweet song" or the "magic" of pure language. See, e.g., Fioretos, "Nothing," 319.

7. That historical and individual particularity themselves constitute the political and ethical thrust of Celan's poetology is an idea worked out at length in the essays collected in Wergin and Schäfer, *Die Zeitlichkeit des Ethos*, especially in Schäfer's introduction (9–17).

8. This second notion, in particular, derives from the poetic tradition culminating in Mallarmé, to whom Celan refers by name in the address (Celan, *Meridian*, 5; Celan, *Selections*, 159).

suggests that contemporary poetry must "remain mindful of its dates" (*die Daten eingedenk bleiben*). In the tentative, questioning mode that characterizes the speech, Celan asks:

> Perhaps we can say that every poem is marked by its own '20th of January'? Perhaps the newness of poems written today is that they try most plainly to be mindful of this kind of date? But do we not all write from and toward some such date? [And which dates do we ascribe to ourselves?]⁹

The twentieth of January is the date on which Büchner's *Lenz* begins; it is also the date of the day of the Wannsee Conference in 1942 on which the implementation and coordination of the "final solution" to the Jewish question was discussed.¹⁰ Celan's choice of a date with a multiplicity of significances, together with his questions about whether writing toward and from such dates might be a general phenomenon (*wir alle*, "we all"), emphasizes that such mindfulness is not a matter of identifying universal dates, rooted in the past and infinitely repeatable, but is always an issue or problem at any particular moment. Rather, poetry must discover the dates from which and to which it proceeds as it develops a mindfulness rooted in language.¹¹

In addition to its reformulation of the mutual shaping of world (history) and language played out in "Die Silbe Schmerz" (The Syllable Pain) this insistence on the particularity of historical finitude puts a significant strain on the intelligibility of poetic language.¹² But—through questioning, paradox, encounter, and exploration—Celan works in the *Meridian* speech to develop a poetics of particularity that, precisely by *way* of its inscription in history and its individual fragility, is able to seek a communicative space with an address or "you":

> But the poem speaks. It is mindful of its dates, but it speaks. True, it speaks only on its own, its very own behalf.
>
> But I think—and this will hardly surprise you—that the poem has always hoped, for this very reason, to speak also on behalf of the *strange*—no, I can no longer use this word here—*on behalf of the other*, who knows, perhaps of an *altogether other*.¹³

---

9. Celan, *Selections*, 162–63.

10. See Celan, *Selections*, 226.

11. Lemke reads this mindfulness of dates as a radicalization of the Heideggerian theme of being-toward-death (Lemke, "Andenkendes Dichten," 94).

12. "It is true, the poem, the poem today shows—and this has only indirectly to do with the difficulties of vocabulary, the faster flow of syntax or a more awakened sense of ellipsis, none of which we should underrate—the poem clearly shows a strong tendency towards silence.

"The poem holds its ground, if you will permit me yet another extreme formulation, the poem holds its ground on its own margin. In order to endure, it constantly calls and pulls itself back from [its] 'already-no-more' [*Schon-nicht-mehr*] into [its] 'still-here' [*Immer-noch*]" (Celan, *Selections*, 163–64).

13. Celan, *Selections*, 163.

That is, despite its historical circumscription, and not only despite but because of its ability to speak only in its own voice or on its own behalf, the poem also seeks an encounter with and speaks—perhaps—on behalf of another, without eliding the alterity of that other: the poem "always acts as a promise of communication, contact, and community; yet it is always equally true that by carrying us to the point of our finite singularity, poetic experience—the experience of language as language—renders mortality possible as the mortality that is ours and that keeps us apart."[14] The very finitude of language and those who speak it is what the I and the other share; the basis of communication is the impossibility of its certainty. Any attempt to elide individual or historical particularity once and for all would, as displayed in "Die Silbe Schmerz," risk repeating the totalizations of thought and voice that culminated in the Shoah; instead, the poet must remember that he speaks "from the angle of [inclination] of [his own creaturely] nature."[15]

Thus the insistence on individual and historical finitude in Celan's *Meridian* speech does not represent a retreat to a hermetic world or to an isolated community of two; instead, poetry "must be read as having a basic role in the political life of those who share a language, as well as in the decisions of history."[16] In terms that recall Hölderlin's insistence on individual experience and memory, as well as Rilke's emphasis on attention to the things of the phenomenal world,[17] Celan describes the kind of poetry

---

14. Schmidt, "Black Milk and Blue," 114. Fynsk extends this point by remarking that according to Celan's reading of "I" and "you," "I may situate myself only in relation to an other, but my reach is toward an otherness of the other that I can never appropriate and that exposes me always to an alterity.... This alterity is marked in the poem—brought to 'speak' there—but its voice is fundamentally unsettling *because always other*" (Fynsk, "Realities at Stake," 177). Echoing Celan's critique of Heidegger's lack of particularity as well as my Cavellian critique of Heidegger's ethical blind spot, Fynsk reflects that Celan's emphasis on the alterity of the other shows that for all his talk of *Mitsein*, Heidegger "failed, in effect, to think through sufficiently the relation to the other in its otherness, and to take the measure of what this might mean for a thought of the historicity of Dasein" (176).

15. Celan, *Selections*, 164. The German is "unter dem Neigungswinkel seiner Kreatürlichkeit" (Celan, *Meridian*, 9). This is not to say that Celan's mindfulness of dates refers only to the murder of Europe's Jews or that he insists that every poet write under the sign of the death camps (although he is critical of those with nothing to say about them); because all poetry, for Celan, writes toward finitude and mortality, "one constricts [the] full force" of Celan's treatments of finitude and death "if one regards him only as a poet of the Holocaust" (Schmidt, "Black Milk and Blue," 124). Such emphasis on particularity also prevents the inference, toward which some scholarship on Celan tends, that writing mindful of the Shoah entails and even enables taking up or over the position of victim or survivor. (In part because of her laudable efforts to return to poetry the historicity Heidegger effaces, Lemke, "Andenkendes Dichten," tends in this direction.)

16. Schmidt, "Black Milk and Blue," 118. Martin Jörg Schäfer also analyzes the reciprocity between intimate and political relations, reflecting that the fleeting intimacy worked out in many of Celan's poems always points beyond itself to a historical conditionedness while, conversely, the calling up of history overturns again and again into the most intimate of relations, that between I and You. Martin Jörg Schäfer, "Zeitlichkeit, Ethos, Poetologie—Zur Einleitung," in Wergin and Schäfer, *Die Zeitlichkeit des Ethos*, 12–13.

17. The poem's fundamental mode is that of individual attention to the singular or particular: "The attention the poem pays to all that it encounters, its *more* acute sense of detail, outline, structure, color, but also of the 'tremors and hints' [a quotation from Büchner's *Lenz*]—all this is not, I think, achieved by an eye competing (or concurring) with ever more precise instruments, but rather, by a kind of concentration mindful of all our dates" (Celan, *Selections*, 164).

that emerges from an encounter between the singularity of the I and the alterity of the other as "the poem of a person who still perceives, still turns towards phenomena, addressing and questioning them. The poem becomes conversation—often desperate conversation [*verzweifeltes Gespräch*]."[18] This conversation—a topos already fraught with uncertainty in Hölderlin—does not refer to an always-already existing other whose answers are taken for granted; rather, the poem must constitute its own conversational space and encounter in its own writing.

Celan does not present this poetics of historical and individual particularity that seeks an encounter in *Gespräch* directly or by way of analytical argumentation. Instead, it unfolds in conflict and dialogue with what reads very much like an analysis of poetic attempts to overcome or deny finitude, figured in the *Meridian* speech as *Kunst* (art). In German, as in English, the word for "art" gives its root to "artificial" and "artificiality" (*Kunst*, *künstlich*, *Künstlichkeit*). In the address, Celan contrasts art with *Dichtung* (poetry), where the former is associated with marionettes, automata, and mechanics, and metrical technique.[19] Perhaps most tellingly for questions of finitude, he characterizes art as "a problem, and, as we can see, one that is variable, tough, long lived, let us say, eternal."[20] Using terms of contrast derived from Büchner's *Lenz*, Celan also underscores the consequences for individual particularity of attention to or immersion in art (an eternal but sterile possibility): Büchner's title character, in an extended discussion of art, forgets himself in what Celan describes as the *Ich-Ferne* (distance from the I) of the artist, with whom he contrasts the historical person ("himself, as a person... the historical Lenz," "he as an I").[21] And finally, in specifically poetic terms, art is full of images and metaphors and tropes (*Bilder* and *Metaphern* and *Tropen*), the very components attributed to Celan's poetry as enabling his ostensible retreat into decorative hermeticism.

Poetry (*Dichtung*), by contrast, interests itself precisely in the historical, particular individual; it is what interrupts art's eternal continuation with a "counterword" (*Gegenwort*) or a "step" (*Schritt*) that constitutes an act of freedom or breaking away from art's grandiloquence and virtuosity.[22] Celan first defines poetry as a name for "the majesty of the absurd which [bears witness to] the presence of human beings."[23]

---

18. Celan, *Selections*, 165.
19. "Die Kunst, das ist, Sie erinnern sich, ein marionettenhaftes, jambisch-fünffüßiges und... kinderloses Wesen" (Celan, *Meridian*, 2; Celan, *Selections*, 154: "Art, you will remember, is a puppet-like, iambic, five-footed thing without... offspring"). Thinking of Cavell's thought experiment of the perfect automaton, one might say that in both Cavell and Celan, what the automaton calls forth is the strangeness or otherness of the human/Other. See chapter 1, "From Knowledge to Acknowledgment."
20. Celan, *Selections*, 155.
21. Ibid., 160–61. In German: "Er, als historische Person," "Er als ein Ich" (Celan, *Meridian*, 6–7).
22. Celan, *Meridian*, 3; Celan, *Selections*, 156. See on this point Philippe Lacoue-Labarthe's analysis that "poetry is the interruption of art. Something, if you will, that 'takes art's breath away'" (Philippe Lacoue-Labarthe, "Catastrophe," trans. Andrea Tarnowski, in Fioretos, *Word Traces*, 132.
23. Celan, *Selections*, 157. There is no good English way to render the extended participial phrase in German: "die für die Gegenwart des Menschlichen zeugenden Majestät des Absurden" (Celan, *Meridian*, 3).

Poetry, then, testifies (the German word *zeugen* means "to bear witness" and also "to beget a child," against the sterility of art) to the presence of the human, the particular, the absurd; art is thus contrasted with the singularity of "the human as that which allows there to be one man or another—*that* man there, the singular—in the here and now."²⁴ Once more by way of *Lenz*, Celan links poetry to the living, the human, and the creaturely, "the 'life of the least beings,' the 'tremors and hints,' the 'subtle, hardly noticeable play of emotions on [the] face.' "²⁵ Poetry, then, seems to abandon as dangerous and destructive the desire to transcend finitude, attending instead to the particularity of the individual and the other, and their embodied life and mortality that are shared in a community of conversation from "I" to "you."

But already in Celan's depiction of *Lenz* the distinction between art and poetry begins to fold in on itself: the words cited in Lenz's program of attention to the creaturely and the finite are precisely those he speaks in the discussion of art that renders him alienated from himself. Moreover, the inanimacy of art takes over the living and the human in Lenz's own example: describing a scene of two peasant girls helping each other put up their hair as more alluring than classical sculpture or Dutch painting, he asserts: "Sometimes one would like to be a Medusa's head to turn such a group to stone and gather the people around it."²⁶ Linking this desire back to the naturalist program (with which Büchner was affiliated) of "expanding art," Celan finds a sinister, uncanny undertone to this expansion, in which art's strangeness grasps or invades what is other to it, "to seize the natural as natural by way of art!"²⁷ The very act of grasping the natural is inevitably ossifying, petrifying, deadly. In his own program that seems to turn away from the artificiality of art, Celan takes up Büchner's challenge to art (*In-Frage-Stellung der Kunst*), a calling into question of art that forms the starting point of poetry: "A challenge to which all poetry [today] must return if it wants to question further."²⁸ That is, he identifies, with Büchner, a calling into question of art without which "poetry today" cannot begin.

I cannot trace here every move toward and away and through the two poles of *Kunst* and *Dichtung* that Celan moves through in the dynamics of the speech, throughout which he repeatedly takes up the theme of turning, both in the vocabulary of artifice (*Tropen*, "tropes," a synonym for Celan's "metaphors" and "images,"

---

24. Lacoue-Labarthe, "Catastrophe," 135.
25. Celan, *Selections*, 158. Phrases in single quotation marks are quoted from Büchner by Celan.
26. Celan, *Selections*, 158; the entire passage is a direct quotation from Büchner's *Lenz*.
27. Celan, *Selections*, 158. Lacoue-Labarthe summarizes this point helpfully: "Art wants to expand itself; it clamors to be expanded. It wants its difference from the things and beings of nature to be effaced. In a way, that which is art's own, which is 'proper' to art (to the *Unheimliche*), is the tendency to mitigate differentiation, and in so doing invade and contaminate everything. . . . Art is, if the word can be risked, generalized 'estrangement'—the Medusa's head, the robots, the speeches—without end" (Lacoue-Labarthe, "Catastrophe," 134).
28. Celan, *Selections*, 159.

derives from the Greek *tropos*, "turn or way") and of poetry.[29] Shortly before the end of the address, Celan returns to the question of art's expansion. He sketches the conflict once more and then offers the answer he had thought to give, only to call it into question:

> *Elargissez l'art!* This problem confronts us with its old and new uncanniness. I took it to Büchner, and I think I found it in his work.
>
> I even had an answer ready, I wanted to counter, to contradict, with a word against the grain [*Gegenwort*], like Lucile's.
>
> Enlarge art?
>
> No. On the contrary, take art with you into your innermost narrowness. And set yourself free.
>
> I have taken this route, even today, with you. It has been a circle.
>
> Art (this includes the Medusa's head, the mechanism, the automaton), art, the uncanny strangeness which is so hard to differentiate and perhaps is only *one* after all—art lives on.[30]

Art—and Celan reiterates many of the negatively connoted terms he associates with it throughout the speech—returns; the path poetry traces toward and away from it is a circle, and the opposition between enlarging and contracting, strange and other, freedom and constraint, collapses. Even in the quest for the human, the techniques and technologies, the desire to exceed the human and "live on," constantly reemerges; poetry and art come into being in constant tension with each other.

In the passages quoted above, the interweaving of poetry and art seems to represent a failure; the "way out" Celan sought turns out not to be a way out but a return to its origin. The very end of the *Meridian*, however, recasts this circular turning and returning, introducing its title image for the first time:

> Ladies and gentlemen, I find something which consoles me a bit for having walked this impossible road in your presence, this road of the impossible.
>
> I find the connective [*das Verbindende*] which, like the poem, leads to encounters.
>
> I find something as immaterial as language, yet earthly, terrestrial, in the shape of a circle which, via both poles, rejoins itself and on the way serenely crosses even the tropics [*Tropen*]: I find . . . a *meridian*.[31]

The attributes of art and poetry fall together: the "tropes" of rhetorical figuration and artistic virtuosity become the tropics of terrestrial turning (*Tropen* means both

---

29. "Poetry is perhaps this: an *Atemwende*, a turning of our breath" (Celan, *Selections*, 162; Celan, *Meridian*, 7: "Dichtung: das kann eine Atemwende bedeuten").
30. Celan, *Selections*, 166–67.
31. Celan, *Selections*, 169; suspension points in original.

"tropes" and "tropics" in German); the circle that was before an image of the futility of escaping art now appears to enable the very encounter in whose name poetry sought to free itself from art. But the path is still "impossible," the path *of* the impossible: poetry can neither free itself once and for all from the alienation of art, nor can the human escape its own finitude, its "radical individuation" and its dates in the eternal repetition of art without also losing itself. Poetry, that is, comes to be not as an escape from or denial of art's striving toward the infinite, but in the very impossibilities that striving uncovers, in the yearnings beyond itself of a single I who seeks a communicative encounter along the meridian of the poem.[32]

Celan thus traces a path for the poem that inhabits this conflict between "mutism's *saying nothing*" and "the saying too much of grandiloquence."[33] The speech's final definition of poetry bespeaks both the uncanniness of art that seeks to transcend or overcome finitude and the finitude itself that yearns for that impossible transcendence: "Die Dichtung, meine Damen und Herren—: diese Unendlichsprechung von lauter Sterblichkeit und Umsonst!"[34] Read one way, this sentence seems to catch poetry in a lie: it is the declaration that mortality and what is in vain are eternal (*unendlich*). In this reading, mortality and "what is in vain" (*Umsonst*) belie art's claims to eternity. But read the other way, poetry is defined as the perpetual *speaking* of that which is mortal and that which is in vain; that is, as the move into the language of art and with art of the human, mortal, and absurd or in vain that makes up Celan's poetic response to inevitable finitude in the face of the catastrophes of language and history. His poetry, perhaps even more than Hölderlin's or Rilke's, is aware of the dangers of the desire to overcome finitude: the absolutism and totalization that can follow from the search for what reaches beyond itself, and the endless self-perpetuation of the poetic techniques and traditions that, in attempting to attain immortality, cut themselves off from the human. This awareness, then, is a particularly acute and self-conscious form of the dissatisfaction with language that can inspire either a quest for certainty (anxious or coercive, as the case may be) or the flight into hermeticism. "Art" in Celan's speech is thus a double figure that both identifies dangers whose internal relation to poetry nonetheless

---

32. In an argument that ends up subsuming individual particularity and history to Heidegger's historico-philosophical schema, Lacoue-Labarthe nonetheless accurately characterizes this internal relation: "Poetry, then, *in effect* says existence: the human. It says existence, not because it takes the opposing course to discourse or because it upsets the *unheimlich* turnaround.... Poetry does not take its place outside art, in some sense supposed to be the other of art or of its strangeness. It takes place in the 'strange place' itself" (Lacoue-Labarthe, "Catastrophe," 138).

33. Lacoue-Labarthe, "Catastrophe," 141–42.

34. Celan, *Meridian*, 11; Celan, *Selections*, 167: "Poetry, ladies and gentleman: what an eternalization of nothing but mortality, and in vain." I give the German only in the main text because Waldorp's translation is problematic in that it reduces the sentence's two possibilities to one and heightens the negative affect; moreover, it does not recognize that *Umsonst*, capitalized, is a noun, not a description of the result of poetry's so-called eternalization. (Nor does "eternalization" capture the sense of speaking in *Unendlich-sprechung*.) I give English versions of the two possible readings above.

prompts dissatisfaction with language, and requires standing attention to the necessity of that dissatisfaction in the inhabitation of finitude.

Perhaps the central claim of this project has been that the questions and struggles of human finitude cannot and must not be answered once and for all; accordingly, any conclusion to it can have only a provisional character. Acknowledgment—the repeatedly attempted and uncertain state of responsiveness to what is separate from me but not inaccessible to me—is not something, once completed, whose results can be adduced, recorded, and then left alone. This insight is expressed in Cavell's call for the "holding open" of the "argument of the self with itself (over its finitude)."[35] Rilke abandons his character Malte's call for a single step that would recast all human relations, instead working out repeated shapings of relationality within the finite plasticity of sonnet form. And Hölderlin, in his own historically specific language, forbids the closing of the arguments over finitude both in his insistence that true harmony of and between subjects is achievable only in poetry and in his poetry's calls for communication and responsiveness. I have hinted at some of the ways in which for Celan this responsiveness moves into the material of language itself, thus enabling a tentative encounter and conversation that registers historical particularity. Such responsiveness likewise fully informs the picture of language *use* rather than reference that I unfolded throughout my readings; the abutment of language and world that changes over time and is a matter of deep convention likewise denies any advance certainties of fit or correlation between language and world.

This view of language foregrounds the powers of lyric poetry to address and register but not to solve once and for all the problems of world orientation peculiar (and native) to human subjects; lyric poetry does this yet more paradigmatically than ordinary language use (or, I would want to say, even than prose texts) because of its attention to all of language's semantic, historical, acoustic, written, and formal components. And these powers ground the ambitious claims that both Hölderlin and Rilke make for lyric poetry, including, among other things, that it can create political communities, that it can recast human relations to death, or that it can unite the sensual and intellectual components of human subjectivity. For both poets, orientations in words *are* orientations in and to the world: "That these words should lay aside their differences and join upon this ground of sense, proposes a world which mocks the squalor and cowardice of our imaginations."[36] The harmonies, dissonances, unities, and conflicts poets create in language both come from and influence the world that language comes from and reaches. In my

---

35. Stanley Cavell, *Disowning Knowledge in Seven Plays of Shakespeare*, updated ed. (Cambridge: Cambridge University Press, 2003), 5.
36. Stanley Cavell, *The Senses of Walden—An Expanded Edition* (Chicago: University of Chicago Press, 1992), 44.

readings of Hölderlin and Rilke I have looked in detail at their poetry to show what kind of world each proposes as a challenge and an invitation to the imagination. And in each case this challenge stands not as an example of a philosophical position worked out elsewhere but as the expression of a yearning most fully articulated in poetry.

For Hölderlin, this yearning is expressed as a call for unification in the endeavor to show the subject to be linked with something outside itself, whether in a religious or political community or in inhabitation of the finite natural world. What Hölderlin's poems acknowledge is that the certainty desired in these unifications is unattainable, but that the desire itself can nonetheless form the grounds of tentative and temporary communication, community, or communion. The acknowledgment of this uncertainty requires responsiveness from the poet to the world, as it is separate from but inhabited by the subject, and to others, represented as separate groups or individuals within poetry. Acknowledgment extends even further in the creation of a space for responsiveness from the reader as she holds together the oppositions and unifications unfolded but not forced or assured across the dynamic temporality of any given poem. Each of the three poems I have read from Hölderlin's late period approaches acknowledgment in a different way on both semantic/thematic and formal levels, and each foregrounds a different element of the struggle to live within human finitude.

The unfulfillable yearning for certainty reverses direction in Rilke: where Hölderlin strove to link the subjects and the world, Rilke's protagonist in *The Notebooks of Malte Laurids Brigge* seeks and ultimately fails to find assurances of precisely *which* elements of the world (human or thing) can provide successful world orientations. Absent such certainty, Malte experiences an alarming degree of openness to the world; what Rilke's subsequent texts work out is that this openness is not only threatening but productive. This openness, appearing in the themes of a recast relation to mortality, to earthly existence, and to embodied subjectivity, informs his *Sonnets to Orpheus* in formal and semantic registers. The program of the figure collects these registers into a simultaneously thematic and formal or even plastic shaping and testing of world orientations. The *Sonnets* investigate relationality as such, asking the reader to investigate the relations between elements of individual sonnets, between sonnets, and throughout the entire cycle.

As my turn to Celan emphasizes, the three poets differ not only in the discourses in which they treat the problems of finitude but in their treatment of language: Hölderlin, for all his emphasis on sensory concretion and the intensity of his formal shaping of language, does not have the same sense of language as a material medium as does Rilke. When Hölderlin discusses unifications of *Stoff* or material with mind/spirit (*Geist*), he is referring almost invariably to content, not to ink on the page or sounds in the ear. Rilke, in contrast, is highly attentive to both, as evidenced by his laments that he has no such plastic medium for artistic work as does Rodin, and by a strange text from 1919, "Ur-Geräusch" (Primal Sound), in which he imagines the noise that would be made if a phonograph needle traced the grooves in a human skull.[37] The arenas in which theorizing about language occurs, to put it simply, change drastically in the century between the two poets and continue into Celan's radical experimentation with poetic/linguistic materiality.

Surveying the developments in lyric poetry and theorization with a very wide lens at the beginning of the twenty-first century, it is surely safe to say that the emphasis on the materiality of language, whether in concrete poetry, in L=A=N=G=U=A=G=E poetry, in transnational or multilingual poetry, or in dialect or noise poetry, has only intensified. Similarly, the search to explain human mindedness has shifted from philosophy to psychology to the physical material of the brain treated in cognitive science or neurology, at least in one of its strains (this is not to say that philosophy and psychology do not go on—productively and provocatively). And I would suggest that poetry has, in some cases, undertaken the task of reminding us that this emphasis on the material may turn out to be anything but brute or determinist. The explanation of definite theses by way of which investigations of material mindedness proceed will need to be transformed by and in the kind of open exploration of mind, language, and world I have argued lyric poetry is perhaps uniquely qualified to undertake. (At least, such explanations will need to be so transformed if they want to tell us anything about the inhabitation rather than the facts of finitude.) Indeed, these material orientations too are uncertain and in need of convening upon, something that the discourses from which they emerge often seem to elide: "Nothing is more human than the wish to deny one's humanity."[38] Whether precisely the problems of finitude I have been investigating find a home in the quests for knowledge of the new millennium and in its poetry is far too large an investigation to undertake here; in any case, whether they do or not will be determined only by addressing contemporary poetry with the same attention and responsiveness that Hölderlin, Rilke, and Celan call for—and seeing whether that poetry answers.

---

37. KA 4:699–704.
38. Stanley Cavell, *The Claim of Reason: Wittgenstein, Skepticism, Morality, and Tragedy*, new ed. (Oxford: Oxford University Press, 1999), 19.

Selected Bibliography

This bibliography lists only the works I have cited directly; it is thus by no means a complete record of every work I consulted in my research, nor does it offer a comprehensive bibliography of the enormous scholarship on the poets I consider. Such bibliographies may be found in the critical editions of Celan, Hölderlin, and Rilke, which I have listed in separate sections below so that readers may easily find their way to the originals of the poems and the translations I cite. All other works are listed alphabetically in "Other Works."

Celan Editions

Celan, Paul. *Der Meridian: Endfassung—Entwürfe—Materialien*. Edited by Bernhard Böschenstein and Heino Schmull, with Michael Schwarzkopf and Christiane Wittkop. Vol. 4 of Paul Celan, *Werke: Tübinger Ausgabe*, edited by Jürgen Wertheimer. Frankfurt a.M.: Suhrkamp, 1999.

———. *Die Gedichte: Kommentierte Gesamtausgabe*. Edited by Barbara Wiedemann. Frankfurt a.M.: Suhrkamp, 2003.

———. *Glottal Stop: 101 Poems*. Translated by Nikolai Popov and Heather McHugh. Hanover, NH: University Press of New England, 2000.

———. *Selections*. Edited and with an introduction by Pierre Joris. Berkeley: University of California Press, 2005.

Hölderlin Editions

Hölderlin, Friedrich. *Essays and Letters*. Edited and translated with an introduction by Jeremy Adler and Charlie Louth. New York: Penguin, 2009.

———. *Poems and Fragments*. Translated by Michael Hamburger. 4th ed. London: Anvil Press Poetry, 2004.

———. *Sämtliche Werke und Briefe*. Edited by Michael Knaupp. 3 vols. Munich: Hanser Verlag, 1992.

———. *Selected Poems of Friedrich Hölderlin*. Translated by Maxine Chernoff and Paul Hoover. Richmond, CA: Omnidawn Press, 2008.

Rilke Editions

Rilke, Rainer Maria. *Briefe an Nanny Wunderly-Volkart*. Edited by Rätus Luck. 2 vols. Frankfurt a.M.: Suhrkamp, 1977.

———. *Briefe aus Muzot, 1921–1926*. Edited by Ruth Sieber-Rilke and Carl Sieber. Leipzig: Insel Verlag, 1937.

———. *Die Briefe an die Gräfin Sizzo: Aus Rainer Maria Rilkes Nachlass*. Wiesbaden: Insel Verlag, 1950.

———. *Kommentierte Ausgabe in vier Bänden*. Edited by Manfred Engel, Ulrich Fülleborn, Horst Nalewski, and August Stahl. Frankfurt a.M.: Insel Verlag, 1996.

———. *Letters of Rainer Maria Rilke*. Translated by Jane Bannard Green and M. D. Herter Norton. 2 vols. New York: W.W. Norton, 1969.

———. "*Letters to a Young Poet*" and "*The Letter from the Young Worker*." Translated by Charlie Louth. New York: Penguin, 2011.

———. *Mitten im Lesen schreib ich Dir: Ausgewählte Briefe*. Edited by Rätus Luck. Frankfurt a.M.: Insel Verlag, 1996.

———. *The Notebooks of Malte Laurids Brigge*. Translated by Stephen Mitchell. New York: Random House, 1990.

———. *Rainer Maria Rilke-Katharina Kippenberg: Briefwechsel*. Edited by Bettina von Bernhard. Wiesbaden: Insel Verlag, 1954.

———. *Rainer Maria Rilke-Norbert von Hellingrath: Briefe und Dokumente*. Edited by Klaus E. Bohnenkamp. Göttingen: Wallstein Verlag, 2008.

———. *Sonnets to Orpheus*. With English translations and notes by C. F. MacIntyre. Berkeley: University of California Press, 1960.

———. *Sonnets to Orpheus; Duino Elegies*. Translated by Jessie Lemont. New York: Fine Editions Press, 1945.

Other Works

Adler, Hans, and Sabine Groß. "Adjusting the Frame: Comments on Cognitivism and Literature." *Poetics Today* 23 (2002): 195–220.

Adorno, Theodor. *Minima Moralia: Reflections on Damaged Life*. Translated by E. F. N. Jephcott. London: Verso, 2005.

———. "Parataxis: Zur späten Lyrik Hölderlins." In *Gesammelte Schriften in 20 Bänden*, 11:447–94. Frankfurt a.M.: Suhrkamp, 2003.

Allemann, Beda. *Zeit und Figur beim späten Rilke: Ein Beitrag zur Poetik des modernen Gedichts*. Pfullingen: Neske, 1961.
Anderle, Martin. *Die Landschaft in den Gedichten Hölderlins: Die Funktion des konkreten im idealistischen Weltbild*. Bonn: Bouvier, 1986.
André, Robert. "Hölderlins Auf-Gabe und die Ode *Blödigkeit*." In *Das Denken der Sprache und die Performanz des Literarischen um 1800*, edited by Stephan Jaeger and Stefan Willer, 55–72. Würzburg: Königshausen und Neumann, 2000.
Baer, Ulrich. "The Status of the Correspondence in Rilke's Work." In *The Cambridge Companion to Rilke*, edited by Karen Leeder and Robert Vilain, 27–38. Cambridge: Cambridge University Press, 2010.
Benjamin, Walter. "Two Poems by Friedrich Hölderlin: 'The Poet's Courage' and 'Timidity.'" In Walter Benjamin, *Selected Writings*, edited by Marcus Bullock and Michael W. Jennings, 1:18–36. Cambridge, MA: Belknap Press of Harvard University Press, 1996.
Bennholdt-Thomsen, Anke, and Alfredo Guzzoni. *Analecta Hölderliana I: Zur Hermetik des Spätwerks*. Würzburg: Königshausen und Neumann, 1999.
Bernstein, Charles. *A Poetics*. Cambridge, MA: Harvard University Press, 1992.
———. "Reading Cavell Reading Wittgenstein." *boundary 2* 9, no. 2 (Winter 1981): 295–306.
Bernstein, J. M. *Against Voluptuous Bodies: Late Modernism and the Meaning of Painting*. Stanford, CA: Stanford University Press, 2006.
Bernstein, Richard J. "Philosophy in the Conversation of Mankind." *Review of Metaphysics* 33, no. 4 (June 1980): 745–75.
Borst, Otto. *Geschichte Baden-Württembergs: Ein Lesebuch*. Edited by Susanne Quarthal and Franz Quarthal. Stuttgart: Theiss Verlag, 2004.
Bosse, Anke. "'Auch die sternische Verbindung trügt': Aspekte der Rilke-Lektüre Paul de Mans." *Germanistische Mitteilungen: Zeitschrift für Deutsche Sprache, Literatur und Kultur* 54 (2001): 1–19.
Brose, Eric Dorn. *German History 1789–1871: From the Holy Roman Empire to the Bismarckian Reich*. Oxford: Berghahn Books, 1997.
Burdorf, Dieter. "Der Text als Landschaft: Eine topographische Lektüre der Seiten 73–76 des Homburger Folioheftes." In *Neue Wege zu Hölderlin*, edited by Uwe Beyer, 113–41. Würzburg: Königshausen und Neumann, 1994.
———. *Hölderlins späte Gedichtfragmente: "Unendlicher Deutung voll."* Stuttgart: Metzler Verlag, 1993.
———. "Mikrologische Lektüre: Am Beispiel eines Bruchstücks aus dem Homburger Folioheft." In *Hölderlin und Nürtingen*, edited by Peter Härtling and Gerhard Kurz, 191–202. Stuttgart: Metzler Verlag, 1994.
Candlish, Stewart, and George Wrisley. "Private Language." In *Stanford Encyclopedia of Philosophy*, Winter 2011 ed. (article published 26 July 1996; substantive revision 29 September 2010). http://plato.stanford.edu/archives/win2011/entries/private-language/.
Cavell, Marcia. *Becoming a Subject: Reflections in Philosophy and Psychoanalysis*. Oxford: Clarendon Press, 2006.
Cavell, Stanley. "Aesthetic Problems of Modern Philosophy." In *Must We Mean What We Say? A Book of Essays*, 73–96. Updated ed. Cambridge: Cambridge University Press, 2002.
———. "The Availability of Wittgenstein's Later Philosophy." In *Must We Mean What We Say? A Book of Essays*, 44–72. Updated ed. Cambridge: Cambridge University Press, 2002.
———. *The Claim of Reason: Wittgenstein, Skepticism, Morality, and Tragedy*. New ed. Oxford: Oxford University Press, 1999.

———. *Conditions Handsome and Unhandsome: The Constitution of Emersonian Perfectionism*. The Carus Lectures, 1988. Chicago: University of Chicago Press, 1991.

———. *Disowning Knowledge in Seven Plays of Shakespeare*. Updated ed. Cambridge: Cambridge University Press, 2003.

———. *In Quest of the Ordinary: Lines of Skepticism and Romanticism*. Chicago: University of Chicago Press, 1988.

———. "Knowing and Acknowledging." In *Must We Mean What We Say? A Book of Essays*, 238–66. Updated ed. Cambridge: Cambridge University Press, 2002.

———. *Must We Mean What We Say? A Book of Essays*. Updated ed. Cambridge: Cambridge University Press, 2002.

———. "Must We Mean What We Say?" In *Must We Mean What We Say? A Book of Essays*, 1–43. Updated ed. Cambridge: Cambridge University Press, 2002.

———. "Politics as Opposed to What?" *Critical Inquiry* 9, no. 1 (1982): 157–78.

———. "Responses." In *Contending with Stanley Cavell*, edited by Russell B. Goodman, 157–76. Oxford: Oxford University Press, 2005.

———. *The Senses of Walden—An Expanded Edition*. Chicago: University of Chicago Press, 1992.

Constantine, David. *Friedrich Hölderlin*. Oxford: Clarendon Press, 1988.

Critchley, Simon. "Cavell's 'Romanticism' and Cavell's Romanticism." In *Contending with Stanley Cavell*, edited by Russell B. Goodman, 37–54. Oxford: Oxford University Press, 2005.

———. *Very Little . . . Almost Nothing: Death, Philosophy, and Literature*. 2nd ed. London: Routledge, 2004.

d'Almeida, Fabrice. *High Society in the Third Reich*. Cambridge: Polity Press, 2008.

de Man, Paul. *Allegories of Reading: Figural Language in Rousseau, Nietzsche, Rilke, and Proust*. New Haven, CT: Yale University Press, 1979.

———. "Patterns of Temporality in Hölderlin's 'Wie wenn am Feiertage . . .'" In *Romanticism and Contemporary Criticism: The Gauss Seminar and Other Papers*, edited by E. S. Burt, Kevin Newmark, and Andrzej Warminski, 50–73. Baltimore: Johns Hopkins University Press, 1993.

Dupré, Louis. *The Quest of the Absolute: Birth and Decline of European Romanticism*. Notre Dame, IN: University of Notre Dame Press, 2013.

Eckel, Winfried. "Bild und Figur in der Lyrik des Symbolismus: Beobachtungen zu Baudelaire, Mallarmé und Rilke." In *Das lyrische Bild*, edited by Ralf Simon, Nina Herres, and Csongor Lorincz, 112–53. Munich: Wilhelm Fink, 2010.

———. "Einzelgedichte 1902–1910." In *Rilke Handbuch: Leben—Werk—Wirkung*, edited by Manfred Engel with Dorothea Lauterbach, 336–54. Stuttgart: Metzler Verlag, 2004.

Eldridge, Hannah Vandegrift. "Forms of Knowledge/Knowledge of Forms: The Epistemology of Goethe's West-östlicher Divan and Cavellian Skepticism." *Goethe Yearbook* 20 (2013): 147–65.

Eldridge, Richard. "'A Continuing Task': Cavell and Skepticism." In *The Persistence of Romanticism: Essays in Philosophy and Literature*, 189–204. Cambridge: Cambridge University Press, 2001.

———. *Leading a Human Life: Wittgenstein, Intentionality, and Romanticism*. Chicago: University of Chicago Press, 1997.

———. *Literature, Life, and Modernity*. New York: Columbia University Press, 2008.

———. "Philosophy and the Achievement of Community: Rorty, Cavell, and Criticism." *Metaphilosophy* 14, no. 2 (April 1983): 107–25.

———. "'To Bear the Momentarily Incomplete': Subject Development and Expression in Hegel and Hölderlin." Special issue, *Graduate Faculty Philosophy Journal* 27, no. 2 (2006): 141–58.
Eldridge, Richard, and Bernard Rhie, eds. *Stanley Cavell and Literary Studies: Consequences of Skepticism*. New York: Continuum, 2011.
Engel, Manfred. "Die Sonette an Orpheus." In *Rilke Handbuch: Leben—Werk—Wirkung*, edited by Manfred Engel with Dorothea Lauterbach, 405–23. Stuttgart: Metzler Verlag, 2004.
———. "Vier Werkphasen." In *Rilke Handbuch—Leben, Werk, Wirkung*, edited by Manfred Engel with Dorothea Lauterbach, 175–81. Stuttgart: Metzler Verlag, 2004.
Fioretos, Aris. "Nothing: History and Materiality in Celan." In *Word Traces*, edited by Aris Fioretos, 295–341. Baltimore: Johns Hopkins University Press, 1994.
Fischer, Michael. *Stanley Cavell and Literary Skepticism*. Chicago: University of Chicago Press, 1989.
Frank, Manfred. "Hölderlins philosophische Grundlagen." In *Hölderlin und die Moderne: Eine Bestandaufnahme*, edited by Gerhard Kurz, Valerie Lawitschka, and Jürgen Wertheimer, 174–94. Tübingen: Attempo-Verlag, 1995.
Franz, Michael. "Hölderlins Gedicht 'Andenken.'" In *Friedrich Hölderlin*, special issue of *Text + Kritik*, edited by Heinz Ludwig Arnold and Andreas Döhler, 195–212. Munich: e:t+k, 1996.
Fynsk, Christopher. "The Realities at Stake in a Poem: Celan's Bremen and Darmstadt Addresses." In *Word Traces*, edited by Aris Fioretos, 159–84. Baltimore: Johns Hopkins University Press, 1994.
Gadamer, Hans Georg. "Anmerkung zu Hölderlins 'Andenken.'" In *Neue Wege zu Hölderlin*, edited by Uwe Beyer, 143–52. Würzburg: Königshausen und Neumann, 1994.
Gaier, Ulrich. "Hölderlins vaterländischer Gesang 'Andenken.'" *Hölderlin Jahrbuch* 26 (1988/89): 175–201.
Gerok-Reiter, Annette. *Wink und Wandlung: Komposition und Poetik in Rilkes "Sonette an Orpheus."* Tübingen: Niemeyer Verlag, 1996.
Gibson, John, and Wolfgang Huemer, eds. *The Literary Wittgenstein*. New York: Routledge, 2004.
Gosetti-Ferencei, Jennifer Anna. *The Ecstatic Quotidian: Phenomenological Sightings in Modern Art and Literature*. University Park: Pennsylvania State University Press, 2007.
———. *Heidegger, Hölderlin, and the Subject of Poetic Language: Toward a New Poetics of Dasein*. New York: Fordham University Press, 2004.
———. "Immanent Transcendence in Rilke and Stevens." *German Quarterly* 83, no. 3 (2010): 275–96.
Groddeck, Wolfram. "Ästhetischer Kommentar: Anmerkungen zu Walter Benjamins Hölderlinlektüre." *Le Pauvre Holterling* 1 (1976): 17–21.
———. "Lebensalter." In *Interpretationen: Gedichte von Friedrich Hölderlin*, edited by Gehard Kurz, 153–65. Stuttgart: Reclam, 1996.
———. "Kosmische Didaktik: Rilkes 'Reiter'-Sonett." In *Gedichte von Rainer Maria Rilke*, edited by Wolfram Groddeck, 203–28. Stuttgart: Reclam, 1999.
Hacker, P. M. S. *Insight and Illusion: Themes in the Philosophy of Wittgenstein*. Rev. ed. Oxford: Oxford University Press, 1986.
Hamacher, Werner. "Parusie, Mauern: Mittelbarkeit und Zeitlichkeit, später Hölderlin." *Hölderlin Jahrbuch* 34 (2004/5): 93–142.

Hamburger, Michael, ed. and trans. *An Unofficial Rilke: Poems 1912–1926*. London: Anvil Press, 1981.
Hamlin, Cyrus. 'Die Poetik des Gedächtnisses: Aus einem Gespräch über Hölderlins 'Andenken.'" *Hölderlin Jahrbuch* 24 (1984/85): 119–38.
Hanssen, Beatrice. "'Dichtermut' and 'Blödigkeit': Two Poems by Hölderlin Interpreted by Walter Benjamin." *MLN* 112, no. 5 (1997): 786–816.
Harrison, Bernard. "Imagined Worlds and the real one: Plato, Wittgenstein, and Mimesis." In *The Literary Wittgenstein*, edited by John Gibson and Wolfgang Huemer, 92–108. New York: Routledge, 2004.
Hayden-Roy, Priscilla. *"A Foretaste of Heaven": Friedrich Hölderlin in the Context of Württemberg Pietism*. Amsterdam: Rodopi, 1994.
Heidegger, Martin. *Erläuterungen zu Hölderlins Dichtung*. Frankfurt a.M.: Vittorio Klostermann, 1951.
Hejinian, Lyn. "Who Is Speaking?" In *The Language of Inquiry*, 30–39. Berkeley: University of California Press, 2000.
Henrich, Dieter. *The Course of Remembrance and Other Essays on Hölderlin*. Edited by Eckhart Förster. Stanford, CA: Stanford University Press, 1997.
———. *Der Grund im Bewußtsein: Untersuchungen zu Hölderlins Denken (1794–1795)*. Stuttgart: Klett-Cotta Verlag, 2004.
———. "Die Anfänge der Theorie des Subjekts (1789)." In *Zwischenbetrachtungen: Im Prozess der Aufklärung*, edited by Axel Honneth, Thomas McCarthy, Claus Offe, and Albrecht Wellmer, 106–70. Frankfurt a.M.: Suhrkamp, 1989.
———. *Grundlegung aus dem Ich: Untersuchungen zur Vorgeschichte des Idealismus; Tübingen—Jena 1790–1794*. Frankfurt a.M.: Suhrkamp, 2004.
———. *Hegel im Kontext*. Frankfurt a.M.: Suhrkamp, 1971.
Henrich, Dieter, with David S. Pacini. *Between Kant and Hegel: Lectures on German Idealism*. Cambridge, MA: Harvard University Press, 2003.
Höhler, Gertrud. "Rainer Maria Rilkes Orpheus." In *Mythos und Mythologie in der Literatur des 19. Jahrhunderts*, edited by Helmut Koopmann, 367–85. Frankfurt a.M.: Klosterman, 1979.
Hornbacher, Annette. "Wie ein Hund: Zum 'mythischen Vortrag' in Hölderlins Entwurf 'Das Nächste Beste.'" *Hölderlin Jahrbuch* 31 (1998/99): 222–46.
Hübner, Götz E. "Nach Port-au-Prince: 'Andenken' als Hölderlins geschichtspoetologisches Vermächtnis." *Le Pauvre Holterling* 9 (2003): 43–54.
Jamme, Christoph. "'Rufer des neuen Gottes': Zur Remythisierung Hölderlins im Georgekreis und ihren Heideggerianischen Folgen." In *Hölderlin in der Moderne: Kolloquium für Dieter Henrich zum 85. Geburtstag*, edited by Friedrich Vollhardt, 80–92. Berlin: Erich Schmidt Verlag, 2014.
Kenny, Anthony. *Wittgenstein*. Cambridge, MA: Harvard University Press, 1973.
Kleist, Heinrich von. *An Abyss Deep Enough: Letters of Heinrich von Kleist with a Selection of Essays and Anecdotes*. Edited and translated by Philip B. Miller. New York: Dutton, 1982.
Krämer, Thomas. *Rilkes "Sonette an Orpheus" Erster Teil: Ein Interpretationsgang*. Würzburg: Königshausen und Neumann, 1999.
Kurz, Gerhard. *Mittelbarkeit und Vereinigung: Zum Verhältnis von Poesie, Reflexion und Revolution bei Hölderlin*. Stuttgart: Metzler Verlag, 1975.
———. *"Das Nächste Beste."* In *Interpretationen: Gedichte von Friedrich Hölderlin*, edited by Gerhard Kurz, 166–85. Stuttgart: Reclam, 1996.

Lacan, Jacques. "The Moral Goals of Psychoanalysis. " Chap. 8 in *The Ethics of Psychoanalysis*, edited by Jacques-Alain Miller, translated by Dennis Porter, 302–10. The Seminar of Jacques Lacan, bk. 7. New York: W.W. Norton, 1992.

Lacoue-Labarthe, Philippe. "Catastrophe." Translated by Andrea Tarnowski. In *Word Traces*, edited by Aris Fioretos, 130–56. Baltimore: Johns Hopkins University Press, 1994.

Lacoue-Labarthe, Philippe, and Jean-Luc Nancy. *The Literary Absolute: The Theory of Literature in German Romanticism*. Edited and translated by Philip Barnard and Cheryl Lester. Albany: SUNY Press, 1988.

Large, David Clay. *Where Ghosts Walked: Munich's Road to the Third Reich*. New York: Norton, 1997.

Laugier, Sandra. "Rethinking the Ordinary: Austin *after* Cavell." In *Contending with Stanley Cavell*, edited by Russell B. Goodman, 82–99. Oxford: Oxford University Press, 2005.

Lefebvre, Jean-Pierre. "Abschied von Andenken: Erörtern heißt hier verortern." *Hölderlin Jahrbuch* 35 (2006/7): 227–51.

———. "Auch die Stege sind Holzwege." *Hölderlin Jahrbuch* 26 (1988/89): 202–23.

Lemke, Anja. "Andenkendes Dichten—Paul Celans Poetik der Erinnerung in 'Tübingen, Jänner' und 'Todtnauberg' in Auseinandersetzung mit Hölderlin und Heidegger." In *Die Zeitlichkeit des Ethos: Poetologische Aspekte im Schreiben Paul Celans*, edited by Ulrich Wergin and Martin Jörg Schäfer, 89–111. Würzburg: Königshausen und Neumann, 2003.

Liberman, Mark, and Geoffrey Pullum. *Language Log* (blog). http://languagelog.ldc.upenn.edu/nll/.

Martinec, Thomas. "The Sonnets to Orpheus." In *The Cambridge Companion to Rilke*, edited by Karen Leeder and Robert Vilain, 95–110. Cambridge: Cambridge University Press, 2010.

McBride, Patrizia C. *The Void of Ethics: Robert Musil and the Experience of Modernity*. Evanston, IL: Northwestern University Press, 2006.

Melville, Stephen. *Philosophy beside Itself: On Deconstruction and Modernism*. Minneapolis: University of Minnesota Press, 1986.

Mendicino, Kristina. "An Other Rhetoric: Paul Celan's *Meridian*." *MLN* 126, no. 3 (2011): 630–50.

Miall, David S. "Experimental Approaches to Reader Responses to Literature," In *New Directions in Aesthetics, Creativity, and the Arts*, ed. Paul Locher et al., 175–88. Amityville, NY: Baywood Press, 2006.

———. "Neuroaesthetics of Literary Reading." In *Neuroaesthetics*, ed. Martin Skov et al., 233–47. Amityville, NY: Baywood Publishing, 2009.

Mulhall, Stephen. "Wittgenstein and Heidegger: Orientations to the Ordinary." *European Journal of Philosophy* 2, no. 2 (1994): 143–64.

Müller-Sievers, Helmut. "On the Way to Quotation: Paul Celan's Meridian Speech." Special issue, *New German Critique* 91 (Winter 2004): 131–49.

Novalis [Friedrich von Hardenberg]. "Monologue." Translated by Joyce Crick. In *Classic and Romantic German Aesthetics*, edited by J. M. Bernstein, 214–15. Cambridge: Cambridge University Press, 2003.

Perloff, Marjorie. *Wittgenstein's Ladder: Poetic Language and the Strangeness of the Ordinary*. Chicago: University of Chicago Press, 1996.

Poiss, Thomas. *Momente der Einheit: Interpretationen zu Pindars Epinikion und Hölderlins "Andenken."* Vienna: Österreichische Akademie der Wissenschaften, 1993.

Pott, Sandra. *Poetiken: Poetologische Lyrik, Poetik und Ästhetik von Novalis bis Rilke.* New York: de Gruyter, 2004.

Prater, Donald. *A Ringing Glass: The Life of Rainer Maria Rilke.* Oxford: Clarendon Press, 1986.

Reitani, Luigi. "'Mit wahrster Verehrung': Hölderlins Rechenschaftsbriefe an Schiller." *Hölderlin Jahrbuch* 34 (2004/5): 143–60.

Reuss, Roland. *"Die eigene Rede des anderen": Hölderlins "Andenken" und "Mnemosyne."* Frankfurt a.M.: Stroemfeld/Roter Stern, 1990.

Richter, Alexandra. "Die politische Dimension der Aufmerksamkeit im *Meridian.*" *DVjS* 77, no. 4 (2003): 659–76.

Riedel, Manfred. "Seinserfahrung in der Dichtung: Heideggers Weg zu Hölderlin." In *"Voll Verdienst, doch dichterisch wohnet der Mensch auf dieser Erde": Heidegger und Hölderlin,* edited by Peter Trawny, 19–49. Frankfurt a.M.: Vittorio Klostermann, 2000.

Rorty, Richard. "Cavell on Skepticism." In *Contending with Stanley Cavell,* edited by Russell B. Goodman, 10–21. Oxford: Oxford University Press, 2005.

Ryan, Judith. *Rilke, Modernism and Poetic Tradition.* Cambridge: Cambridge University Press, 1999.

———. *The Vanishing Subject: Early Psychology and Literary Modernism.* Chicago: University of Chicago Press, 1991.

Ryan, Lawrence. *Hölderlins Lehre vom Wechsel der Töne.* Stuttgart: Kohlhammer Verlag, 1960.

Santner, Eric. *Friedrich Hölderlin: Narrative Vigilance and the Poetic Imagination.* New Brunswick, NJ: Rutgers University Press, 1986.

———. *On Creaturely Life: Rilke, Benjamin, Sebald.* Chicago: University of Chicago Press, 2006.

———. *The Royal Remains: The People's Two Bodies and the Endgames of Sovereignty.* Chicago: University of Chicago Press, 2011.

Schäfer, Martin Jörg. "Zeitlichkeit, Ethos, Poetologie—Zur Einleitung." In *Die Zeitlichkeit des Ethos: Poetologische Aspekte im Schreiben Paul Celans,* edited by Ulrich Wergin and Martin Jörg Schäfer, 9–17. Würzburg: Königshausen und Neumann, 2003.

Scheuer, Hans Jürgen. "Verlagerung des Mythos in die Struktur: Hölderlins Bearbeitung des Orpheus-Todes in der Odenfolge 'Muth des Dichters'—'Dichtermuth'—'Blödigkeit.'" *Jahrbuch der deutschen Schillergesellschaft* 45 (2001): 250–77.

Schiller, Friedrich. *On the Aesthetic Education of Man.* Translated with an introduction by Reginald Snell. Mineola, NY: Dover Publications, 2004.

Schmidt, Dennis J. "Black Milk and Blue: Celan and Heidegger on Pain and Language." In *Word Traces,* edited by Aris Fioretos, 110–29. Baltimore: Johns Hopkins University Press, 1994.

Schmidt, Jochen. *Hölderlins später Widerruf in den Oden "Chiron," "Blödigkeit" und "Ganymed."* Tübingen: Max Niemeyer Verlag, 1978.

Schoolfield, George C. *The Young Rilke and His Time.* Rochester, NY: Camden House, 2009.

Schuster, Jana. "'Tempel im Gehör': Zur Eigenbewegtheit des Klinggedichts am Beispiel des ersten der Sonette an Orpheus von Rainer Maria Rilke." In *Textbewegungen 1800/1900,* edited by Matthias Buschmeier and Till Dembeck, 354–73. Würzburg: Königshausen und Neumann, 2007.

Scimonello, Giovanni. "Benjamin, Adorno und Hölderlin: Interpretation der Ode 'Dichtermuth/Blödigkeit.'" In *In Bildern Denken: Studien zur gesellschaftskritischen Funktion der*

Literatur, edited by Giovanni Scimonello and Ralph Szukala, 11–32. Bielefeld: Aithesis Verlag, 2008.
Stanitzek, Georg. *Blödigkeit: Beschreibungen des Individuums im 18. Jahrhundert*. Tübingen: Niemeyer, 1989.
Steiner, George. "Heidegger, Again." *Salmagundi* 82/83 (1989): 31–55.
Stierle, Karlheinz. "Die Identität des Gedichts—Hölderlin als Paradigma." *Poetik und Hermeneutik* 8 (1979): 505–52.
Storck, Joachim W. "Leben und Persönlichkeit." In *Rilke Handbuch: Leben—Werk— Wirkung*, edited by Manfred Engel with Dorothea Lauterbach, 1–25. Stuttgart: Metzler Verlag, 2004.
Szondi, Peter. "'Überwindung des Klassizismus': Der Brief an Böhlendorff von 4. Dezember 1801." In *Hölderlin-Studien: Mit einem Traktat über philologische Erkenntnis*, 85–104. Frankfurt a.M.: Insel Verlag, 1970.
Thoreau, Henry David. *Walden*. New York: Penguin Books, 1986.
Uffhausen, Dietrich. "Bevestigter Gesang: Hölderlins hymnische Spätdichtung in neuer Gestalt." In *Neue Wege zu Hölderlin*, edited by Uwe Beyer, 323–45. Würzburg: Königshausen und Neumann, 1994.
Urion, Marilyn Vogler. "Emerson's Presence in Rilke's Imagery: Shadows of Early Influence." *Monatshefte* 85, no. 2 (Summer 1993): 153–69.
Waibel, Violetta. "Kant, Fichte, Schelling." In *Hölderlin-Handbuch: Leben—Werk— Wirkung*, edited by Johann Kreuzer, 90–106. Stuttgart: Metzler Verlag, 2002.
Waters, William. "The Elusiveness of Things in Rilke's *Dinggedichte*." In *Das lyrische Bild*, edited by Ralf Simon, Nina Herres, and Csongor Lorincz, 320–36. Munich: Wilhelm Fink, 2010.
———. "The New Poems." In *The Cambridge Companion to Rilke*, edited by Karen Leeder and Robert Vilain, 59–73. Cambridge: Cambridge University Press, 2010.
Wittgenstein, Ludwig. *Philosophical Investigations/Philosophische Untersuchungen*. Translated by G. E. M Anscombe. 3rd ed. Malden, MA: Blackwell Publishing, 2001.
———. *Über Gewissheit/On Certainty*. Edited by G. E. M. Anscombe and G. H. von Wright, translated by Denis Paul and G. E. M. Anscombe. New York: J. & J. Harper Editions, 1969.
Zorach, Cecile Cazort, and Charlotte Melin. "The Columbian Legacy in Postwar German Poetry." *German Quarterly* 65, no. 3/4 (1992): 267–93.
Zuberbühler, Rolf. *Hölderlins Erneuerung der Sprache aus ihren etymologischen Ursprüngen*. Berlin: Erich Schmidt Verlag, 1969.

INDEX

acknowledgment, 15, 48, 202–3
   in Hölderlin, 45, 51–52, 58, 87–88, 115–17
   in Rilke, 129, 131, 137, 141–43, 156, 165, 192–93
   vs. avoidance, 21n, 26, 137–39, 156
   vs. knowledge, 3, 22–26, 28–33
Adorno, Theodor, 3, 6n, 92n, 107n, 191n
aestheticism, 6, 125
alienation, 1, 16, 30, 130n, 201
Andreas-Salomé, Lou, 120
anxiety, 5n, 31, 50–56, 63–65, 69–70, 84–87
Austin, J. L., 7n, 18, 35, 39n, 40–41

Baudelaire, Charles, 126n, 191
Benjamin, Walter, 91n, 92n, 94n, 194
Bernstein, Charles, 7, 17n, 19n, 22n, 35n, 37, 88, 192
Brentano, Clemens, 48, 50n

Cavell, Stanley
   The Claim of Reason, 18–19, 22, 24–27, 35–37, 41, 55n, 142–43

Disowning Knowledge, 17n, 21n, 26n, 137, 140, 202
In Quest of the Ordinary, 20, 30, 48, 51, 84
Must We Mean What We Say? 4–6, 22–24, 34–36, 42
"Politics as Opposed to What?," 7n, 38
"Responses," 18–19, 26, 31
The Senses of Walden, 28–31, 33–34, 119n, 202
Celan, Paul
   Die Meridian (The Meridian), 194–202
   "Die Silbe Schmerz" (The Syllable Pain), 8–14, 196–97
Cezanne, Paul, 121n, 125
Columbus, Christopher, 9–10, 12–14, 86, 112n
convention, 6–7, 27, 33–41, 88, 164, 192–94, 202
Critchley, Simon, 21, 24n, 30, 40, 49
criteria, 23, 35–37, 41, 135, 142n

de Man, Paul, 3, 33n, 38–39, 165n
Derrida, Jacques, 3, 37
Descartes, René, 2, 17n, 19

Emerson, Ralph Waldo, 6n, 28–31, 33, 48
empiricism, 6, 119, 123–25, 127n, 136
everyday, the. *See* the ordinary

Fichte, Johann Gottlieb, 48–49, 52–55,
    58–59, 63n, 66, 119

George, Stefan, 120–21, 125
Goethe, Johann Wolfgang von, 28n, 48

Habermas, Jürgen, 22n
Hausenstein, Wilhelm, 162–63, 165
Heidegger, Martin, 3, 18, 24n, 30–33, 49n,
    133n, 194–97
Hegel, Georg Wilhelm Friedrich, 47–49,
    52, 64n
Hejinian, Lyn, 41n, 192
Hellingrath, Norbert von, 65n, 121–22
Henrich, Dieter, 44n, 45n, 47n, 49n,
    51, 65n
Hofmannsthal, Hugo von, 120, 124–25
Hölderlin, Johann Christian Friedrich
    biography, 45–47, 85–86
    influences, 47–52, 54–55
    Nazi reception of, 122n
    works
        "Andenken" (Remembrance), 79–83,
            107–17
        "Blödigkeit" (Timidness), 71–73,
            90–95
        "Das Nächste Beste" (What Is
            Nearest), 73–79, 95–106
        "Das untergehende Vaterland…"
            (The declining fatherland…), 64
        "Dichtermuth" (The Poet's Courage),
            91–83
        "Fragment of Philosophical Letters,"
            59–61
        "Ground of the *Empedocles*," 63
        "Hälfte des Lebens" (Half of Life), 90
        "Lebensalter" (Ages of Life), 90
        Nachtgesänge (Night Songs), 89–91,
            95, 106, 115–16
        "On the Different Modes of Poetic
            Composition," 62
        "Sein, Urtheil, Möglichkeit" (Being,
            Judgment, Possibility), 58–59, 63

"Seven Maxims," 61–62
"The Standpoint from Which We
    Should Consider Antiquity,"
    62–63
"When the poet is once in command
    of the spirit…," 64–70, 89
Husserl, Edmund, 30–31

idealism, 6, 44n, 48–49, 51–57, 84, 87

Kant, Immanuel, 18–20, 28–29, 41, 47–49,
    51, 58–60
Klee, Paul, 162–63, 165

Lacoue-Labarthe, Philippe, 49–50,
    198–99, 201
Laugier, Sandra, 35, 39–41
Levinas, Emmanuel, 24n, 137n
linguistics, 4n, 40n

Mach, Ernst, 119, 123–24
modernism, 6, 123n, 124n, 162, 164n
modernity, 1, 17, 51, 131, 162n, 191n

Nancy, Jean-Luc, 49–50
Niethammer, Immanuel, 48, 50, 59n
Novalis (Friedrich von Hardenberg),
    48–50

ordinary, the, 27–34, 88n, 144, 160, 167,
    182, 185
ordinary language philosophy, 7n, 22–24,
    35, 40–41

Pater, Walter, 119, 124
philosophical poetry, 6n
Plato, 34
poststructuralism, 1, 38–39, 137
pragmatism, 18–22
psychology, 5n, 123–24, 204

rationalism, 16–19, 28n, 88
reference of/by language, 3–5, 34–39,
    42, 202
relativism, 3n, 16, 18–21
Rilke, Rainer Maria
    biography, 120–23, 157–58

influences, 119–21, 123–27
works
   Aufzeichnungen des Malte Laurids Brigge (*The Notebooks of Malte Laurids Brigge*), 21n, 30n, 119, 121, 127–40, 157, 172–73, 190–92, 202–3
   "Brief eines jungen Arbeiters" (The Letter from a Young Worker), 142, 144
   "Das Ur-Geräusch" (Primal Sound), 203–4
   Duineser Elegien (*Duino Elegies*), 121, 141, 145, 157–60, 162, 168n, 169, 178
   Fünf Gesänge (*Five Cantos*), 121–22
   Neue Gedichte (*New Poems*), 125–27, 157, 163n
   Sonnets to Orpheus I. 6, 149–50, 174–77
   Sonnets to Orpheus I. 8, 150–51, 177–80
   Sonnets to Orpheus I. 9, 151–52, 180–82
   Sonnets to Orpheus I. 11, 147–48, 167–71
   Sonnets to Orpheus I. 12, 148–49, 171–74
   Sonnets to Orpheus II.12, 152–53, 182–85
   Sonnets to Orpheus II.18, 153–54, 185–88
   Sonnets to Orpheus II.28, 154–55, 188–90
   "Testament" ("Das Testament"), 141
Rodin, Auguste, 120, 123–25, 203
romanticism, 6, 18, 48–50, 124
Rorty, Richard, 7n, 18–22, 27, 39n

Schelling, Friedrich Wilhelm Joseph, 47–49, 52n
Schiller, Friedrich, 48–49, 54–55, 66
Schlegel, Friedrich, 47–48, 50
scientism, 16–17, 21–22, 204
Shakespeare, William, 17n, 21n, 26, 137, 140n
Shoah, the, 11–12, 194–97
skepticism, 17–22, 37–40, 43–44, 51–52, 137, 140, 146
   external world skepticism, 27–29
   other minds skepticism, 22–27, 55

Thoreau, Henry David, 28–30, 33–34, 88

Wittgenstein, Ludwig, 2–4, 5, 7, 18–19, 25, 27, 29–34
   grammar and use, 4, 34–42
   Philosophische Untersuchungen (*Philosophical Investigations*), 4n, 166n
   Tractatus Logico-Philosophicus, 4n5
   Über Gewissheit (*On Certainty*), 4–5
Wordsworth, William, 45, 48

www.ingramcontent.com/pod-product-compliance
Lightning Source LLC
Chambersburg PA
CBHW030825230426
43667CB00008B/1388